Clint Eastwood

A M E R I C A N   C U L T U R E

Cutting across traditional boundaries between the human and social sciences, volumes in the American Culture series study the multiplicity of cultural practices from theoretical, historical, and ethnographic perspectives by examining culture's production, circulation, and consumption.

Edited by Stanley Aronowitz, Nancy Fraser, and George Lipsitz

8. Paul Smith, *Clint Eastwood: A Cultural Production*
7. Maria Damon, *The Dark End of the Street: Margins in American Vanguard Poetry*
6. Virginia Carmichael, *Framing History: The Rosenberg Story and the Cold War*
5. Elayne Rapping, *Movie of the Week: Private Stories/Public Events*
4. George Lipsitz, *Time Passages: Collective Memory and American Popular Culture*
3. Alice Echols, *Daring to Be Bad: Radical Feminism in America, 1965-1975*
2. Nancy Walker, *A Very Serious Thing: Women's Humor and American Culture*
1. Henry Giroux, *Schooling and the Struggle for Private Life*

CLINT EASTWOOD

A CULTURAL PRODUCTION

PAUL SMITH

American Culture, Volume 8

University of Minneasota Press
Minneapolis
London

Published by the University of Minnesota Press
2037 University Avenue Southeast, Minneapolis, MN 55414
Printed in the United States of America on acid-free paper

Library of Congress Cataloging-in-Publication Data

Smith, Paul, 1954-
Clint Eastwood : a cultural production / Paul Smith.
p. cm. — (American culture ; v. 8)
Includes bibliographical references and index.
ISBN 0-8166-1958-1 (hc : acid-free paper)
ISBN 0-8166-1960-3 (pb : acid-free paper)
1. Eastwood, Clint, 1930- —Criticism and interpretation.
2. Motion pictures—Social aspects—United States. 3. United States—Popular culture. I. Title. II. Series: American culture (Minneapolis, Minn.) ; v. 8.
PN2287.E37S6 1993
791.43'028'092—dc20 92-34015
CIP

This book is dedicated to my two sisters; I miss you.

Contents

Acknowledgments

This book has its most distant origins in a class on Clint Eastwood that I taught at Miami University, Oxford, Ohio, in 1983. My first acknowledgments are due to the students there who took the class seriously and who seemed to be going out of their way to donate their best ideas, especially Mary Erickson. The course had the support of my colleagues, Paul Sandro and Pete Martin, and my writing of the book has been marked by good memories of working with those two dedicated scholars and teachers of film.

I have had the benefit of help in my research from Jeff Miller, Claire Rivlin, Ed Costello, Matt Jameson, Elizabeth Cronise, Greg Bolton, and Paula Rosky, for which I'm most grateful, and I also thank Patryk Silver for helping me overcome some practical exigencies. Bruce Jenkins of the Walker Art Center, Minneapolis, also helped me with invaluable information.

Some parts of the book were delivered as lectures at the University of Strathclyde, Scotland, and the University of Türkü, Finland; I thank Alan Durant for his hospitality in the first instance (as well as for our long friendship and risibly intermittent correspondence), and I thank Jukka Sihvonen and his colleagues, Martii Lahti and Pirjo Ahokas, for giving me the opportunity to sample the culture of Finland.

A version of one section has been published as "Action Movie Hysteria, or Eastwood Bound," in *Differences* 1 (1989): 88-107. I thank Elizabeth Weed and Naomi Schor for soliciting, editing, and publishing that piece. Parts of another section appeared in an essay "Pedagogy and the Popular-Cultural-Commodity-Text," in *Popular Culture,*

Schooling and Everyday Life, edited by Henry Giroux and Roger Simon (Bergin and Garvey, 1989), 31-46, and first appeared in *Curriculum and Teaching* (Australia) 3 (1988): 9-19. The section on *Bird* was first tried out on audiences at Fordham University and Miami University, thanks to the kind invitations of Patricia Clough and Pete Martin.

My friend and colleague, Kristina Straub, read early pages of some of the book and in that context as well as many others has offered me insights—upon which I hope to have acted and to act—not just into my writing but into things that are more important. Sharon Willis has also played a crucial part in helping me to understand what I wanted to write, and I am grateful to her for many other things besides. Tom Conley encouraged the project from the outset with his astute commentary, for which I thank him.

Introduction

Clint Eastwood stands over the supine and wounded body of a black man, pointing his trademark Magnum .44 at him and daring him to move for his gun. The camera gives a view from beneath Eastwood, almost from the point of view of the man now in his control. A viewer might register the characteristic sneer on Eastwood's lips, the brow furrowed almost vertically, those small and undemonstrative eyes, the general hardness of this lined and weathered face, the roughness of the material of his jacket. This is an image that has in a sense escaped from the film from which I take it (*Dirty Harry*) in the twenty years since that movie's release. It is a scene that might be said to epitomize Eastwood's presence—the kind of figure he cuts—in the realm of film images; certainly it epitomizes Harry Callahan, the character for which Eastwood is undoubtedly best known. The image has escaped into a realm of meanings beyond the realm of that particular film.

This book is to a large extent concerned with the way that such images have resonated in and with American culture and history during the last twenty or thirty years; it is concerned with the nature of the meanings that are circulated in public discourses and how those meanings are related to films, and with the question of how such meanings are related to the cultures that we inhabit in North America. I shall be concentrating on Eastwood and his films in part because of their sheer popularity and thus their significant role in these cultural discourses. By popularity, I do not just mean that a lot of people pay to see his films—though, of course, it is the case that over the last thirty years few if any of the cultural products of Hollywood have been so well and so consistently patronized by filmgoers. But equally (or more), I am pointing out that the films and, indeed, the man himself are the object of almost incessant attention from other parts of the culture: Eastwood and his films are constantly taken up in television, magazines, newspapers, everyday conversation, even in classrooms, and thence constitute part of what we might call the ongoing conversations that our cultures hold with themselves. Those conversations help construct the meanings by which and in which people—"we," as the multifarious agents in those cultures—actually live.

So it is to the circulation and exchange of such meanings and to specific possible ways of acting in and understanding the social world in the United States over the last quarter of a century that this book mainly addresses itself. If it seems at first blush that I shall therefore be concentrating on the films' reception at the expense of their production, that is not quite the case—even if, throughout, I shall certainly be trying not to forget that movies and movie stars are particular kinds of commodity, produced for profit under the particular conditions of a specifiable stage in the history of U.S. capitalism. But this does not imply by any means a lack of emphasis on the films themselves, which have their own unique strategies and modes for the production and circulation of meanings. Indeed, part of my task here will be to try to forge a way of talking and theorizing about the social relations of Hollywood production without ignoring the films as individual texts that call for or provoke (in me, certainly) specific acts of interpretation. Much more will be suggested about these underlying strategies and assumptions in the course of my discussions, and I shall be trying to do more than just hint as I go along at what I think is at stake in adopting any of them. At this point I want only to comment upon the organization of the book and to explain a few of the terms that I use in it.

Fundamentally, the book is not highly organized in any traditional academic mode. It does, however, follow a route that I can only call a narrative—a route and a narrative that are partly historical and/or chronological and partly dictated by questions of genre; there are sections on, for instance, the "Dirty Harry" movies, and these sections appear after a discussion of westerns only because Eastwood first became prominent in the Hollywood industry and in the cultures at large because of his westerns. At the same time, I shall be mixing up the chronological frames and genre patterns, when necessary, in the hope of producing a feasible narrative—which is a construct made from what are inevitably my own fantasies of Eastwood's career. Also—and helping me to disorganize a little further—I shall be allowing myself the license to digress from particular discussion of the films and their meanings into issues that might appear to have little immediate relevance. It is probably true that my motives in all this are partly loutish ones, the desire to stage a petty rebellion against the rather oppressive notion of the well-organized academic book. At the same time I shall be trying to make something textually interesting and effective out of my refusal of that notion, and something also that textually signals the complexity and multiplicity of the issues that I think watching any film can evoke.

In fact, part of the refusal of the form of the academic book has been encouraged by the simple fact that, while I was writing it and talking about it, many people who are not academics expressed a certain degree of interest in it. I often had the sense that their interest was as much a product of surprise as anything else: surprise that the apparently highbrow immovable object that the intellectual is often assumed to be should deliberately attempt to meet the irresistible force of the determinedly popular (and even populist) work that Eastwood is understood to produce. In hearing that kind of interest and surprise I gained a lot of clues about what I could be writing and how. At the same time, the book tries to engage a whole range of issues that arise in the academic study of film and popular culture, even while I deal unequally with Eastwood's films (that is, some are barely mentioned, while others are dealt with at length). Among the results of these strategies is that there will be excursions into what might appear to be the most abstruse of theoretical discussions and the most fanciful of interpretative flights. I cannot apologize enough to readers who will find this mixing of registers, emphases, and concerns obnoxious; I can only hope that they will ultimately feel that at least I do it with a modicum of grace and poise.

I hope too that readers will recognize that I have tried to write the book in such a way that those who might ordinarily suspect or disdain the academic (as I think Eastwood himself does) will still be able to read it with some enjoyment and profit, and certainly without great difficulty. At the same time, there are some terms that I use consistently that might need some explanation in advance, and I hope that my discussing some of them in the next few paragraphs will be helpful.

Part of the intellectual interest I had in writing the book derived from a sense that media scholarship and its theoretical arms have in recent years become unable to deal convincingly with the sustained body of work of any figure like Clint Eastwood—that is, a popular and highly successful single figure or personality in the business of producing movies. There are, of course, many journalistic and popular accounts of the careers of such people (including several on Eastwood himself, which I deploy at various moments in this book). But most such accounts tend to assume that the achievements, failures, meanings, or nature of the work can be explained by reference to that individual as their punctual origin. This is the everyday version of the so-called auteur theory, which posits that individual workers in the film industry generate a body of work that in various ways is symptomatic of and expressive of their personality. Film theory has long since rejected the auteur theory as a working device, and I think rightly. At the same time, nothing has replaced this theory as a way of enabling the consideration of a body of work that is discursively attached to a particular name and popularly understood to "belong" to that name. This book is, at one level, an attempt to see what can be done with such a body of work and its cultural designations without replicating the mistakes of auteur criticism. Thus the term *auteur* is more or less a negative one in this book, even though I am trying to give a narrative of the career and work of one "name."

I do not, of course, deny that Eastwood as producer and director of and actor in a broad range of films has agency in their making, nor that he might have had particular aims, intentions, and even agendas. Rather, I am interested in the way that what are taken in an everyday fashion to be "his" utterances are articulated with other discourses and ideologies. These are what I call the presignified discursive formations that constitute the availabilities and possibilities of—the freedoms and constraints upon—any of "Eastwood's" utterances. Glimpsed as the always complex and overdetermined relation of a cultural artifact to the culture that it inhabits, these discourses depend upon what I call, drawing on Gérard Genette (1969) and Tzvetan Todorov (1977), cinematic and cultural codes of verisimilitude. That is, the discourses of film, no more nor less than the discourses of the broader cultures, are limited—and limit themselves—as to what can be said or uttered. That those limitations change and alter over time is of course a historical question, and thence I refer occasionally to the notion that a particular film or utterance lives among cotextual histories. I mean by that phrase the ensemble of ever-shifting discursive possibilities that cohabit with any particular text in a given culture at a specific moment. For me cotextual histories implicate the processes of both the production and the reception of a text or utterance.

The specificity and variability of the cotextual histories of any text render that text interpretable, of course, and usable by its readers—and obviously not just by its academic reader but by popular audiences, too. Current film and cultural criticism and theory appear to me (even if I am being a little reductive in saying this) to want to celebrate an almost limitless freedom of interpretation, use, and pleasure on the part of audiences when faced with a text. Especially prized by many contemporary critics is the process whereby audiences transform or refunction a text in aid of what are assumed to be their own resistant uses and pleasures. This moment or movement in criticism has, I think, many problems attendant upon it—some of them empirical ones. Fundamentally it can be seen as a reaction against some earlier forms of cultural criticism that are understood to posit spectators as helpless dupes in front of texts, or as unknowing victims of the capitalist system, which produces commodities for entertainment and pleasure. Particularly demonized from among those older forms of cultural criticism are the Frankfurt School theorists; Theodor Adorno, especially, seems to me to be badly understood in this regard—not to mention that his work is often read with little attention, if at all. While I would not try to elide the fact that audiences use, take pleasure in, and sometimes resist the commodity texts of capitalism (indeed, some of my own uses, pleasures, and resistances are openly at play in this book), I cannot yet imagine that one can ignore their ideological function, nor underestimate, as Adorno puts it, the culture industry's mode of proclaiming: "You shall conform, without instruction as to what; conform to that which exists anyway, and to that which everyone thinks anyway as a reflex of its power and omnipresence" (1990, 133).

What I suggest and try to demonstrate throughout this book is the ultimately rather simple proposition that this function of the culture industry is always dialectically bound up with audience reaction and that, even if there is no predictable transcendent moment in that dialectic, a film or any other kind of cultural text directs a certain set of possibilities toward its readers. Thus I often stress what I call the intendment of the text—the semiotic and ideological pressure that it puts on its readers to interpret it in a particular and circumscribed way. *Intendment* is, of course, a word drawn from legal discourse, and I sometimes want to exploit the force of that origin. At other moments I refer to what the text profers. The word *profer* is a conflation of—or perhaps a pun on—the English words "offer" and "prefer" and the French word *proférer*—to utter. The conflation suggests, then, that the text offers the reader preferred meanings. The text cannot, of course, *guarantee* that those meanings will be recognized or taken up, but at the same time, it seems to me that readers are unlikely to be able to ignore their proferring, or their intendment, in most instances (see Smith 1988a, especially chap. 2).

The channels by which a text's proferrings or intendments are relayed are not confined to the text itself. I make use throughout of the term *tributary media* to point to the discursive arenas whereby the Hollywood text is, in effect, advertised and amplified, where its meanings are explicated and reinforced, for viewers and potential viewers. Among the tributary media I include particularly television and journalism and their functions as what we call "reviewers" of texts that Hollywood has produced. It becomes daily more and more inescapable that many television programs (such as *Entertainment Tonight*) and many media-oriented magazines (like *Movieline*), as well as the traditional newspaper and magazine practice of film reviewing, are all part of the Hollywood text. Similarly, the media attention given to stars in interviews, features, gossip columns, and so on, is in effect a service to the Hollywood industry that, even if it is not always directly paid for by the industry, disseminates the intendments of both particular texts and the industry in general. What used to be thought of as the critical function of the tributary media is really at this point risibly small, but in any case I would argue that that function scarcely ever exceeds the service (or tributary) function of those media.

One of the many marks of the compliance of the tributary media with the aims of the Hollywood industry is their general acceptance of particular aesthetic ideologies—for instance, their insistence on dividing "entertainment" from "art," or their abiding by and even attempting to enforce codes of both cinematic and cultural verisimilitude in terms of what is and is not permitted to be uttered in the realms of politics, sexuality, violence, and so on. Perhaps the most important area of compliance or complicity is around an aesthetic of "realism." Throughout popular and journalistic discourses on film there runs an assumption that a film can or should be judged in part by assessing its proximity to some putative set of likelihoods, resemblances, and believabilities; an assumption, that is, that a film should be verisimilitudinous.

There are many philosophical and aesthetic—not to mention political—questions and criticisms that can be brought to bear around this assumption, and some of them will emerge through the course of the book. But for the moment I want to underscore my own assumption that a cultural demand for—and a concomitant expectation of—a loosely defined "realism" in a film is met by the product in particular ways, which are not simply diegetic but also narrational. The "world" that a particular film will assume and set up, make to look real, believable, and readily available for its audience's comprehension is what I call its diegetic world, the world in which its story will be told. Indeed, the diegetic construction that a popular film will offer an audience is a precondition for its narrative to make sense or become intelligible. But I will be suggesting throughout that narratives themselves—the stories constructed and proferred within given diegetic frames—are also devices of verisimilitude. In other words, it is not just the superficial "realism" of a film's diegetic construction that construes that film's verisimilitude, but also the narrative itself.

Subaltern Spaghetti

Sergio Leone's trilogy of so-called spaghetti westerns—*A Fistful of Dollars* (1964), *For a Few Dollars More* (1965), and *The Good, the Bad, and the Ugly* (1966)—whatever their merits as movies, constitute an undoubtedly important and almost unique moment in the history of Hollywood cinema. Even though they were financed primarily by European capital, were shot in Italy's Cinecittà studios and on location in Spain, and used a mostly Italian work force, they have had a significant impact on the shape, style, and potentials of American movies ever since. Their importance is partly a function of the fact that they are the best-known instances of the production of what has been the only major and sustained revision of that central Hollywood movie genre, the western, that has ever been undertaken outside Hollywood and largely without its capital. These movies are also, of course, what constitute not so much the start of Clint Eastwood's career (which dates back to 1955 and includes small parts in a number of minor movies, as well as a long regular stint in the television series *Rawhide*),[1] but certainly the beginning of his status as a major international star.

Spaghetti westerns, made not just by Leone but by many other Italian directors in the 1960s, also mark the full-fledged emergence of Italian cinema onto the international commercial market after World War II. The Italian film industry had for all intents and purposes been taken over by U.S. concerns almost immediately after World War II: in 1946 alone the Italian domestic market had been flooded by something like six hundred American movies (Guback, 24). Despite several attempts between the war and the early sixties on the part of the

Italian industry and government to curb this influx, and despite the various legal restrictions that were placed on the use in Italy and remittance to the United States of American capital in those years, the staple product on the Italian movie market remained the American one.

Domestic Italian movie production did not cease, of course, and indeed a huge number of films have been made in Italy since the war, rising to an average of two hundred a year in the sixties (Frayling, xiii). But often these movies were made with and by American directors, actors, and workers; they regularly used American production money that could not be readily remitted back to the United States because of postwar currency and trade restrictions or that had been variously channeled through European-based production companies. It was a common experience for Italian film workers, like Leone himself, to have labored on many movies, only to have their work subsumed under the name of someone else for purpose of export, or credited only under pseudonyms in an attempt to persuade European audiences that these were "authentic" American movies. This happened to Leone when he apparently directed *Sodom and Gomorrah* (1962), a film that was credited in the United States to the director Robert Aldrich. Leone in fact claims to have worked as assistant director on nearly sixty films before he made his first feature, *A Fistful of Dollars* (Cumbow, x)—and that movie too was initially credited under the pseudonym Bob Robertson in order to make it more salable in the Italian and European markets.

A Fistful of Dollars was by no means the first Italian western produced under these conditions: Bondanella suggests that a couple of dozen westerns had been made at Cinecittà before Leone started making that movie in 1963 (253). It is not exactly clear why westerns became the genre of choice, or why they should have been so successfully manufactured in the Italian context. One explanation of their preeminence is offered by Bondanella, who claims that the American production system was simply unable to meet the market demand for westerns during a period of relative retrenchment and economic difficulty in Hollywood (254). This explanation seems likely to be wrong. Most histories of the western will point to a decline in its production in the 1950s that far exceeds the general Hollywood trend of slumping production: "As a percentage of all films made [westerns] went from 27 percent in 1953 to a mere 9 percent in

1963" (Buscombe, 48). And despite a late 1950s boom in westerns on television, the declining fortune of movie westerns has continued into the 1990s, with only a very few being produced or becoming successful in the American market.

In other words, the western's central role in American moviemaking has steadily been reduced since the 1950s, and the status of audience demand for westerns is highly questionable. Thus a more likely explanation than Bondanella's for the offshore production of westerns in the 1960s is Hollywood's eagerness to maintain a genre that, even while becoming less popular in the United States and while facing too stiff a competition from television, nonetheless remained an important commodity on the world market. Its importance was not just economic, but also symbolic: that is, outside North America the western remained in the 1950s and 1960s—and to an extent still remains—the very epitome of American filmmaking for many audiences, and also corresponded to the imaginary that world audiences had or have of America.

The relative cheapness and efficiency of producing westerns for non-American audiences from within the solid infrastructure of the Italian industry could only have been enticing to American producers. They would have had the additional incentive of thereby finding a way to deploy the American capital that was still often trapped in Europe's postwar economies, and a not irrelevant factor might also have been the ready availability of state guarantees and subsidies in Italy, especially after 1965 (see Guback, 150-52). Also, the Italian industry was practiced at the cheap production of popular movies for both European and non-European markets, specializing in epics based on Greek and Roman mythology or Biblical stories, action espionage movies, and a brand of horror movie. The industry was additionally well placed in that many of its workers had served as apprentices to a variety of American filmmakers, as Leone had.

In this context where the hegemony of American interests had been consistently powerful over the years since World War II, and where the workers in the Italian industry had always had their work constrained by the models of American production, it is scarcely surprising that in their adoption of westerns—perhaps the quintessential American genre—Italian filmmakers effected changes that can be read as a certain kind of resistance to their masters. At one level the spaghetti western must be understood through its status as a product of a dependent economy, one engaged in a day-to-day struggle to accommodate not only the economic but also the cultural consequences of military defeat in World War II and of subsequent American regulation of markets. When the spaghetti westerns were released in the United States, critics (though not so much audiences, as will be seen later) were exceptionally disparaging, by and large thinking of them as "cold blooded attempts at sterile emulation" (quoted in Frayling, 121).[2] Yet in the context I have sketched out, the project of emulation might not accurately describe what the filmmakers were doing. Rather, the particular kinds of operation done on the American western by the spaghettis might best be grasped as the response—or, more strongly, the riposte—to colonizing models on the part of what can effectively be called a subaltern culture (that is, a culture whose structures and formations on many important levels are provoked by and forged in the shadow of a more dominant culture).

One way in which the subaltern's riposte can be made is by a cheapening of the product in various ways. Economic "cheapness" is not, of course, the only aspect in which this riposte can be seen, though it is certainly an important aspect. In the instance of the spaghettis, when the American critics pronounce them "inauthentic," their view focuses less upon the economic aspect and more primarily upon exactly those features of the movies that are the *consequences* of the system of cheap offshore production that American capital had instituted: the displaced locations in Spain, different standards and registers of acting, and generally low production values in sound recording and image quality. At the level of plot and action, the critics found the spaghettis to be intolerable mutations of the real American thing and often resorted to the idea that these movies could only be parodies. However, while there may well be an element of parody in the spaghettis, it is perhaps just as important to grasp them as deliberate transformations—rather than inept mutations—of the Hollywood western.

The transformations that Leone's trilogy operates upon the genre of the western are many and exist at several different registers. First of all, simply as non-American products that garner worldwide audiences and make radical adjustments to a crucial American genre, they already thereby stand as a kind of challenge to the American film industry. The three Leone films were indeed not distributed in the

United States until several years after the appearance of *Fistful*, a delay that cannot be entirely explained by the copyright difficulties surrounding the relation of *Fistful* to Akira Kurosawa's movie, *Yojimbo* (see Frayling, 287). Perhaps the central problem for the American distributors was reflected in the kinds of reviews the films received in the U.S. press, which are mentioned above. The hostile reviews can be read as symptoms of a kind of protectionist xenophobia (and even racism) that the American media have scarcely ever shied away from in many contexts. They may equally be a reaction to an overt resistance in the product itself, a product that effectively interrogates the American industry's confidence in its sole ownership of the "rights" to one of its historically most privileged genres.

In some ways the subaltern appropriation of the western teaches a lesson about the relative complacency of the Hollywood industry in relation to that genre, to its significations, and to its supposedly quintessential Americanness. Despite the massive historical and economic significance of the western, Hollywood has chronically and more or less unquestioningly regarded it as a formula product. Leone himself suggests that American filmmakers "have never treated the West seriously. . . . It was this superficiality that struck and interested me" (quoted in Frayling, 94). It is not quite clear from this quotation what Leone might imagine it should mean to treat the West seriously, but his own resistance to the product of the western seems to be enacted by carrying the logic of the western to extremes: he exploits and intensifies the superficiality of the Hollywood treatment of the West by making his films both closer to the *vraisemblable* of the West and also more distant. The films are closer in ways that I will discuss later, such as in their depiction of historical elements that had hitherto usually been missing from the Hollywood product (e.g., the Mexican/Spanish constituents of the West, the presence of bounty hunters, and so on); Leone also claims that they are more historically "accurate" than Hollywood films.[3] Yet they are more distant in terms, for instance, of their extreme and almost cartoonish violence, or in their deployment of references to European heroic figures like Ulysses and Hercules. Again this is a procedure that is reminiscent of the way in which subaltern or colonial agents will not only lionize the American product or artifact but also at the same time turn it to different signifying ends and social functions within their own cultural systems.

Not only that, but the ease and economy with which the Italian films work changes on the western and make themselves popular and successful underscore a certain crisis in the American film industry in the 1960s, which Leone exploits. That crisis is a complex one, which, at its simplest level, marks the response of the industry to its somewhat lean years in the late fifties and its conscious attempt to construct a new American cinema. Suffering the collapse of the studio system, the rise of the package unit system, and the competition of television, the industry reformulated its practices in the sixties, resulting in the rise of a new kind of auteur system in the "New Hollywood."[4]

Filmmakers like Leone play an important role in this crisis for many reasons, but not least because their mode of economical filmmaking stands against the tendency of Hollywood to spend increasingly large amounts of money on the always uncertain and speculative production of blockbusters. Leone himself is again an interesting commentator here. Reflecting on his apprenticeship with American directors, he says, "I cannot say that working with the great American directors was a dazzling experience: for one thing the Italians I worked with were old professionals who knew their job very well; for another, it is easy to make films as the American directors do, if you have vast budgets, kilometres of film footage, several cameras, and several crews who often do all the hard work" (quoted in Frayling, 100).

A more economical mode of making films is derived from this kind of insight, and is later to have significant effect on the films of Eastwood, too. As we shall see in a later section, Eastwood is to become renowned within the American industry for his ability to make highly successful movies relatively cheaply and always at least within budget. Eastwood's career as a director and producer begins within a few years of the success of the trilogy and follows his experience in several international productions that he perceived as wasteful and uneconomical (i.e., *Where Eagles Dare*, *Paint Your Wagon*, and *Kelly's Heroes*). At the same time as he was participating in such high-budget movies, he was experiencing the opposite kind of production by acting in several low-budget, cost-conscious movies (such as *Hang 'em High*), especially those directed by Don Siegel (*Coogan's Bluff*, *Two Mules for Sister Sara*, *The Beguiled*, and finally *Dirty Harry*). Such movies as these constitute as it were the underbelly of the carefully contrived star-director system of the New Hollywood and its connivance with an increasingly large "art movie" market. That is, these movies are seen as merely the *popular* counterpart of Hollywood's movement toward redefining itself; given that the New Hollywood constitutes on the part of the industry and the tributary media an aspiration toward an American "art" cinema, based on a handful of directors elevated to the condition of "auteurs," it is perhaps not all that surprising that these movies rarely get mentioned in accounts of that part of Hollywood history.[5]

Frayling makes a rather substantial list of the referential elements that Leone's trilogy foregrounds, which are by and large neglected ones in classic Hollywood narratives and which help these movies displace the traditional signifying nexus of Hollywood westerns. In several senses this displacement is quite literal: the offshore nature of production and the on-location shooting in Spain rather than in the United States, for example. But equally, as Frayling remarks, they tend to foreground "aspects of American history in which Hollywood had rarely shown interest" (127). Primarily of interest here is the emphasis on the place in the western's culture of Mexican and Hispanic elements and histories. The displacement of the Hollywood history begins with a displacement of its geography or topography, as the southwest frontier and territory across the border into Mexico become the locale of choice for Leone's version of the western.

These relocations are epitomized perhaps by the tiny collection of little whitewashed mud buildings and the narrow alleyways of Agua Caliente in *Few Dollars*, and can be easily contrasted to the collections of wooden buildings and wide-open main streets that have become the authorized version of the western town through countless Hollywood movies. Beyond these tiny towns, the landscapes of Leone's films are more or less desert and deserted; these locations contrast with the landscapes punctuated by glorious natural monuments (Monument Valley being the type here), mountains, hills, and valleys that provide the site of Hollywood's West. The whitewashed cinematography of Leone's landscapes replaces (or resists) the harder hues of the standard Hollywood western.

These Hispanic towns and desert places become the stage for dramas in which the presence of Mexican and Hispanic culture is fundamental. This emphasis is announced in the first frames of *Fistful*, where No Name rides into the town. Here, as elsewhere in the trilogy, the culture is also marked by its religious signs. In *Fistful* the religiosity is foregrounded by No Name's active sympathy for the victimized Hispanic family, whose wife, Marisol, is kept as the property of the Rojas, separated from her husband and young son. As an ordinary version of the holy family, they are thrown into conflict with the independent caudillo regime of the Rojas and are finally liberated by No Name. The organizational system of the Hispanic lands offered in the trilogy is not quite the full-blown *caudillaje* of Latin American culture, but it is similar, giving not only a sense of the nature and origin of the power wielded by the Rojas family or Indio's outlaw gang in *Few Dollars*, but also and more simply a description of the quasi feudalism of the southwestern frontier, by which backdrop the lawlessness of the protagonists becomes motivated.[6]

The autochthonous cultural history of this kind of feudalistic arrangement is mixed with the Hispanic cult of Catholicism, and produces a novel locale in which the dramas of the western plots will be played out, but in a now necessarily quite unfamiliar form. For Hollywood, the social organization of the American West ideally bears no relation to autochthonous culture but only to a liberal Northern European paradigm of civic life; equally, the religious guide for that kind of organization is less the Catholic church than the spirit of Protestantism. Occasionally the history of the western has allowed itself an alternative to this liberal-Protestant tradition when it has depicted the supposedly mystic and pantheistic tradition of Native Americans, but generally speaking the only possible civilizing force for Hollywood's West has been this particular strand of the European tradition: thus Leone's depiction of an alternative and competing tradition is almost literally a sacrilegious intervention.

Leone's extended treatment of a Hispanicized West and of Mexican culture and characters, then, constitutes one aspect of his resistance to the American western, and this resistance at what might be thought of as the level of historical verisimilitude is intimately related to the changes in the standard western narratives that Leone effects. By and large the American product has chronically been confined to two kinds of situation: first, where the cowboy hero rides in to adjudicate an internal conflict between various elements of the liberal-Protestant civilizing force (often settlers pitted against big business)—a conflict that has to be settled by his applying the principles of natural rather than civic justice; or second, where the civilizing force is set the task of taming the wilderness and its native peoples. Leone's movies can be said to take one or the other of two approaches in relation to those standard situations. Either they can be understood as turning the first situation of internal conflict into a much broader conflict of cultures, by recalling the effective silencing of Hispanic culture by the Anglo culture; or—and perhaps at the same time—his movies can be seen as redefining the "other" for the Anglo culture so that, instead of Indians,[7] the competing force becomes the bedrock Hispanic culture. Indeed, there is an almost complete absence of Indians in the trilogy; symptomatically, the Hispanic character Tuco in *Good, Bad, Ugly* is called upon to underscore this absence when, testing out guns in a store that he is about to rob, he fires at and destroys three wooden Indians, the only representations of Native Americans to appear in these movies.

Whether one reads Leone's trilogy in the first or second way, or both at once, it is clear that he has worked to effect a radical shift in the paradigms of the western. One consequence of this shift is simply the visual preeminence of Hispanic characters in the trilogy. Frayling explains this emphasis in part by suggesting that the peon figure might reflect the Italian cinema's interest in its third-world market (57). While this is probably correct, nonetheless one can only wonder what audiences in those markets might have thought about the fate of such characters. That is, the simple underscoring of the Hispanic culture and presence by no means amounts to a proposition of its dominance; Rojas and Indio are both defeated and killed by the white man in ways that are quite familiar and predictable; Tuco, although not killed, is controlled, humiliated, and finally abandoned by the aptly named Blondie. Nonetheless, the centrality of the Rojas family and Indio and his gang underscores the transformations that Leone makes. While those characters might still play roles that are in many ways familiar (Rojas as the metonym for an "Indian" chief, Indio as the equivalent of the leader of some band of outlaws), Tuco in *Good, Bad, Ugly* is a spectacularly radical novelty, and the narrative fate of these characters does not totally vitiate the way in which Leone makes them take center stage.

In all of these ways, then, Leone's movies are posed against the idea of the westerns that has prevailed both before and after them. But his transformations are probably most commonly understood at other levels. That is, these movies have often been taken as significant interventions into the history of the western in terms of their visual style or their mise-en-scène, or in terms of their plot structures and their view of the western hero. Clint Eastwood's construction and development as a star is heavily dependent on these shifts, and in many ways both his acting career and his directorial style have for nearly thirty years been indelibly marked by Leone's films.

At the simplest level the transmutation of the classic western plot is accompanied by a major alteration in the figure of the hero-protagonist. Much has been made of how the spaghettis are part of a general move in the 1960s toward a debunking of various heroic myths and figures in cinema, where the "white hat" cowboy of traditional Hollywood turns into an antihero, working less for the community than for himself, rendering his violence less acceptably motivated and less righteous than in previous movies. The shift is emblematized in the making of the trilogy by Leone's decision to cast as his amoral antihero precisely a figure whose previous career has been largely taken up in playing a quite ordinary and likeable cowboy, Rowdy in *Rawhide*, who, despite his name, is not especially rowdy. Leone's account of his intentions in casting Eastwood in this way claims that it was the fact that Eastwood himself is "slow, calm, rather like a cat" (quoted in Frayling, 146) that helped forge the performance in the trilogy, but he also suggests that the transformation of the Rowdy character, who was "a little sophisticated, a little light," was part of his aim. He forces the same kind of transformation later with the all-American star, Henry Fonda, in *Once upon a Time in the West*, by turning him into an amoral contract killer—apparently delighting in seeing the figure whom he identified with Abraham Lincoln turned into one of the ambiguous heroes of the spaghettis.

But ultimately it is Eastwood himself who most readily stands for the spaghetti westerns, and this is the result of the radically subversive manner of Leone's directorial work. In some ways what is interesting about the way Eastwood is deployed is not so much the production of an antihero, but the production of a particular kind of masculinity, which Eastwood as actor lives with for the rest of his career. Effectively what Leone does to the standard hero of the western is to turn his self-sufficient and calm toughness into a kind of ritualized, stylized, and heavily gestured masculinity (about which more will be said later in this book). The formality of Leone's work underscores this ritualism: Leone peppers his work with portentous close-ups of faces, costumes, and gestures that do not so much signify the internal qualities of the classic cowboy, the "real man" of the Hollywood imaginary, as construct instead a mere exterior, a purely physical demeanor that stands in for masculinity itself.

It is perhaps in *Good, Bad, Ugly* that this ritualizing is most prevalent. At the level of visual style, the film figures the repetitious lighting and relighting of Blondie's cheroot, fetishizes his ritual gun cleaning, and heavily foregrounds the tiny gestures of hands on guns. Also, at another level, the film reflects a slow forging of a bond between Tuco and Blondie by stressing their habitual giving to and taking from one another, their bond being most firmly sealed when Blondie gives Tuco a cheroot. In most instances the ritual significance is signaled by the use of close-ups that intervene into the action sequences of the films as a way of slowing them down and adding weight to them. They can also be extremely fetishizing shots, marked not so much by their significant content or their functional role, but by their slow consideration of some aspect of the male body. Perhaps the most fulfilled of the many such shots is at the climactic moment of *Good, Bad, Ugly* where Blondie, Tuco, and Angel Eyes set up for their three-way corrida duel. The camera closely regards Blondie as he places a stone (on which is supposed to be written the name of the grave they are all seeking) on the ground, and the shot lingers for several seconds over the slow movement of the hand to the ground. Directing himself, Eastwood replicates this kind of ritualism, which he learned from Leone. In *Outlaw Josey Wales*, for instance, Wales is constructed as a particular presence by the movie's stress on his repeated habits and tics. Particularly, there, his habit of repeating the same phrases in several different situations and his penchant for spitting out chewed tobacco bespeak two parts of his masculinity—his reticence in the face of emotional situations and his ruggedness.

This ritualizing of the protagonist's presence works in tandem in the trilogy with Leone's innovative use of close-ups and extreme close-ups to destroy any sense of the characters' interiority. The celebrated sequences of extreme close-ups, deployed especially in climactic scenes of confrontation such as the corrida duel at the end of *Good, Bad, Ugly* and the gunfight between No Name and Rojas at the end of *Fistful*, function first as intensifications and finally as elisions of the Hollywood method for narrativizing reactions. Leone replaces the classic shot/reverse-shot sequences by an equally formalized sequence of frontal facial shots—sometimes focusing in very tightly on just the eyes—which altogether belie the tradition of reaction shots. That is, the reactions proferred by these sequences are utterly minimal. Any dramatic tension generated here derives, indeed, from the fact that the Eastwood figure never shows any reaction at all to the situation, while his lack of emotion is significant only in relation to the tiniest registrations of agitation on the part of his adversaries. That is, the mark of a loser is any sign of anxiety in these close-ups; Eastwood, always the winner, has to do no more than remain impassive.

Leone has claimed that his use of close-ups is a result of his rejection of his apprenticeship with American directors: "I was at the side of directors who applied all the rules. . . . I reacted against all that." Yet he also rather strangely suggests that "close-ups in my films are always the expression of an emotion. . . . I'm seeking, first and foremost, the relevant emotion" (Simsolo 1973, 30). It is difficult to see how Leone's claim that he is after the emotion is carried through. Most of the close-ups are of static and impassive faces; their significance is often simply the ugliness and idiosyncrasy of the faces. Otherwise, when the faces move it is a sign of weakness and imminent defeat. So emotion is scarcely the issue, but rather this revision of Hollywood helps Leone subtract from the interiority of character, offering instead the placid and almost spectral presence that finds its ideal owner in the figure and face of Clint Eastwood.

This ritualized depiction of the protagonist has the effect of structuring a presence rather than a fully developed character in the classic sense. Leone has in fact said of Eastwood in this regard, "I looked at him and I didn't see any character . . . just a physical figure" (quoted in Cumbow, 154). His laconic and even animal aura is emphasized by the fact that relatively few words come from his mouth; those that do are delivered flatly and almost sotto voce. Critics, both at the time and since, seem never to have been especially impressed or convinced by the way Eastwood comes across in this format, and indeed the reputation of his acting has never been good. Eastwood's attempts in these films to be "just a physical figure" have encouraged the view that he is in a sense a nonactor.

What it would mean for a movie actor to be called a nonactor and how Eastwood himself both performs and transforms this in later movies are issues that will be taken up in later sections. For the moment, it can be said that the function of this presence is to articulate itself to the dominance of the white protagonist over the "native" surroundings and characters, while at the same time rarely allowing that white dominance to lay claim to the moral superiority that it accrues to itself in other westerns. Here the brooding and tutelary presence of Eastwood's white protagonists is offered as a threatening kind of armory of physical and mental acumen ready to be unleashed on any target. It might not be going too far to say that Leone's resistance to Hollywood in this sense constitutes exactly a critique of the white dominance that is fostered and celebrated in other westerns. The emptying out of the moral codes of the western hero and their replacement by a simple powerful presence working for its own selfish ends is openly insulting to the American tradition; it at least, as Frayling says, "conflicted with the implicit moral message audiences expected from the classic western formula" (256).

In these and many other respects the Leone movies in which Eastwood stars effect a huge change in what audiences will watch under the heading "western." The most remarkable thing about their popularity in America as elsewhere (a popularity that seems to be abiding, to judge by their popularity in video stores and their almost perpetual presence on television) is that at the same time they counter generic expectations, refuse the "moral messages" of which Frayling speaks, and in general stand as a kind of resistance to and questioning of this crucial Hollywood genre. Indeed, it would not be an exaggeration to say that they equally question the integrity and the consistency of the imaginary that American culture has chronically constructed around the western and its concomitant ideologies.

Interestingly enough, it is a filmmaker from a subordinate economy, film industry, and culture who makes these interventions. Leone's personal history has something to do with this, of course. As he himself explains:

> In my childhood, America was like a religion. . . . I dreamed of the wide open spaces . . . the great expanses of desert, the extraordinary melting pot. . . . The long, straight roads . . . which begin nowhere, and end nowhere, for their function is to cross the

> whole continent. Then real-life Americans abruptly entered my life—in jeeps—and upset all my dreams. . . . They were no longer the Americans of the West. They were soldiers . . . materialist, possessive, keen on pleasures and earthly goods. . . . I could see nothing that I had seen in Hemingway, Dos Passos or Chandler. . . . Nothing—or almost nothing—of the great prairies, or of the demigods of my childhood. (Quoted in Frayling, 65)

But Leone's interventions and their subsequent effect on Hollywood and, particularly, on the career of Clint Eastwood are not simply the effects and results of measuring a personalized myth of America against some version of reality. His recollections of the soldiers shattering his dream of America must be added to many other factors—including his own dissatisfied view of the American filmmakers—to help explain his invention of a new western style. If his movies constitute, as Frayling has suggested, a "critical cinema," they are equally importantly born from a particular cultural and economic context where what I have been calling a resistance to the American product is simultaneously a resistance to American hegemony in all spheres.

The resistance that Leone mounts to Hollywood westerns is in fact pushed further—or at least, is made more overtly a political gesture—in later spaghettis with other directors and writers. Leone's resistance is, by the above account, an economic and cultural one that in most ordinary senses refuses to actually name an overt political position. In later spaghettis, however, the transformation of the American western comes to be attached to a rhetoric of left-wing politics. It is this space that Leone has opened up for the spaghettis by cracking the generic codes that had hitherto existed almost unquestioned in Hollywood products. The naming of a brand of political commitment that has been effectively removed from the Hollywood product (if indeed it was ever there) becomes clearer in movies such as *A Bullet for the General* (directed by Damiano Damiani, 1967) or *Compañeros* (directed by Sergio Corbucci, 1970), where the allegorical reading I have hinted at in Leone is made absolutely overt: that is, for example, such spaghettis use the "peon/gringo" conflict to comment upon the relationship between the South (the "Third World") and the United States—an allegorical commentary that had especial relevance at the time of the Vietnam War but that by no means limits its ambit to that conflict.

Leone's movies do not undertake the kind of overt anti-American and anti-imperialist commentary that films by Corbucci or Sergio Sollima, for example, do. Yet his work does have the considerable merit of deliberately debunking the moral superiority of the western hero by exposing the emptiness of his character and the egotism of his violence and by foregrounding the presence of the culture and the people who are his historical victims. They also simultaneously withhold from him the standard excuse for his violence: that is, the rationale that he is working for the best interests of the community. Leone's films remove, then, the rationalized motivations for the cowboy, which have always suggested that violence is something to be unproblematically and usually unreflexively engaged in as a result of the attempt by anticommunity forces to disrupt or encroach upon proper communities. Leone's protagonists ride off at the end of his movies leaving no community behind them, and thus what they dispense with is the Hollywood shibboleth that the violence of the gunfighter will lead to a reinvigoration and regeneration of community. Although this is an ideology that seems even now to guide the conduct of American life and foreign policy in addition to the plots of westerns, it is one that Leone overtly rejects when he describes the West—home of that ideology—as nothing more than the "reign of violence by violence" (quoted in Frayling, 135).

And yet these are movies that remain steadfastly at the stage of a critique of Hollywood's representations, without attempting to usher in any political message. So, for instance, while the Hollywood theme of the "civic responsibility" of the western hero is dismantled, it is not replaced by any other kind of political awareness. Thus in *Fistful*, No Name's actions appear to be guided by no civic sensibility. Throughout this movie No Name stands between a white family on one side, the Baxters, who are nominally the representatives of the law (Baxter is the town's ineffectual sheriff), and on the other side a Mexican family, the Rojas, and their entourage of lawlessness. He plays the two families off against each other, driven only by the profit motive and by a growing sense of personal vengefulness. At the end he specifically rejects the idea of playing a similar role poised between the Mexican and the American governments: "The Mexican government on one side and maybe the American government on the other, and me smack in the middle? Too dangerous." Any more generally political role for the man is thus evidently eschewed.

Similarly, although it is the case that Leone's movies bring back to the fore the Hispanic "other" in the West and Southwest, in that sense uncovering a part of the history of America that Hollywood has left not only unmythologized but actually unnoticed, the most overt political tendencies here are in fact quite compromised. In *Fistful*, the Rojas *caudillaje* is clearly proferred as a worse prospect than that of the Baxters having control; accordingly No Name's actions veer toward a favoritism for the gringo family. Indeed, on this and other levels the racism of the trilogy is quite marked. The leading Hispanic characters are presented in a wildly racist manner. Indio in *Few Dollars* is given as a psychopath, dopehead, and sadist, his manic laughter supplying a running accompaniment to the film's regular violence. Although Tuco in *Good, Bad, Ugly* survives his encounter with Blondie, in relation to the white man—who is, after all, embarked upon the same project of stealing Union gold—he is more overtly greedy, vicious, excitable, double-crossing, and dirty. Eli Wallach's role as Tuco calls upon him to produce an extended series of childish or hysterical tantrums, culminating appropriately in the final shot of the film, where, in mimicry almost of the boy Joey calling after his hero in *Shane*, he yells names across the landscape after Blondie who is riding away into the hills.

Each of these interventions into the Hollywood imaginary is, then, partial and indeed ambivalent. But in that regard they might be constitutive of what we could properly call a postmodern intervention. That is, I have tried to suggest here a small narrative: Hollywood's attachment to the fixities of its genres, and its confidence in the inviolability of its privileges in relation to those genres, is resisted as a result of the fact that, first of all, the product itself is, as it were, "dumped" on dependent markets, and that the production of the genre is handed over to the cheap productive facilities and labor attendant upon those markets. This sort of context, where the dependent economies first of all fetishize the American product and then, under the shadow of a disillusionment, transform it to their own uses, is a familiar one in what we sometimes call the postmodern global economy. The process is perhaps most interestingly illustrated in cinema by the movie *The Perfumed Nightmare* by the Filipino filmmaker Kidlat Tahimik; there the central, quasi-autobiographical character begins with abject fascination for America and its products, but slowly goes through a disillusionment caused by his insights into the cultural and economic imperialism of America. The film is exemplary in this context in that the process of its own production reflects the turning back of the American product on itself: the film was financed by the use of American gasoline credit cards (Tahimik, 1989).

While what I am calling the subaltern commodity often contains a critique of or a riposte to the dominant culture, it is not all that often that we see the product return in transformed condition to affect and alter production in America. But this is what I am suggesting has happened with the spaghetti westerns, whose return to America—unwanted as it might have been by the industry and by the critics, guardians of the industry's interests—constitutes a challenge and a resistance to the domestic industry, especially since the films proved so popular with American audiences. The ambivalence of Leone's view of the United States is related to this narrative, but even in that ambivalence we can see in operation a postmodernist assault on the settled midcentury modes of the dominant culture of Hollywood. Because Leone's movies differ from some of the other spaghettis in that his do not offer an overt oppositional politics, their reception is in a sense tolerated and even exploited. Yet the way in which the later spaghettis proceed to open up the political discourse that underpins Leone's transformations points to the danger inherent in this process for the domestic industry.

In part because of their popular reception these movies have had an immense and complex effect on film production in the United States. Not the least aspect of their importance is their responsibility for the rise of Clint Eastwood to major stardom; equally, they bring up difficult questions for an industry that had hitherto appeared relatively comfortable with its working definition of its privileged genre, the western. In the next sections I will first try to show the cultural importance of those questions about genre, and then examine the process by which Eastwood himself—in some sense a collaborator in Leone's moment of resistance because of his starring role—progressively disavows that resistance while still exploiting certain of its effects.

Genre

The spaghetti westerns stretch to the limits what Steve Neale calls "generic verisimilitude" (1990, 47). That is, their relation to the texts that together are commonly understood to constitute the genre of westerns is a relation of resistance and in a way dissent: they *are* westerns, but unexpected ones, and to judge by their critical reception, which I have mentioned before, they are ones that are unwanted in some respects. And yet the fate of westerns in the years following the American success of the spaghettis is in many ways dependent upon the nature of these very movies. In the following section I will look at the way in which Eastwood's westerns in particular constitute a particular formation of response to them. For now, it might be as well to suggest something of the historical and theoretical confusion that occurs around the notion of genre, in order to point out the relation of genre to the cultural and social imaginaries which give rise to it and to which it contributes.

In the success of the spaghettis we might see an instance of what the Russian Formalist, Viktor Shklovsky discerns as a frequent event in the life of a genre. That is, Shklovsky maintains (at least in relation to literary genres) that genres are regularly shifted, altered, and renewed through the displacement of dominant instances by what he calls their "junior branch" (Erlich, 260). The junior branch is often constituted in texts that do not display an absolute conformity to codes of generic or cultural verisimilitude (that is, to broadly defined cultural standards of what constitutes the real, the likely, the possible, and so on). These are texts that are frequently of largely popular appeal or that emerge from a nonsanctioned arena of culture: clearly this is the case with the spaghettis, whose unacceptability to the critical guardians in the tributary media and whose popularity with general audiences almost epitomize the social relations of a genre's "junior branch."

According to the Formalists, such texts often come to reanimate a genre that is in the process of losing or has already lost its cultural effectivity. As with the western, effectivity and cultural significance can be lost after much repetition of standardized formulae and codes. This is especially the case with the production of cinema, where generic conventions, formulae, and codes are called upon to bear the weight of massive repetition. In addition to that repetition, there is the fact that genres as it were migrate; that is, particular structures and even fundamental tropes of an established genre can be "disguised," to use Robert Ray's term, by being deployed in the absence of some other signal generic factors. For instance, Ray cites *Casablanca* as a disguised western because its protagonist replicates the role of a western hero and the narrative structure mimes familiar westerns, even while the movie's diegetic world has been displaced from the nineteenth-century American West to Morocco in World War II (Ray, 1985).

Ray's notion of disguised genres does as much as anything to point up the fact that genre lives not by repetition alone; rather it subsists, as does the whole of Hollywood production, in a dialectic of repetition and difference. That is, the Hollywood product must not be simply or only a repetition but must also ring some discernible changes on previous products. Product differentiation is in this sense perhaps more crucial an element in the film industry than in any other, while at the same time the industry depends utterly upon the recognition of any product as appropriate and as belonging—as, finally, *not* different. This tension leads to a situation in which what Neale calls "regulated difference, contained variety, pre-sold expectations" (1990, 64) is the order of the day.

In an early essay on genre Neale has noted how those expectations are themselves "double" for both audiences and for the professionals who make and sell the product: "As far as genre is concerned, expectations exist both to be satisfied, and, also, to be redefined. There is thus, so to speak, a double layer of expectation. One level concerns the meeting of a set of basic conventional requirements, the other concerns the necessity for novelty and difference" (1980,

54). Either level of expectation is, of course, guided by previous products, by the ways in which those products have been received (i.e., critically or at the box office), and by the particular conventions that have accrued to them. Texts that successfully adhere to social and cultural codes of verisimilitude are in Northern culture likely to be understood—at least critically—as products superior to those that "merely" meet the requirements of generic verisimilitude. Thus, genres such as horror or science fiction tend to carry with them less cultural capital than, say, psychological dramas. Neale surmises that this is because the propensity to adhere primarily to generic verisimilitude allows movies to "sidestep, or transgress broad social and cultural regimes." At the same time, it seems to have been the case throughout the history of Hollywood that the attempt is made to have movies conform to both generic and cultural codes, creating a situation in which a given movie can be understood as "realistic" and in which the constituent elements and structures of genre are fused with and become part of more general cultural ideas of what is real, likely, or possible.

Westerns have chronically been a privileged site of this fusion, since part of their function has been to construct within certain very tightly conceived syntagmatic functions a repeated narrative about the formation of American culture: a narrative "about" the nineteenth century and westward expansion that by and large stands in for and allegorizes in the American imaginary other "origins" or formations—such as the first white exploration and exploitation of America in the fifteenth and sixteenth centuries, or the political founding of the republic in the eighteenth. This narrative, repeated with small variation over and over in the generic ways of westerns, becomes a huge part of American imaginaries and ideologies of real history, indeed of the realities and possibilities of America and life itself. Thus westerns are often thought to bear an especially privileged—almost "official"—relation to American history and, indeed, American ideologies.

Few commentators on westerns have failed to address this relation in one way or another. Some of the most influential criticism on westerns has treated them in terms of the "myths" or "mythologies" that they seem to present for the American cultural imaginary and for American social life and history.[1] Other critics, more averse to the idea that there is some essential "Americanness" that is laid out and repeated in the culture's texts, have seen the shifts and changes in the western genre as reflections of specifiable social and historical formations in the United States.[2] In either form of criticism, it seems agreed that westerns say something quite direct either about or to America's view of itself. This conviction is not contradicted, of course, by the way in which a public figure like Ronald Reagan could adopt various and numerous poses drawn from the westerns during his time as president; Reagan's 1988 campaign in the western states on behalf of his eventual successor, George Bush, demonstrated this particularly well in its overdetermined use of cowboy motifs.[3] Nor is it contradicted by the fact that the general rationale for reactive violence given by prespaghetti Hollywood westerns is repeated in American justifications for the military devastation of Iraq in 1991. And just as presidents have enjoined the discourse of westerns, so the makers of westerns have sometimes deliberately attempted to link their movies with governmental discourses: one thinks here especially, perhaps, of John Wayne's sacrificial screech of a movie, *The Cowboys* (1972), which directly takes on the task of exhorting America's "boys" to their patriotic duty of militarism.

And yet the story of this reflected or mythological American imaginary is not so static or direct as it is sometimes given to be by critics and scholars. Nor are this narrative and its variations quite simply a matter of some gross and almost unmanageably huge ideological formation (America) trying out new arrangements within a delimited field. Rather we must take account of the fact that the genre always addresses itself, as much as it addresses any cultural imaginary, to the production of what are effectively contested fields of meaning, since audiences cannot be relied upon to simply "buy" a movie's interventions. Leone's movies are an interesting case in point here because their displacement of generic verisimilitude is put to the service of a displacement of the cultural imaginary that inhabits the generic conventions. Leone's westerns set up a larger gap between themselves and previous products than is easily tolerable in a single increment.

All of this tends to suggest that genre is an element that is quite tightly construed and effectively operates at two levels (the level of professional domestic production and the level of the tributary media's reception and replication of the text), but less so at the third (the level of audience reception). Audiences appear capable of tolerating quite large product differential—rather larger than the industry predicts and than the tributary media would seem to like. In that sense, even if genre in some way guides audience's expectations, it is less powerful and important for them than is generally held, and at the same time it is an element of production that is held in place by the industry and its guardians. Here I am perhaps following Neale's emphasis when he calls for a view of genre that will see it less as an aesthetic formation and more as "an industrial/journalistic term" (1990, 50).

Equally, one might suggest that genres themselves exhibit a degree of flexibility (partly by virtue of the industry's insistence upon and its need for product differentiation) but that generic verisimilitude can also be pushed to the point of becoming unworkable, or unserviceable, in relation to cultural and social regimes of verisimilitude. That is, while any text's relation to a genre is one of both similarity and variation, certain texts that will attach themselves to a given genre—or that will profer themselves as belonging to that genre—can act to push the genre beyond the functions that it is intended to fulfill, beyond the gates that it is supposed to guard, and beyond the complicity of verisimilitudes. I have been proposing Leone's movies as instances of how this works, although at the same time there is a paradox here with Leone's movies—a paradox that could perhaps have been introduced only by an alien's treatment of the genre: that is, as his movies counter or resist the imaginary of social and cultural verisimilitudes, Leone is actually led to make claims for them on the grounds not so much of their historical verisimilitude, but on the grounds of their historical *accuracy*. In other words he intends to take at its word the genre's claim to represent American history, and in doing so he paradoxically disrupts the American imaginary of history.

I am suggesting, then, that the notion of a genre is a matter of imaginaries—social and cultural, as well as textual. One might add further that part of the reason that the idea of genre is such a problematic one is that a genre is itself a phantasmic structure. Logically, that is, genres are a kind of post factum construct: there is never a "pure" textual instance of a genre, and there is never an act of reception that can be said to follow perfectly the outlines of genre. Critics are often led to understand genre as a hypothetical set of readerly expectations that are activated or not in a given reading circumstance. But these expectations are, of course, themselves variable in different readerly circumstances, so it can be argued that genres themselves respond only to particular interests in particular circumstances. Thus any text that is intertextually drawn into genre relations in an act of reading has an existence that is in a sense eccentric to those expectations. Leone's westerns will be read according to different intertextual relations wherever they are exhibited, and so any notion of genre that would include the expectations and intertextual relations of varied readers in Italy and the United States, for example, would ultimately end up describing such a complexity of relationships that it would become useless and probably contradictory. Equally, the question of what actually constitutes a genre might founder upon the fact that a given text can be exhibited in many different contexts and even different media: the experience of watching *Fistful* at home on video or on broadcast is different from watching it in a cinema, and so on.

This is, of course, to say little else than this: that in addition to the fact that different texts can render the genre's functions unstable, so too the sheer diversity of reading experiences and expectations will always tend to exceed any possible definitions of genre. We might indeed begin to suspect that the establishment of genres—either through the industrial media's production, or through journalistic and even scholarly consideration—is a device for closing down the range of reading experiences for any particular audience.

The attempt to impose genre on the part of popular media serves what is on the face of it an interest other than what, in the literary-critical field, E. D. Hirsch produces as a concern to reach culturally "valid" readings (1967). Yet the assignation of a movie to a genre in the popular culture industry, of course, serves a purpose that is related to consumption and reception. The industry attempts to isolate and reach a particular audience and its interests by imposing a particular preinterpretation on the movie. John Ellis has called one aspect of this imposed preinterpretation the film's "narrative image," which is, most simply, "the film's circulation outside its performances in cinemas" (1982, 31). The narrative image, constructed by advertising and other activities in the tributary media, first assigns a film to a genre or gives it a brand name, and then indicates what Ellis calls its particular "enigma," answers to which will be found in the film itself. The narrative image is perhaps most often and at its simplest found in visual advertising, and there the assignation of a movie to a genre is often the prime concern.

For the industry a great and continual difficulty is to sell movies that fall between or outside the apparent genres that they have created. This difficulty most likely can help explain the belated American distribution even of *Fistful*, a movie that is ostensibly close to the American industry's idea of a western but that exceeds that idea in significant ways. This construction of a potential audience through the assignation of genre labels is, as I suggested, primarily a marketing device, yet there is still, in industry practice, a reliance upon an at least covert notion of "correctness" and "validity"—not just in audience interpretation insofar as certain cultural and ideological meanings are promulgated through the establishment of genre expectations, but equally in production, where professional codes and values are called into play by members of the filmmaking crew, all the way from makeup person to director and producer.[4] So, even while genres and their definitions are theoretically illogical and in practice unwieldy, they are still recognizable parts of both the production and reception processes of the filmic experience; and, importantly, they derive from and serve the ideological interest of delimiting and closing down readings, making readings "correct" and "valid" and allowing intendments to operate effectively. And at the same time they provide frameworks by which the makers of film work by speaking necessarily to the history of other texts onto which they attempt to impose order and coherence. In these ways, genres are part of the concrete self-understanding of the industry, guarded and replicated by the tributary media, consumed by the audience.

Where any discourse is most delimited and circumscribed by its own regulations and conventions, moments of change will become of paramount interest. The change will always be referable both to intratextual innovations and rearrangements and to changes in what Bennett and Woolacott call "reading formations"[5] and what I call cotextual histories. The Leone westerns have constituted a particular moment of change, disruption, uncertainty, and even resistance to the Hollywood genre. Eastwood's own westerns, to which I shall now turn, are made after the spaghettis and in a context where the imposition of the generic guidelines has been forcibly relaxed by the insurgence of a "junior branch"; the response of Eastwood's westerns, I shall argue, is to attempt to right the wrongs that Leone has seemed to have done to the genre, and thence to reassert the dominance of the paternal branch over the junior one.

Restitution

Christopher Frayling notes that *Hang 'em High* in 1968 is "the first Western made in Hollywood to cash in on Eastwood's 'Dollars' image—and cash in it did, to the tune of $17 million" (284); it is also the first movie made under the auspices of Eastwood's own production company, Malpaso, which was started up that year. In many ways the film is a literal return to Hollywood for Eastwood. Although the image of the grim and ruthless Eastwood, playing Jedediah Cooper, continually evokes the spaghettis and alludes to them, by and large the movie takes very little from the spaghetti trilogy at other levels. *Hang 'em* operates within the thematic parameters and with a mise-en-scène that are traditional for the western even if they are exactly what Leone's movies tended to eschew. Specifically, the movie takes Eastwood's spaghetti image and turns it to account within the framework of more traditionally American concerns than the Leone movies wanted to deal with.

The central thematic issue in *Hang 'em* is the familiar western conflict between the civic law and some sense of natural law, and that theme is conducted around the equally sanctioned twin themes of the sacralization of property rights and the right of revenge. The conflict between natural and civic law gives energy to the revenge theme of the movie (whereas in Leone all revenge is motivated, if at all, only by a fairly ruthless desire for wealth and is turned to a kind of amoralism that exceeds the parameters that traditional westerns have established), and the same conflict informs the film's dissertation on ownership and property.

Hang 'em thus begins with a dispute over the ownership of some cattle with which Cooper is traveling—a dispute that gets Cooper hung and almost killed by a lynching party. The movie throws in a gratuitous illustration of general lawlessness by having one of the lynch party, Reno, take Cooper's saddle as he's about to be hung; Reno says, "I like to see justice done, but I'm taking the saddle," and someone else then takes Cooper's wallet. Cooper is saved from a hanging death by a representative of the Oklahoma civic law, Marshal Bliss, and taken to the nearest town. There he is exonerated of any wrongdoing by the local law officer, Judge Fenton, and persuaded to become a marshal for this judge, who describes the lawlessness of Oklahoma Territory in 1889—seventeen marshals and one court to cover seventy thousand square miles—to appeal to Cooper's sense of civic responsibility. Despite his once before having been a lawman, Cooper takes the position in the hope of using it to avenge his lynching.

Thus the main action of the movie's narrative stems from Cooper's steering a course between, on the one hand, his own determination to get revenge and to exercise his rights under natural law and, on the other hand, the judge's zeal in imposing the civic law. The narrative allows for and seems finally to want to vindicate both courses in a fairly uneasy mix. Cooper zealously goes about exacting his revenge, but also and at the same time becomes a conscientious law officer. His conduct responds not only to his own sense of justice but also to the judge's question, "You a law man or ain't you?" The film can keep these contradictions in play only by dint of the presence of the judge, whose excessive enthusiasm for mass public hangings is a point of ambivalence in his drive for law and order. The fact that his penchant for hangings is offered as a kind of extremism helps the movie to downplay the contradictory tendencies of Cooper's own actions. But even the judge's monomaniacal behavior is justified before the film's end. His rationale for the extremity of his actions is that Oklahoma is not yet a state, that it is understaffed, and so on, and his conclusion is that a certain ruthless rigor must be maintained *pour encourager les autres*. Cooper's role at that point is to remind the civic law of the merits of mercy as he insists upon leniency and fair treatment for two teenage criminals and also for the oldest and feeblest member of the gang that had lynched him.

Cooper's narrative is almost impossibly contradictory: he carries out his "natural" revenge, and yet maintains himself as a good law officer who can even act as a restraining influence on the excesses of civic law. The presence of this contradiction is underscored by the differing points of view of the film offered in two 1968 reviews. In the *New York Times* Howard Thompson says that the movie "not only makes sense but actually promotes good old-fashioned law abidance." On the other hand, the *Variety* reviewer suggests that it is nothing but "a rambling tale which glorifies personal justice, mocks and derogates orderly justice."[1]

However, *Hang 'em*'s incoherent position might seem less incoherent if seen in light of one of the central claims that Richard Ray makes about the history of American movies: namely, that one of the central "thematic paradigms" of Hollywood is the statement of the possibility that incompatible positions can be resolved (1985). As Ray also suggests, and as *Hang 'em* exemplifies, Hollywood is fond of proferring texts whose intendment is both to warn against a reckless exercise of "natural law" in the name of civic virtue and at the same time to glamorize and heroize the outlaw protagonist over the "official" protagonist (in this case, Cooper over Fenton). We can see resonances of this paradigm again in many years of American foreign policy, perhaps particularly in the eighties, when America both claimed to staunchly uphold international law and ignored it at those points where a more "natural" justice could be invoked to rationalize violence: for instance, the bombing of Libya or the mining of Nicaraguan harbors. These events of the eighties are perhaps paradigmatic moments where the fusion of cultural and generic verisimilitudes has taken hold and become effective in the conduct of the everyday life of the state.

There is an attempt, as Ray's generalization suggests there would be, to mediate the incompatible positions of Fenton and Cooper at the end of the movie. The movie ends so that no one man can be considered to be the embodiment of law. Fenton cannot because of the blindness induced by his attachment to the letter of the law, and Cooper cannot for the opposite reason. But that apparent standoff in the movie's intendment is modulated by the fact that Cooper's personal vengefulness and his outlaw role in general are both elements of the privileged kind of narrative in those westerns that bring up this kind of issue. Thus it would seem, as the *Variety* review makes clear, that the "do-it-yourself, subjective type of justice" is vindicated in the movie's outcome.

In some ways the two reviews that I have quoted reflect perfectly the conflict of the movie as it imports the Eastwood figure from the Leone movies and inserts that figure into a standard American narrative framed by the dispute between civic and natural law. The amoral and independent figure that this movie supposedly exploits—Leone's "invention"—has its only affinities with the figure of the outlaw and/or the "natural" hero within the American framework and so cannot be easily drawn into or under the civic law in the way that this movie attempts to do. Quite apart from the standard ambivalence that constitutes the history of Hollywood westerns in relation to the problem of civic and natural laws, Ted Post's movie here muddies the issue further by, in a sense, misappropriating the Eastwood figure. It could be said that "the first Western made in Hollywood to cash in on Eastwood's 'Dollars' image" actually demonstrates a severe misunderstanding of that image even as (or because) it tries to domesticate it. Another way of saying this is to suggest that Post's movie accidentally resists the resistance that the Leone trilogy had effected.

Certainly, both of the reviewers I have quoted see *Hang 'em* as bearing some kind of skewed relation to Leone's movies and to their Eastwood icon. Thompson says with some evident satisfaction that this movie is "unlike those previous sadomasochistic exercises on foreign prairies where the grizzled Mr. Eastwood stalked around in a filthy serape, holster-deep in corpses" (and it seems especially important for this reviewer that Cooper is properly shaven here). The *Variety* reviewer, ironically enough, thinks of *Hang 'em* "as a poorly-made imitation of a poorly-made Italian imitation of an American western"—the logic of the subaltern product returning to the dominant economy and altering it becomes almost abyssal in that formulation.

The next western that Eastwood stars in, *Joe Kidd*, was directed in 1972 by John Sturges, who had already directed a number of well-respected, or at least well-known, westerns.[2] This movie had the advantage over *Hang 'em* in the sense that the Eastwood image that it could draw on had by then been proved in other realms and other films. That is, the allure of Eastwood's tough and laconic persona seems to have been consolidated by his appearance in *Dirty Harry* the previous year rather more than altered by his appearances in

Play Misty for Me and *The Beguiled* and other such movies, where he plays roles that are more hysterical. Certainly in general terms his reputation—and his box-office success—had been enhanced enough that he was named "Male Star of the Year" by the National Association of Theater Owners, an award that was given while he was filming *Joe Kidd* (*Film Facts* 25 (1971): 423). Thus the tough guy role was already beginning to stereotype Eastwood performances, and the setting of the classic western (this one filmed in New Mexico) invokes its lineaments.

The main action of *Joe Kidd* begins when several Mexican-Americans, led by Louis Chama, take over and burn a courtroom in protest against the legal theft of their land by big business; Kidd is in the courtroom at the time, having just been given a short jail term for drunkenness and disorderly behavior. Kidd helps the magistrate escape when the Hispanic protestors attempt to take him hostage as they leave. Although Kidd at first will not join a posse to go after Chama and his gang, he later rides out against them after learning that they have taken revenge on him for helping the law by raiding his homestead. However, at that juncture he rides out, not as part of a legal posse, but as the hired tracker and guide for a party led by the land baron, Frank Harlan. The audience is made aware that Kidd would not be going against Chama's people but for the attack on his own land. The hunting down of Chama and the confrontation between his group and Harlan's constitutes the central action of the rest of the narrative, which is marked by several shifts in alliances reminiscent of the ups and downs of *The Good, the Bad, and the Ugly*. Kidd makes apparent his dislike of Harlan, his men, and his tactics; Harlan disarms and contains him; he escapes to join Chama's group, only to become angry at and disillusioned by Chama's tactics; he finally takes Chama to face trial after defeating Harlan's gang in order to do so.

At the same time as taking the new western icon into this movie, Sturges draws him into a narrative that again plays out the drama of the opposition between natural and civic legality and also draws him into a number of other elements of the standard western revenge narratives. For instance, Kidd's decision to go after the bad guys is "correct" in Hollywood terms, since it plays out the rule that says that the hero must have a personal reason to turn to violence, that reason having been supplied by Chama's attack on his homestead: before that he has stated that he has "nothing against Louis Chama." Yet the standard rules are complexified here because Kidd's going after Chama does not serve the interests of any particular community. Rather, Kidd quite explicitly joins up with the normal bad guys of westerns, the land baron Harlan and his crew of hired killers. However, as Harlan's crew does finally turn out to be the bad guys, this would logically leave Kidd working in the service of the community of the wronged settlers. In this case, though, those wronged settlers are the Hispanic people who have had their land stolen. The movie cannot quite allow the white outlaw hero, Kidd, to throw in his lot with them. Instead, he throws in his lot with just one of them, a woman whom he effectively steals from Chama, and meanwhile he turns Chama over to the civic law.

This narrative caused one reviewer to rail that "Joe Kidd, in his single-minded purpose of turning the corrupt Mexican over to a corrupt justice, is demonstrably mad." That reviewer could be said to have missed the logic of the film in one sense. That is, the film is caught between on the one hand its ability, inherited from the spaghettis, to name the wronged community as Hispanic, and on the other hand its inability to cross the cultural verisimilitude of having a white American hero unequivocally lend his political support to Hispanics, especially violent ones. The film in fact goes out of its way to make it clear, by discrediting Chama, that Hispanics cannot constitute an authentic wronged community. The only moment of overt politics in the film, apart from the initiating irruption of Chama's gang into the courtroom, comes when Kidd and Chama discuss the latter's willingness to allow the hostages Harlan has taken to be shot while Chama himself stays free. Chama at this point suggests that his cause needs martyrs, while Kidd thinks that he should hand himself over to the law and address his grievances through the legal system.

Here we have a most unlikely confrontation in many senses: most of all it is rather contradictory that Kidd, who has already hired himself out to the real bad guys as a way of satisfying his own desire for revenge, should become the upholder of civic law. It would perhaps be going too far to suggest that we have here a confrontation between the bankruptcy of the liberal-Protestant when faced with a political issue and the supposed ideological bankruptcy of the Catholic. Nonetheless, that cultural element is present in the confrontation, if only because Leone's films have left it there as a possibility. The white

American imaginary of the violent nonwhite other always includes the idea that his politics is irrational and betrays a lack of respect for the lives of others. It is this imaginary that permits Kidd to continue in the "madness" of turning Chama over to the corrupt white law, rather than joining him to help address the grievances of the Hispanics as he would, by Hollywood logic, if these settlers had been white. To put a final twist on the contradictions of this scene, it is soon followed by a moment where Kidd, making for the town with his prisoners, sends one of the Latino band ahead into what he knows is likely to be an ambush; the Latino is promptly killed and Kidd's own respect for the lives of others fully demonstrated.

So while this film is akin to *Hang 'em* in its task of importing, polishing, and exploiting the image of Eastwood, it differs in the sense that the logic with which it involves itself is more complex. Whereas in *Hang 'em* there was simply a bad fit between this highly connotated antihero image and the theme of civic/natural justice, this movie gets itself into difficulty because it has broached, and got very close to, the themes of minority race and ethnic rights in this country. The space that is opened at the beginning of the film with Chama's claiming of his and his people's rights cannot be sustained in terms of cultural verisimilitude, even if the spaghettis have helped enable such a topic at the level of genre formation.

The principal symptom of the film's desire to bury the issue once it has been mooted is to discredit the personality of Chama as leader of the rebels, attacking him as the evil seducer of misguided people (much in the way that various other nonwhite leaders, such as Qaddafi, Arafat, Noriega, and Saddam Hussein, have consistently been personally vilified in American policy and its tributary media). But most of all, the movie's script simply caves in to the cultural impossibility of having the white hero fight for a nonwhite and politicized community: all he can do is steal that community's exotic woman and deliver the men to what is recognized to be a corrupt system of white justice. In that light, the *Saturday Review* writer does see something correctly about this movie when he complains that "one might suppose from the first reel or so . . . that we are off into another of those movies that pick at scabs on the American conscience. . . . With similar injustices to the American Indians fresh on our minds, *Joe Kidd* prepares us to be wholly sympathetic to the plight of yet another minority group . . . but the script (by Elmore Leonard) forgets all about this aspect of the story" (*Film Facts* 25 (1971): 423).

The way in which westerns in particular, and Hollywood films in general, relate to cultural imaginaries, or to what I have been calling social and cultural verisimilitudes, is not, of course, a process of reflection (where the films would be understood as "imitating" a preexistent set of meanings); nor is it the case that movies directly install particular cultural imaginaries in the heads of viewers. Rather this is a dialectical process and one that is complexified further by the fact that the cinema not only has a relation to cultural imaginaries but also incessantly addresses its own "internal" history. This double relation of the cinema often leads to a kind of disturbance in a particular text at a particular moment. Here *Joe Kidd*'s relationship to what, by 1972, has come to constitute an important and new element of the genre of the western—that is, a discourse on minority history and rights—interferes with its execution of other elements in that history to create a kind of uneasiness and even incoherence. That incoherence is likely to be exacerbated by cotextual histories, such as the issues to which the *Saturday Review* alludes related to Native Americans—"fresh in our minds" in 1972 because of various incidents involving Native American activism, including the occupation of Alcatraz Island by the Indians of All Tribes in 1969, the work of the American Indian Movement, and activism by other Native Americans such as the Pomo Indians in the early 1970s.[3] One might add that the film can well be understood also as a kind of prescriptive allegory for the winding down of the war in Vietnam, where the lesson is precisely that the white male hero is no longer obliged to fight for the community of men of color, even though he can still take their women as a kind of price for his dangerous cooperation.

The introduction into *Joe Kidd* of the discourse of minority rights constitutes, then, a disturbance that has finally to be denied and elided by the film's narrative because, however much the recent history of the genre can be said to have enabled such a discourse, Hollywood film's more general aim of fusing generic with cultural verisimilitude has become compromised by it. In other words, certain things cannot be said in the generic format—or can be said in only partial, confused, or incoherent ways—if they cause cultural verisimilitude to be stretched beyond certain limits. To say this is probably not very surprising, since to do so is merely to point, in effect, to the ideological functioning or complicity of generic forms. While it is certainly not useless to remark this once again, my more particular aim here is to show how that ideological functioning or complicity cannot be regarded as fixed or as a given. That is, genre formation (or what some critics would, wrongly I think, call the evolution of genre)[4] is continually in flux or in process, open to the vagaries of particular films and filmmakers, but equally to the cotextual histories that surround and interact with particular texts. As I have suggested before, there is never a pure textual instance of a genre—and most certainly, the latest instance is not the definition of the genre. Rather a particular genre is the arena in which meanings are proferred, elaborated, and then contested within certain confined limits. When those limits are stretched or threatened, the genre itself comes under intense pressure and its effectivity at the ideological level is potentially weakened. In talking about the string of Eastwood westerns, then, I want to construe a narrative that will suggest the instability of the western genre's grip, or the limits of its workability.

This issue of the discourse of minority rights is important, not just because it has a direct political referent, but because its appearance helps to illuminate the fragility and vulnerability of a whole history of the western. The almost complete silence of Hollywood westerns on the question of minority rights is a remarkable historical phenomenon, especially since the logic of these texts is to champion the rights of white homesteaders, farmers, and assorted other individuals on the grounds that they have natural rights, not bestowed by earthly government but deriving from the very nature of man. The partisan clarity of the traditional western is staggering in that respect: it effectively argues, mostly without shame, that the white man is the only true owner of those natural and inalienable rights.[5] Where any contrary suggestion is mooted by a particular film, that film will rapidly compromise the putative coherence and authority that it might inherit from its generic antecedents. Such is the case with *Joe Kidd*.

The grip of the white male protagonist, representative of the liberal-Protestant project, is not necessarily threatened by the mere presence of the minority other, or simply by the presence of that other history. Indeed, one remarkable feature of Eastwood's Hollywood westerns is that they often depict that presence and even recognize its status. In addition to the presence of the Hispanic community in *Joe Kidd*, *Hang 'em* includes representation of the relative integration of African-Americans, Native Americans, and Hispanics into the life and working routines of the West. A later Eastwood western, *High Plains Drifter*, pointedly contrasts the white townsfolk's view of "Indians" and Mexicans as "goddamn savages" with the Eastwood figure's sympathetic and even charitable treatment of them. The film that is, in my assessment, Eastwood's central western text, *Josey Wales*, is so in part because of its more than usually forthright treatment of issues of race and minority. Yet even there, the integration and cooperation among and between races is possible only under the tutelage of Wales as enlightened community maker. In other words, the representation of racial difference and even disturbance is a feasible project within the western genre, but the emergence of racial minorities into any overt political independence or agency exceeds the possibility of the genre because it exceeds the cultural imaginary of white America.

This fact receives a certain kind of confirmation and commentary in Eastwood's rather ambiguous and yet jingoistic movie, *Bronco Billy* (1980), a comedy about the survival of the western spirit in contemporary America in the shape of a traveling Wild West show. There Eastwood as Bronco Billy is the paternal figure who organizes and defends a ragtag community of social misfits (including notably an African-American and a Native American), all of whom are united in their faith in his vision and all of whom are authorized precisely by it and it alone. The film makes no bones about the necessity for Billy's control over this community of diversity: he refers to himself as "head ramrod" on many occasions, and is perpetually invoking his own authority in a way that often makes him look petty and boorish. The comic treatment of this figure in *Bronco Billy* resonates back upon the same kind of figure in *Josey Wales*, where the patronizing nature of his tutelage is revealed without irony.

The paternal and patronizing function of these white male protagonists is part of a general defense necessitated by seeing rights attaching to minorities in a world that the white man nonetheless keeps on ruling. As a thematic element in westerns the role of paternity has chronically been most important, but I would suggest that it comes to attain greater than usual importance in Eastwood's westerns, in part because both generic and cultural verisimilitudes demand the disavowal of the threat that minorities come to represent both in the late sixties and onward. That is, the stress on paternity becomes a way of asserting that both the genre and the white male will continue to rule, will settle all claims, and be the dispenser of rights; most of all it guarantees that he will hand on those powers to the next white male. It is also not incidental, at the level of generic process, that Eastwood's movies in this sense reinsert what many critics have seen as a traditional "Oedipal" obsession in the genre of westerns, a structure that became dissipated or dispersed in the sixties and which seems to be utterly absent from the spaghettis.

Eastwood's *High Plains Drifter* (1973) is only the second movie and the first western that Eastwood himself directs, and it constitutes an interesting response to the kind of confusion and incoherence that the Post and Sturges westerns had exhibited. That is, it seems to seek to clarify and distill the essence of the No Name figure through a highly aestheticized mise-en-scène, while at the same time eschewing or eliding some of the problems that those first two post-Leone westerns had produced for themselves. The location is no longer the Hispanicized frontier with its political problems, but a white town in the California Sierras. The movie's plot is again a return to generally recognizable paradigms: it is a revenge plot, where the outlaw hero works for the community against a gang that had held it in thrall. At the same time, there is a twist in that the hero's revenge is in a sense to be taken out on the townsfolk themselves. Thus, while he becomes their champion against their enemies, the requisite personal motives for his action involve punishing the townsfolk, whose crime is that they apparently allowed the criminal gang to kill his brother who had been sheriff. In other words, the showdown with the gang is a prerequisite for his revenge on the townfolk.

Yet even this twist is in the service of the movie's attempt to reinstate the classic moral messages of the genre, since it is effectively a lesson in civics that he teaches them, demonstrating to them the need for communities to stand up for themselves against evil and the turpitude of being complicit in wrongdoing by standing by and simply watching it. As he trains the citizens to stand up against the criminals—whom they had previously hired and come to rely upon, only to find these professional protectors turning against the town—the stranger gives them a civics lesson about self-defense. The lesson is that when, out of weakness or complacency, communities hand over the defense of what they own and earn to professionals, they run the risk of weakening themselves further. As with so many previous westerns, the concern here is a message that addresses itself in part to the U.S. Constitution's Second Amendment.

At the level of its plot, then, the movie marks a return to some of the commonplaces of Hollywood westerns. At the same time it takes on the full brunt of the task of integrating the No Name character, with all his style and connotation, into the Hollywood plot. The stranger's role here is to act once more as the agent and instigator of responsible community action and ideology—a far cry from the role of No Name in the Leone trilogy. In this sense at least it might be right to suggest, as François Guérif does, that *High Plains* constitutes "a final farewell to the spaghetti western" (96), and is a movie intended, he implies, as a gesture of exorcism. It can certainly be agreed that the stranger here is a polished and even distilled version of that character. Eastwood's directing of himself heavily emphasizes the rhythmic slowness and ritualized behavior of the protagonist in a way that Leone only approaches (with this effect reinforced by the contrast caused by the fast and almost staccato editing of action scenes). My sense that this is what is achieved is perhaps in part a consequence of the almost perpetual presence on screen of Eastwood's image in this movie. The repeated long takes of his slowly moving body and the close-ups of the formality of his behavioral rituals and of the almost total impassivity of his squinting face compose by far the bulk of the film's shots, and their overall effect is to offer the Eastwood body as an object of contemplation and objectification in a way that Leone does only sporadically. In other words, this is a highly formalized representation of Eastwood's body, which is itself a gesture of restitution, literally putting the white male demigod back into the center of the screen.

Perhaps a particularly telling example of how Eastwood's directing produces this aestheticization of the protagonist (of his own body, indeed) in conjunction with a return to Hollywood modes is in the use of shot/reverse-shot sequences. These standard Hollywood devices (which, as I mentioned earlier, Leone has already tried to transform for his films) regain their place as a staple formal element under Eastwood's direction. In most Hollywood productions the reverse shot would be used to allow a character to play a verbal or gestural reaction to the previous shot. The way that Eastwood uses it here is to present simply an impassive and unspeaking visage, an objectified image of his own face or body. I take this to be an instance of how Eastwood attempts to exploit the power of the image that Leone has bequeathed him, while melding it back into the traditional array of devices in which Hollywood cinema has been constituted. Other stylistic devices that Eastwood uses here and in later movies have the same effect of reinforcing this intense emphasis on the physique, physiology, and form of the protagonist. For instance, this movie makes extensive and repeated use of backlighting for interior scenes: interiors are dark to the point that the actors are not necessarily clearly seen; however, the mass of the actor's body is grasped as an indistinct yet dominating and heroic form in the visual field. The cinematographer for *High Plains*, Bruce Surtees, has over the years turned this backlighting habit into a trademark on Eastwood films, formally subventing the significance of the emphasis on shape rather than substance, physique rather than interiority.

There are many other formal aspects of this film that are notable and that help produce what is perhaps one of the most highly styled and crafted westerns of any decade, but certainly of the 1970s. While Eastwood's arrival as an accomplished and intelligent director is one of the film's points of interest, for me its main effect is to have brought the image of Eastwood established in the Leone movies into a more recognizable Hollywood frame. One way to mark this is by looking at the way in which the film reintroduces an "Oedipalized" narrative of the sort I spoke about above. The centering of the white male protagonist in the narrative and on the screen in a way that is extreme—and that has even caused Eastwood to be charged with narcissism[6]—establishes him as a kind of paternal specter in the movie; and this patronal role is inspissated by two aspects of the narrative in particular—the stranger's relation to the character Mordecai and his dealings with the movie's two women characters.

Early in the movie, after the stranger has ridden into town and introduced himself by shooting down three men, he encounters a young woman of the town, Callie (played by Marianna Hill), who deliberately bumps into him and insults him. By way of response he carries her away and rapes her—this is what he calls a "lesson in manners." The film's other woman character, played by Verna Bloom, is somewhat older than Callie and is the wife of the local hotelier; throughout the movie she demonstrates a certain recognition of and sympathy with the stranger whom she eventually sleeps with. The two women are set in a familiar contrast: the young woman is given by the film as hysterical, the other as more measured and finally full of integrity. The protagonist's simple task is to demonstrate, by applying the perfection of his masculinity, which of these is the mother and which is the whore.

The stranger's relation to these two women is intently watched by Mordecai (played by Billy Curtis), a dwarf who is continually mocked and generally disdained by the townsfolk but whom the stranger, when he is given control of the town, names sheriff. Mordecai becomes the son who watches the father at work, and to whom the father's power is handed on. Perhaps the most striking narrative strategy that ties Mordecai to his protecting father is the repeated presentation of Mordecai watching the stranger in his interactions with the two women. The rape scene at the beginning of the movie is intercut with shots of Mordecai watching from the periphery. His observing this primal scene is not a traumatizing experience, but rather one that inaugurates his admiration for this father. Mordecai later demonstrates his ability to understand the logic of his father's masculinity by explaining why Callie is angry after the rape—"because you didn't go back for more."

The father and son are linked together also by their sharing of a common vision, or rather of a common memory. There are three flashback sequences in the movie, each delivering part of the narrative of the townsfolk's original crime of watching the former sheriff being whipped to death by the Carlin gang. The first of these flashbacks comes to the stranger as he rests early after his arrival in Lago. But the second comes to Mordecai later in the movie and fills in details that had been enigmatically omitted from the first. Mordecai's flashback is a kind of traumatic childhood memory, in sharp distinction to his view of the stranger raping Callie. In this more pained memory, he is shown taking shelter under a sidewalk in order to escape being hit by one of the townsfolk, and from that vantage point he has a close-up view of the attack on the sheriff. The third flashback completes the relay between Mordecai and the stranger by allowing the latter to add some final pieces of information to the whipping sequence. By means of this relay the two are united, as I suggested, in a common vision, father and son sharing the same history and the same affects.

Mordecai's role as the stranger's son throughout the movie is marked in other formal terms as well. Early in the film the stranger

Father and son in *High Plains Drifter*

lifts Mordecai up to his own height, and thereafter the camera regularly shoots Mordecai from below to emphasize his promotion. At one other interesting point he is seen sitting with his new father, his head at the same level as the stranger's, watching a pair of Hispanic carpenters at work fulfilling the latter's instructions. There we have the scenario that I have been suggesting has been a central element of Eastwood's westerns. On the frontier that the white father reclaims, the proper relation of center and margin is reestablished: the Mexican workers are to be sympathized with, of course (in contrast to the town priest, who talks about charity and kindness to his "brothers and sisters," the stranger gives the local Native Americans fabrics and candies that they otherwise could not afford), but the oppressed do not even begin to emerge into the narrative as agents; rather they remain only marginals or menials in the diegesis, people to whom the largesse and tolerant benevolence of the whites should be directed. Thus, this becomes a properly hierarchized frontier that the father can then exhibit for the benefit of his smaller and admiring companion.

It seems to me important that this quite perverse family—

avenging and enigmatic father, intuitive and stolidly sympathetic mother, and the little man as son, with the "other woman" hysterically on the periphery—is established in a movie that belongs to the narrative I am setting out here: the narrative whereby a particular historical resistance to the western genre has to be recuperated and where the genre has to be as it were restored. The Oedipalization of the westerns of the fifties (that is, of the time immediately before the genre's relative demise) cannot be restored to exactly its prior state by 1973, but the paradigm is certainly reestablished in this movie, and I am suggesting that this reestablishment is part of a trajectory undertaken with and by Eastwood to reassert ownership—ownership of the genre and ownership of history.

It is, then, too naive to think of *High Plains* simply as Eastwood's "farewell to the spaghetti westerns" without recognizing that what is at stake in that movie and his other post-Leone westerns is a determination to reverse the effects of the spaghetti westerns: in short, the restitution of a genre. The two westerns that Eastwood makes after *High Plains* can both be seen as outcrops of that project in different ways. *Outlaw Josey Wales* (1976) is perhaps Eastwood's most important and achieved western, and can be understood equally as a self-conscious intervention into the process of the western genre's formation; *Pale Rider* (1985) is Eastwood's last western and is in many respects an homage to—even a remake of—*Shane*, George Stevens's 1952 movie, which in many critical registers is "often taken to be a distillation of the whole Western genre" (Buscombe, 207). Eastwood's intervention into the western genre ends, then, with a repetition, or reaffirmation, of one of its central texts.

It is not irrelevant to note that *Josey Wales* was made just after the end of the Vietnam War, at a time when America had so recently and violently been reminded of the deep divisions of ideology and culture that have chronically subsisted as one part of the ideological motto, *e pluribus unum*. *Josey Wales* in many respects—and like so many other American movies, of course—is an optimistic tale of the construction of one community from the many. It is easy to think about the movie in the context of the then recent history of the Vietnam conflict, since it is set during the immediate aftermath of the American Civil War. The war has displaced Josey Wales and destroyed his family and homestead, and in the aftermath Wales leads the search for a new community and for new values of cooperation on the frontier. The fundamental narrative structure of the film is picaresque, as Wales, escaping from Union Redleg forces, proceeds from Missouri to Texas, gathering a diverse collection of other searchers under his wing as he goes along.

The movie is thus concerned with the restitution of community values after their disruption by war. Its moral in this respect is perhaps best represented at the end when the leading character in the pursuing Redleg gang, Fletcher (John Vernon), refuses a final showdown with Wales by pretending that he does not recognize him and suggesting to him that the war is best regarded as finished. Here Eastwood underscores the movie's assertion of the importance of community by suggesting that Wales will not then ride away into the sunset (as the classic gunfighter hero would do once he has saved the community), but will actually return to the fledgling community that he has traveled with and protected throughout the film. He in fact literally *does* ride into the sunset in the last shots of the film, but much has been previously made of the need for him to keep the sun behind him in order to have an edge over the enemies who pursue him, and by virtue of that his turning toward the sun here appears to be a twist on the hackneyed ending of the classic western.

But whether audiences are supposed to assume that he returns or not, Wales's important achievement is to have patronized the building and settling of a community in their American paradise. That community is a relatively diverse one: it includes Lone Wolf and Little Moonlight, two Native Americans from different peoples; Grandma Sarah, a once bigoted Union supporter who learns the benefits of tolerance and community; her blonde granddaughter (Sondra Locke); and also a peripheral but supportive group of white and Hispanic citizens from a town near to this new community's farm. Wales has helped the two Native Americans escape from the hardships and dangers of the post–Civil War territories, and has rescued the grandmother and granddaughter from comancheros. He himself has escaped from various types of hunter (the Redlegs, principally, but also bounty hunters and the like), and not only protected his group from the Union forces but also negotiated a living settlement with the Comanches who inhabit the land where the community's farm is located. The travails of the journey and the impress of danger persuade the travelers of the need to put aside their prejudices and their racial and regional differences in order to live together. They are led even in this by Wales himself, who, for instance, appears to hold no ill will toward the grandmother's anti-Confederacy bigotry.[7]

An important aspect of this settling and the nurturing of an apolitical (or what American media and politicians like to call "nonpartisan") tolerance and cooperation is that it should be prepared to defend itself. Wales's negotiations with Seven Bears, the Comanche chief, stress this. The Wales community has, of course, no originary claim on the land, but the land had been previously settled by Grandma's son; but, of course, it is land that is in the middle of Native American territory, wrested from them in the first place. The pact between the two fighting men is the result merely of a private negotiation between two individuals, rather than between two communities as such or between two representative legal entities—an epiphenomenal moment in the American media's historical habit of synecdochally turning whole peoples into the men who temporarily rule them.

The stress on this synecdochalized male figure implies a second important aspect of this movie: that is, for the continued security of the community, the strong central male must reproduce himself. The logic that *Josey Wales* sets out thence demands the romantic liaison that develops between Wales and the character played by Sondra Locke, the granddaughter Laura Lee. Wales had lost his wife and son in the Civil War lawlessness—and it is notable that in the early scenes depicting this loss, the film begins by showing Wales and his young son in their Jeffersonian idyll, the mother being no more than glimpsed as she is killed by the marauders. Subsequently, in his flight from the Redlegs, Wales loses a second "son," the boy Jamie, who alone of the Southerners that Wales has joined sustains his stand against the Union treachery. Jamie is wounded and loses his life on the trail, after an incident where he actually gets to call Josey "Pa." Having lost these two sons Wales must now not only regenerate the civilization that has been mauled by the war, but must also reproduce himself. As I noted before, it is strongly suggested in this movie that Wales returns to his community rather than riding away into the hills; his return would be a return to Laura Lee and to the prospect of reproducing himself with the young blonde teenager who has already recognized her future in him.

Insofar as this suggestion is made, it would represent a significant shift in the standard western paradigms where the hero precisely cannot return since he is forever alienated from the communities that he saves because of his profession. Westerns of the fifties are especially morbid on this count, filled with reflections upon the death or outmoded nature of the gunfighter, and upon his inability to actually become part of the community that he saves. Eastwood's movie appears to suggest, in keeping with its general moral message that "the war is over," that the hero can indeed return. Here again, the generic verisimilitudes and constraints are stretched in order to allow this film to deliver a notion that would have particular resonance at the moment of its manufacture.

If, as I suggest it does, *Josey Wales* makes that kind of intervention into the paradigmatic structures of westerns, this is consistent with the insight that the genre should be understood as a process, and that part of that process is the attempt to respond to the changing pressures of cultural verisimilitude at any given moment in history. The movie is a highly accomplished blending of the demands of the genre itself for repetition and difference, and yet also it seems to be able to turn the differences to account within the context in which it finds itself. That is, it reassumes or repeats the load of the western's traditional form of utterance and thereby stakes a further claim on behalf of American ownership of the genre. The final western that Eastwood has made, *Pale Rider*, finishes this narrative of restoration and reclamation in an overt and almost overdetermined way.

Eastwood's most confident contribution to this generic restabilization or rehabilitation (at least, until the 1992 release of *Unforgiven*)[8] comes in 1985, almost ten years after the intervention that *Josey Wales* constitutes and approximately two decades from the moment of his own emergence as a centrally important figure in the process of the genre's formation. The release of *Pale Rider* is a certain kind of market risk: according to a marketing executive at Warner Brothers, the film's distributor, "Everybody was nervous about a Western working" (*USA Today*, 2 July 1985, D1). The fact that the movie was yet another huge box-office success for Eastwood[9] belied the industry's caution about westerns, a caution that perhaps failed to recognize the continual effort that Eastwood personally had put into recuperating the genre from its relative demise.

The industry's fear of the western in the 1970s is perhaps reflected by the dwindling number of entries after 1972 in Phil Hardy's useful encyclopedia, *The Western*, and even the few that Hardy cites are characterized by their inability to ring changes on the western tradition in any way that would attract audiences. In 1980 an article in *Variety* (25 June, 7) noted (in relation to *Urban Cowboy* and Eastwood's own *Bronco Billy*) the difficulty that westerns encountered at the box office and gave credence to "the theory that the cowboy angle, whatever the trappings and no matter how up-to-date, constitutes a b.o. liability." The actual reasons for this collapse in the western can easily be imputed to the increasing production of what Robin Wood has called the "incoherent" texts of the seventies (Wood, 1986). The paradigmatic elements available to filmmakers had multiplied, and genre guidelines had broken down in ways that I have suggested. Perhaps also relevant here is the western's loss of its longest-serving protagonist, John Wayne, who died in 1979 after having spent the 1970s making increasingly bitter, morbid, and politically jingoistic westerns.[10] Many of the westerns of the later 1970s are comedies or parodies, almost literally the last laugh in the playing out of the vein of Hollywood's attempt to meld the western with European-style art movies (*Butch Cassidy and the Sundance Kid* [1969] or *McCabe and Mrs. Miller* [1971] are good instances of this moment).

However, despite this history and despite the industry's cautious approach to the western, the mid-1980s might well have seemed an ideal moment for a revival of the western as a central plank in the Hollywood edifice. The public discourse of the Reagan presidency was self-consciously and determinedly posed as a return to those "traditional American values" that were supposed to have disappeared from the civic life: the "values" of individualistic autonomy and civic self-defense, with a concomitant devolution of powers to individuals and local communities, widespread xenophobia and racism, selective views of history that take white hegemony as the unquestionable standard, and so on. There are many possible points of articulation between the public discourses of Reaganism and the habitual ideological profferings of the western, and these articulations were often made quite explicit by Reagan himself. More than loosely associated with the Hollywood industry, and indeed with westerns particularly, Reagan in many of his public remarks and often in his physical trappings and demeanor made overt allusion to this American tradition.[11] In this period, with its ideological discourse of a "return" to some supposedly essential Americanness, the industry's nervousness about westerns abated at least enough to allow some gestures toward the rehabilitation of the western.

The almost simultaneous release of Eastwood's *Pale Rider* and Lawrence Kasdan's *Silverado* in the summer of 1985 can be understood, then, as another opportunistic attempt to fuse the Hollywood product with the cultural discourses of the moment. Kasdan's movie is devoted to what the *New York Times* (7 July 1985, H1) described as the "mythic archetypes that form an American morality play, and Mr. Kasdan says it is in that sense that he tried to use them." In the same article Kasdan himself is quoted as suggesting that his use of these "archetypes" is a crucial part of his effort to make a "primer" for "a whole generation [that] grew up without westerns," a movie that "is trying to say that these are real values." Kasdan's remarks on his motives for this revival are so convoluted and couched as to become contradictory; of the relation of his revivalism to the contemporary discursive situation he says:

> I don't deny that we're in a period of a lot of frustration about impotence. . . . You feel other people are controlling your life internationally—American right and might is frustrated and you don't know what to do about it. That may touch a nerve in audiences today, but that's not where this film came from. It came from the fact that I liked westerns and missed them. But why did I like them? That may be the link. What excited me was the enormous potential and energy. I'm living in this society. I feel the frustrations too.

Kasdan's remarks betray some awareness that the close propinquity of the "values" of the western and those of the discourses of mainstream culture (this is the moment of the cultural shibboleth that says that America in the post-Vietnam era of the 1970s and 1980s is frustrated and disaffected by the waning of its influence and erosion of its power) can become articulated through the medium of "audiences." The notion implied here is that audiences (whoever they may actually be) will at least grasp the resonances between what they hear (and perhaps believe) about America's status and position and the archetypal values that are being promoted by the revival of the western. Although Kasdan tries to deny that the political discourses of his culture actually motivated his intervention into the western genre, he is clearly aware that his film could reinforce them. And when he then talks of more particular aspects of these "mythic archetypes," he actually renders himself more complicit with this process than he appears to want to: that is, speaking of the centralizing and heroizing of the white male protagonist of the western, he says that "those are things important for kids. I think they're still positive and I'm not cynical or sophisticated about that. . . . A strong man who can be compassionate and caring and makes a moral choice at critical moments is essential to our idea of ourselves as Americans."

Perhaps the most disturbing thing about this cultural fascination with the "strong, . . . compassionate and caring" male guardian that Kasdan thinks is "essential" is the way he is seen as precisely an archetype. That is, as with all propositions of archetypal value, or of mythical attribute, the distinctly ideological nature of the construct is elided when thought of in those terms. Kasdan here seems to be aware that in attaching to such an image he might be understood as being complicit with a particular ideological stance, but immediately denies it by rather naively proclaiming, "I don't think you have to be a conservative to honor that quality." It should scarcely need pointing out that in fact the precise function of such an image is conservative in all of its aspects; the more important point here is to see how the use of such archetypes and myths immediately entails the denial of political or ideological effects. Even though Kasdan glimpses the idea that to make a western in 1985 has some definite political resonance, he simultaneously denies this by imputing the transcendence or the essential (and therefore nonpolitical) nature of that gesture.

Addressing the same kind of questions about why he would choose to make a western at that particular historical juncture, Eastwood is much more cautious in his response. That is to say, his answer reaches for the same transcendent and essential justification as Kasdan's but does not allow the same glimpses of the political consequences: "There aren't any intellectual reasons for it; it's instinctual," he claims (Simsolo 1990, 152). This response, turning the issue at hand into a matter of essential (instinctual) and personal volition, is reinforced later in the same interview. The interviewer suggests that perhaps he needs to make a western every now and then "because westerns are the real roots of American cinema"; Eastwood responds that "perhaps it's because my own roots are there." Eastwood's description of the decisions in such a personalized manner and as a matter of pragmatism is perhaps nothing more than a disavowal of exactly the kinds of political and cultural connection of the western that Kasdan less guardedly addresses. At any rate, his film is clearly no less "an unabashed embrace of the values of the old Westerns" (Kasdan) than *Silverado*. Certainly, as the film's reviewer in the *Progressive* is at pains to point out, both "*Pale Rider* and *Silverado* try to persuade us that we have never lost the simple and straightforward values of the mythic Old West. Look here, these films declaim, America is America again" (Sept. 1985, 38).

Each of these movies has in its way tried to grapple with and pin down the genre, but the special gesture of *Pale Rider* is, as I've mentioned, to look back over one of the classic westerns, *Shane*. Despite the disclaimers of one of the screenwriters, Dennis Shyack (*New York Times*, 21 July 1985), the similarities between the two films are so obvious that they cannot be ignored. There are several variations worked on particular moments in *Shane* that underscore the similarities even in their difference. For instance, in *Shane* the gunslinger hero cooperates with the homesteader in getting rid of a particularly troublesome tree root on his land; in *Pale Rider* the tree root is changed to a massive boulder. This is in accordance with the fact that Eastwood's film has set its hero between corporate and independent mining interests, in place of the classic situation where he would be set between corporate and independent agricultural interests; in other words Eastwood sets his drama on that stage of the frontier, Sierra Nevada mining country, that, according to Frederick Turner's well-known genealogy of the West, comes after the homesteader stage. But in both cases the drama is structurally the same in that the clearing of the obstacle is to bespeak the bonding of the hero with the ordinary man who is attempting to turn his staked claim to profit; in *Shane* the tree has hitherto stood in the way of cultivation, and in *Pale Rider* the removal of the rock leads to the discovery of the settler's first sizable recovery of gold ore.

There are many other instances in this film that both stress a relationship of similarity to *Shane* and yet mark a distance from it to some extent. Perhaps the most interesting is the later film's replacement of the homesteader's son, Joey, by the gold prospector's daughter, Megan. In *Shane* Joey had supplied a somewhat standard Oedipal element of the western, being the young white male for whom a real or earthly father must be replaced by the ideal father, by the avenging and all-powerful white male who comes to save him and then ascends into the hills. *Pale Rider* complicates this fundamental relationship by changing the gender of the child. Megan's attachment to the hero thence becomes an overtly sexual one in a way that Joey's cannot be. There is a rather fraught sequence in the early part of *Pale Rider* where the young girl in effect asks her new "father" to make love to her, becoming angry when he will not. This helps retrospectively to make overt the sexual dimension to *Shane*'s narrative that the latter cannot fully acknowledge. This dimension comes to the fore again when the gunfighter saves Megan from rape by the son of the prospector's antagonist, Lahood. It emerges again when he sleeps with Megan's mother, making explicit a relation between the hero and the subhero's wife that is only hinted at in *Shane*.

The more overt sexualization of the narrative that *Pale Rider* presents still leaves the almost paradigmatic shape of the *Shane* narrative intact, but intensifies what I'm loosely calling the "Oedipal" structure of that narrative. It is true that in removing the son Joey, *Pale Rider* sacrifices a certain kind of emphasis on the idea that the western community can be safely handed on to a male heir who has understood the civics lessons that the gunfighter comes to deliver. But something else is gained by the substitution of a daughter. That is, the girl's adoration of the gunfighter and the mother's explicit submission to him bespeak an ordering of things that more fully or extensively implicates the ideal masculinity of the protagonist. Whereas Joey's adoration had to remain at the level, literally, of hero worship, the protagonist in *Pale Rider* instead achieves the consent—in several registers—of the women of the frontier. In traditional western paradigms, the women characters tended to represent a continual ambivalence about the violent course of the menfolk. But here Megan already is won over: she acts the part of a dutiful son in that she has no problem with the violence of her prospective savior and desired lover—indeed, she is reading aloud from *Revelations* and implicitly calling for the violent angel of death when the pale rider, pat on cue, appears for the first time. Her mother, Sarah, does at first have objections to the menfolk's determination to confront Lahood's gang, but these qualms are effectively swept aside after she has consented to a night with the stranger. As with the hotelier's wife in *High Plains* (also called Sarah), her initial "womanly" objections to violent behavior turn to complicity at the behest of the stranger's masculine power.

The way in which the women of Eastwood's westerns, epitomized by these two in *Pale Rider*, as it were endow the protagonist with an overtly sexualized rectitude constitutes an important strand in those westerns and feasibly has consequences in terms of the reception of Eastwood as star. Eastwood's star status, that is, is based not only upon the simple heroism that a Joey could enjoy, but also on a heterosexual contract that both produces and depends upon feminine compliance and complicity with the image of masculinity that is shown. There are no reliable industry studies of the gender breakdown of the audiences for Eastwood movies (any more than there are studies conducted around race and ethnicity), but tributary media discussion of Eastwood often revolves around his image for women spectators: even as he approaches his sixties, Eastwood appears to be regarded as a sex symbol in many contexts, and certainly in his younger years a large part of his following consisted of women who found him attractive. It is difficult to speculate about the value of the kinds of popular journalism surveys and polls in which that sort of result emerges, but it is not difficult to see that their results must have been affected by the way in which a movie like *Pale Rider* transmogrifies generic formulae in order to profer (and thus perhaps manufacture) women's consent in this intensified lionizing of the "archetypal" hero.

If this is one way in which the movie is related to cultural codes and discourses—effecting or affecting them through an active rearrangement of generic possibilities—*Pale Rider* also offers an instance of how the genre can be refined to accommodate burgeoning but already existent social discourses that it has not normally attended to. Here I am alluding to the discourse of liberal ecology that circulates within *Pale Rider*. Within the voluminous literature on the American West, questions of ecology, conflicting ideas of land use, considerations of the notion of wilderness, and so on, are persistent and even central. Yet, with few exceptions, westerns as such deal with ecological questions in only gingerly and sporadic fashion, by and large displacing them onto the familiar power struggles between homesteaders and land barons, communities and railroads, settlers and "Indians," and the like. Rarely do westerns place concern with the land itself, or concern about the effects of land use, at the forefront of their discourses.

This is strange in some ways, given that part of the ideological and cultural significance of the West resides precisely in its imaginary status as wilderness and in its potentialities as a locus for contemplation and spiritual renewal. It would seem that those qualities of the West, which appear mostly as figurations in painting or perhaps in literary texts, give way to the demand for narrative action in western films. As they disappear, so does the possibility of directly commenting upon ecological questions. But perhaps more crucial than that, it would also seem to be more simply the case that for most of the history of the western the ideological concern for the cultivation of the West is at odds with and has no room for the more romanticized strain of American thinking that sees the West as a place of wilderness and solitude.

The absence in westerns of what is elsewhere a continual clash of ideologies surrounding this issue and the absence of ecological issues in general install the idea of the West unproblematically on one side of a particular dichotomy: between, that is, the idea of the West as an objectifiable resource, or set of resources, for the advancement of American communities and interests, and the idea of the West as the territory of ecological sanctity or of recreation and meditation. Michael Rogin describes this same dichotomy when he suggests that "there is a division at the center of American politics between a nature-become-commodity, which separates men in civil society, and a virgin land, which purifies and unites them" (1987, 177). And yet westerns implicitly argue that even the "virgin land" must be cultivated, exploited, and used—if only for the production of use-value. At any rate there is no ecological sanctity as far as most of the western film tradition is concerned, but only the possibility of exploitation; most westerns thus will confine their interest to suggesting what kind of exploitation is civically most preferable.

Eastwood's movie is no different in that respect: its suggestion is that a small community of independent miners is preferable to the technologized corporation exactly because it is a community. The task of the preacher-gunfighter in *Pale Rider* is to exhort that community to look after itself and defend itself, and to empower it to live as a kind of epitome of the Jeffersonian small republic of virtuous citizens. In this sense the movie merely repeats the emphasis of *Shane* and any number of other westerns. Its difference, however, is to have added to this ideology of virtuous and self-sufficient community the notion that such a community is simply better for the land. Where corporate abuse of lands has been mooted in other westerns it has been in terms, for instance, of using up too much water so that smaller settlers cannot survive, and thus is treated as a question only of property and competing rights and powers. The Eastwood movie, on the other hand, permits itself to sermonize about the preference for the Jeffersonian over the Madisonian economy in purely ecological terms.

Thus, for instance, the movie spends some time depicting the "rape of the land" of which Lahood's massive hydraulic technology is guilty, this rape being echoed by Lahood's son's attempted assault on Megan after he has proudly pointed out to her all of the rapine technology that his father has put in place. Scenes of the moonscape effects of Lahood's methods are juxtaposed with the quiet industry of Hull Barret and his companions working by hand. The visual effects are perhaps more powerful than the prose of the novelized version of *Pale Rider* (by Alan Dean Foster [London: Arrow Books, 1988]), but the latter has the leisure to make the sermon more overt; commenting on the water cannons used to flush ore, the novel says, "A cannon that spat water instead of fire was not a sign, as one might think, that the world had been turned topsy-turvy. For one thing, its blast was just as destructive as any weapon in the army's arsenal, and considerably more consistent" (53).

The entry of this kind of concern into westerns is, as I have said, relatively novel and is an articulation of a more general cultural concern about the West as such; that is, a concern that the land that the westerns had more or less unproblematically considered as a resource might become an irreplaceable resource, or a literally priceless one. These kinds of concerns were at a particularly high pitch in the early 1980s, during the tenure of Ronald Reagan's secretary of the interior, James Watt, but had been provoked in the 1970s by huge numbers of litigations in the courts over environmental resources. *Pale Rider* seems to want to intervene into this context, and to want to weigh in on the side of moderate and communal use or exploitation of land and resources. Such an argument is made in part on the grounds that this is consonant with the communitarian autonomy that the ideology of westerns has chronically promoted. At the same time its rhetoric—its specific appeal to the dangers posed to the land itself—constitutes, I would argue, a development in the genre and acts as a kind of response to and reinforcement of some of the available social and cultural codes.

In the two ways that I have been discussing, then—in relation to the general issues of sexuality and ecology—this film provides an instance of how the process of genre formation operates. I am not intending to impute these changes and accommodations to any specific agent; certainly, I am not positing Eastwood himself as "auteur" here. Indeed, one of the aims in trying to isolate these processes in a series of films involving one particular man is to bypass any such "auteur" notion; it seems possible to do that here in part because Eastwood does in fact take on a variety of functions in relation to the manufacture of any of the movies I have been discussing—producer, director, actor under his own direction, actor under Leone's or Post's or Sturges's direction, or whatever. This is not to suggest that Eastwood's own views or his own volition are not somehow present in these films. Indeed, as far as the introduction of the ecology issue into the genre is concerned, it is quite possible that the rhetoric of *Pale Rider* expresses a view that Eastwood holds or has held. In some ways, as we shall see later, Eastwood's tenure as mayor of Carmel in 1986 might suggest that this is the case. Equally, one of the few times that Eastwood has performed for the tributary media would also seem to support that view: in 1987 he appeared in a series of television messages produced by the Department of the Interior and aimed against the ecological abuse of public lands.[12]

However, my interest here has been less in what Eastwood himself might be assumed to be "expressing" and rather more in the way that the series of movies in which he is involved is necessarily caught up in another kind of narrative—a narrative that involves a process of shifts and alterations in a dialectic between, on the one hand, these cultural products, their histories and their generic address and, on the other hand, the cotextual histories that constitute the culture in which these films are both manufactured and consumed. As a series of gestures these movies can be understood as helping to produce that dialectic, of course, pushing its meanings and its processes toward something in particular, namely toward a restitution of a genre that Hollywood thinks of as having been damaged in the context of an America that sees itself as having been weakened.

At the Smithsonian

There is a moment in *Bronco Billy* when the obnoxious upper-class heiress, who is unwillingly traveling with Bronco Billy's band of contemporary "cowboys and Indians," gets into an argument with Billy and is promptly removed from the truck cab and deposited at the roadside. What she has done to deserve this is to suggest that Billy is "nothing but an illiterate cowboy." Having got rid of her, Billy warns that "no one talks like that about a cowboy."

It is apparently true, even after the effective demise of westerns as a continuing Hollywood project, that you cannot say things like that about cowboys, or—to extend the point—that you cannot question the wholesomeness and integrity of the ideological tradition that he embodies. In case there were any doubt on this score, the limits of what is allowed to be said about the West were reaffirmed by both popular and official reactions to an exhibition on the American West at the Smithsonian Institution in Washington in 1991. "The West as America: Reinterpreting Images of the Frontier" presented a selection of art made between 1820 and 1920 that addresses the westward expansion of the nineteenth century. These works included many paintings and photographs that have become central to the popular American imaginary of what the West looked like and its sense of what the true history of the West might be. Much of the work exhibited, by artists and photographers like Charles Schreyvogel, Frederic Remington, or Charles Russell, has become the fodder of mass reproduction this century. In that role, and by dint of their use in education and entertainment, these images have consequently done much to forge those "mythical" and "archetypical" notions of the West to which many Americans give credence.

However, the aim of this exhibition was exactly not to reinforce those myths and archetypes, but rather to the contrary, to historicize them. The artworks were accompanied by interpretative texts that attempted to explain how "these images are carefully staged fictions" that served—and continue to serve—the function of justifying and rationalizing what is recognized by many historians as a quite ruthless and uncontrolled colonizing enterprise.[1] In other words, these interpretative texts continually stressed the fact that the work upon which they commented had profound ideological dimensions. Some of them explicated the complicity of the artists with white America's vindication of its right to expand wherever it wished and by whatever means. Some went into detail about the destruction of Native American cultures that the westward expansion inevitably entailed. Some offered unflattering psychoanalytical interpretation of the impulses of the artists in making such works. All were condemned from a variety of sources, both in public and in the Institution's visitors book.

The public attack on the show was led by various senators from western states who confessed themselves shocked and appalled that a publicly funded museum should have so thoroughly—and indeed, aggressively—interrogated the standard popular versions of such a crucial moment in American history. The charge was joined by various dignitaries such as Daniel Boorstin, former librarian of Congress, who wrote in the visitors book that this was a "perverse, historically inaccurate, destructive" show; and the bourgeois historian, Simon Schama, who complained about the exhibition's "relentless sermon of condescension."[2]

It would seem that a good number of the less well known visitors who wrote in the exhibition visitors book concurred. Flushed with America's recent "victory" over Iraqi foes in the Middle East war, and having been coached to now name the enemy at home by means of the rash of media denunciations of the "politically correct" (PC) delusions of the nation's campus intellectuals, this portion of the public produced comments such as the following: "This show is just another banal exercise in the 'politically correct' 'oppression study' movement." . . . "Deconstructionist B.S." . . . "reflects a contemporary, Eastern, left-wing, revisionist view of U.S. domestic history. It does America no good." Various newspapers stirred up and egged on the attacks with commentary such as the following from the *Washington Post*: "With the sort of tortured revisionism now so stridently de rigueur in academia, [the exhibition] effectively trashes not only the integrity of the art it presents but most of our national history as well, reducing the saga of America's Western pioneers to little more than victimization, disillusion, and environmental rape." There are, in fact, other meanings to which the exhibition deliberately "reduced" this phase of American history (a phase rather curiously described by the reviewer as "most of our national history"), including the affirmation and installation at that time of a Madisonian vision of bourgeois political economy over possible alternative visions of America, and also including the wanton destruction, massacre, and cheating of Native Americans and their cultures that was part of that process, as well as the pandemic racism implicit in both the history itself and in these representations of the history.

The interesting aspect of the various attacks on the exhibition is not so much the indignant denial of any of the particular aspects of the "revisionist" history it is accused of proposing. Rather, what the attack betrays is simply the continued inability of white American culture to recognize that its imaginary of its own history is not invulnerable—even if that imaginary has been elevated to the status of myth, archetype, or essence. As was clearly the case with Lawrence Kasdan's remarks surrounding *Silverado*, the central point about the construction of such myths, archetypes, and essences is that they should deflect anything that might be described as a political dimension to history. In other words, in American public discourse and ideology, historicizing is the equivalent of "politicizing." And, as has often been pointed out, to politicize is in this context to undertake some illegitimate or simply unseemly exercise designed in some way to undermine "America."

The eagerness that is so often exhibited in American culture to either ignore or transcend "politics" (as in the turning out by Congress of "bipartisan"—that is, supposedly nonpolitical—agreements and decisions) is symptomatic of an urge toward a single legitimating narrative of civic life that will designate the past as a glorious and fixed heritage. Such a single narrative tends, of course, to be reinforced by the process of genre formation (at least, this is the case if we are talking of genre in Hollywood cinema), which, as I have suggested, is the process by which repetition and difference are accommodated one to the other. However, it is important to underscore that the differences that are accommodated in that process are not the differences that would be produced by competing or contestatory narratives, but differences that are already within the purview or the possible paradigms of an already prescribed cultural verisimilitude. Such a set of cultural discourses and ideologies, while not totally circumscribed and while certainly not impervious to change and modification, is kept in check or maintained within certain boundaries by the apparatuses of a capitalist culture in both its privately owned and its state aspects. In that light, it remains crucial to remember that, even if the array of elements allowable through a sense of what I am calling cultural verisimilitude is broad, it is nonetheless exclusionary, and that the legitimizing, or the making viable of these elements, is dependent upon firm ownership of the means by which they can be disseminated.

Thus it seems pertinent to remark that many of the objections to the exhibition derive from a sense that a publicly funded institution like the Smithsonian should not be assailing or questioning the single narrative. Any publicly funded institution in this country is presumed either to be, or to have the obligation to be, nonpolitical, since one of the political functions of the single narrative it is authorized to disseminate is precisely to support the ideology that politics can be transcended into a single narrative. This logic, which is of course circular and which demands and entails a repression of other narratives, is the warrant for remarks such as that of Alaska senator, Ted Stevens: "Why should people come to your institution and see a history that is so perverted? I don't think the Smithsonian has any business, or has ever had any business, developing a political agenda."

The perversion of history that Stevens complains of consists in the very act of introducing competing narratives through the process of interpretative historicizing. That process is condemned as "politicized" while its condemners heroically claim to have no political agenda. The narratives which that process unearths remain largely unheard—and if they are heard, they are thought of as dismissable. Thus official white American culture is still by and large unable to hear a narrative that suggests that its civilization is founded upon the lives of its victims and upon the ruins of their cultures, particularly Native American ones. No one, not Leone, nor the Smithsonian, is allowed to talk like that about a cowboy.

Homesteaders

I guess I am a capitalist.
—Clint Eastwood

By 1968, due to the huge popular success of the spaghetti westerns, Clint Eastwood had become a major star and box-office draw, and he has, of course, remained so to the present. His films—certainly nearly all those in which he has performed and most of those which he has directed—are simply and phenomenally successful in industry terms. As of January 1988 (up to and including the release of *Heartbreak Ridge*), no fewer than twenty-eight of the pictures in which Eastwood has appeared were included on *Variety*'s list of all-time domestic hits. According to *Variety*'s figures, those films made returns of almost $457 million in the United States and Canada, beginning in 1964 with, appropriately enough, *A Fistful of Dollars*, and even many of the older ones continue to bring in significant profits: for instance, *Every Which Way but Loose*, after having netted $48 million in the first three years of its release, added almost another $4 million between 1981 and 1988.

It is hard to think of another Hollywood figure of the last quarter of a century who could be the catalyst for such consistent box-office earnings. And these earnings are all the more astounding when set against the cost of most of Eastwood's movies. His directorial debut, *Play Misty for Me*, was budgeted at less than $1 million and has brought in about five or six times that amount in domestic returns since 1971. This is a ratio that is probably about the norm for his work—although the earnings for his most successful movie, *Every Which Way but Loose* (1978), relatively expensive to make at $3.5 million, come in at about $87 million worldwide, a staggering 2500 percent return.[1] Even the more expensive movies in which he has been involved, like *Firefox* and its $18 million budget, turn significant profits.[2]

These figures bespeak a form of industry practice that is, to say the least, unusual. The combination of a top-rank star with low-budget pictures is perhaps the most remarkable indicator of Eastwood's productions. Beyond that, the sizes of the budgets that Eastwood and his colleagues work with are minimal by the ordinary standards of the industry, where, today, a first-run movie with a major star would be an anomaly if it cost less than $25 or $30 million to make. Part of the explanation for the unusual nature of Eastwood's practice derives from his having worked almost exclusively for his own production company, Malpaso, since the late 1960s. From 1970's *Kelly's Heroes* onward, Eastwood has not worked on a film that does not include either his own or Malpaso's name in the production credits. And since the mid-1970s, when *Thunderbolt and Lightfoot* (1974) was released by United Artists and *The Eiger Sanction* (1975) by Universal, Eastwood and Malpaso have had what appears to be an exclusive distribution arrangement with Warner Brothers.

Malpaso was formed in 1968 while Eastwood made what was only his second American movie after the Leone trilogy, *Coogan's Bluff* (1968). It seems that the company was initially conceived as a way of lessening Eastwood's personal tax burden; that is, Malpaso was effectively an incorporation of Eastwood himself, and a way to exploit his earnings potential. To undertake such an incorporation was, and is, scarcely an unusual step for actors, actresses, directors, and producers in the industry. Many stars form corporations to further their own interests as commodities, but usually such companies are limited to the function of hiring out the star to other interests, or occasionally developing properties in which they are especially interested (like Burt Reynolds's company, BR Productions, which is not actually a production company as such). Only a few such companies venture into the realm of production in the way that Malpaso did in the early seventies—Robert Redford's Wildwood would be another instance—and fewer still have the record of longevity and consistent popular success that Malpaso can boast. The kind of relationship that Malpaso has had to the major corporate interests of Warner Brothers is also not the norm for such companies, and perhaps has a modern counterpart only in Woody Allen's erstwhile arrangement with United Artists (see Bach).

At any rate, by the early 1970s Malpaso had become a full-fledged independent production company. Its evolution from a tax-saving device into Eastwood's private production company appears to have been influenced primarily by the actor's experience in making various movies in the early 1970s. Eastwood starred during those years in a number of different kinds of film, including several high-budget movies intended to be blockbusters like *Where Eagles Dare* (1969) and *Kelly's Heroes* (1970). He also worked for several different major producers and distributors—United Artists (who had been the U.S. distributors of the Leone movies), Universal, MGM, and Paramount. At the same time, his Malpaso projects were attached for a while to Universal and for a while to United Artists. In the course of all these projects Eastwood seems to have developed a critique of some of the standard practices of the industry that led him to a more and more determinedly independent stance and to the increased use of Malpaso as a base for his own ideas about filmmaking practices.

The root of Eastwood's dissatisfaction with the standard procedures of Hollywood filmmaking derives from several insights. The first of these—or at least, the one that seems to be most frequently stated in his own and others' accounts and upon which the figures mentioned above act as a commentary—is the sense that Hollywood filmmaking is unconscionably wasteful. That is, the multimillion-dollar budgets that are authorized for production of even the most negligible movie are in Eastwood's view excessive, and Malpaso comes to be dedicated to the proposition that box-office successes can be made without such gargantuan budgets. The waste of which Eastwood complains is corrected in Malpaso productions in ways that I shall come to in a moment, but they are exacerbated in the normal Hollywood procedures of distribution and exhibition. The wasted parts of the $17 million budget for *Paint Your Wagon* and, relatedly, that movie's inordinately long shooting schedules seem to have particularly bothered Eastwood[3] and provoked him toward the expansion of Malpaso.

Equally, Eastwood thinks of several of his films in the early seventies as having been badly or wrongly treated by the controlling distributors. This complaint extends from the studios' reluctance to allow directors final cut (as in MGM's refusal to allow Brian Hutton to oversee the final version of *Kelly's Heroes*) to their unwillingness or inability to properly handle and promote certain films. Eastwood's relationship with United Artists, for instance, ceased after they had, in his view, mishandled *Thunderbolt and Lightfoot*.[4] Similarly, Eastwood had complaints about Universal's handling of *Breezy*, a film that he had directed but not starred in and that was simply a box-office failure.[5] The relationship with Universal ended definitively in 1975, after the release of *The Eiger Sanction*, and Eastwood and Malpaso worked thereafter almost exclusively with Warner Brothers, who, presumably, had recognized the wisdom of giving Eastwood virtually free rein in production and of aggressively promoting and distributing his work—although it might be observed that by 1975 Eastwood's movies more or less sold themselves, and Warner's decisions must have been quite easy to reach.

In terms of the actual production of his movies, Eastwood has what some observers like to think of as a minimalist approach to film. This is perhaps because of his initiation into the industry through the stripped-down production methods used in the Italian industry, and perhaps because of his early work in television; but the central explanation he himself gives is of seeing big studio budgets go to waste in the making of films such as *Paint Your Wagon*. As his longtime friend and colleague in Malpaso, former production chief Robert Daley, once put it, the central aim of a company like theirs is to "survive in a frightening industry by putting all the money on the screen, not in expense account luxuries and other wasteful practices."[6] While such expense account profligacy as Daley points to is common in the industry, cutting it down is only one way in which Malpaso saves money. The more general project of "putting all the money on the screen" has informed a series of procedural options which Malpaso has adopted and consistently carried through since the mid-1970s or even earlier.

The most important and effective of these procedures is probably the determination to shoot movies in such a way that they stay within budget and within schedule. This is achieved through the combination of a number of factors, notably the decision to shoot on location whenever possible. It is reported that "between 1970 and 1974 the company spent only 6 of more than 200 shooting days on a soundstage or back lot; [in 1985], although Malpaso can afford to do otherwise, that percentage pretty much holds up." This tendency has become more marked in Hollywood production since the 1970s, and

Malpaso's setting the example and its subsequent success may well have been influential in that regard.

I shall say more in the next section about some of the other factors as they involve shooting and editing; in the meantime there are other options on the production side that are significant. For instance, from the outset of production, Malpaso attempts to save money by careful acquisition and development of properties. That is, most of Malpaso Productions' stories and screenplays are taken from sources which do not automatically command the high prices of, for example, a Robert Ludlum story. One exception to this was perhaps their purchase of a Craig Thomas best-seller for *Firefox*. Some scripts have been elaborated from amateur sources, such as the story for *The Enforcer*, which was, apparently, "written by two northern Californian youths who gave it to the *maître d'* at Eastwood's restaurant" (*Variety*, 15 Sept. 1976, 30). But most of the scripts and stories used are developed by Sonia Chernus, who has been involved with Malpaso since its inception, having previously worked on stories for *Rawhide* when Eastwood was appearing in that TV series. (Chernus was also, incidentally, the creator of television's Mr. Ed.) A number of different screenwriting credits crop up several times in the history of Malpaso—the names of Dean Reisner, Richard Tuggle (who also directs *Tightrope*), Michael Butler, Dennis Shyack, and Jo Heims, the last of whom was a close collaborator of Eastwood's at Malpaso until her death, having once been his secretary.

The repeated employment of known and trusted names in other areas, too, is a Malpaso trademark and indicates the company's commitment to the idea of forging close and continuing relationships with its creative workers. This is perhaps clearest at the level of directors and cinematographers; in the latter category, Bruce Surtees was for many years the first choice as photographer on Eastwood movies and latterly that role seems to have fallen to Jack Green. In terms of direction, Eastwood himself is Malpaso's principal director, but people like Richard Tuggle, Buddy Van Horn, and James Fargo have signed Malpaso pictures, and worked on others even where Eastwood is credited with the direction. Eastwood has considered part of the function of Malpaso to be the encouragement of such directors, and he was responsible for giving, among others, Michael Cimino his first opportunity as director (on *Thunderbolt and Lightfoot*). Work on Malpaso sound tracks has been given predominantly to Lalo Schifrin or Lennie Niehaus, with the former appearing to have had the contract on the "Dirty Harry" movies. This habit of hiring known quantities and family and friends also carries over to casting. Sondra Locke, Eastwood's companion for many years, has of course starred alongside him in a number of movies, and his daughter Alison and son Kyle have played substantial parts in *Tightrope* and *Honky Tonk Man*, respectively. A quite sizable list can be drawn up—including the names of Geoffrey Lewis, Harry Guardino, Sam Bottoms, Jack Thibeau, Bradford Dillman, and George Kennedy—of actors who have been hired several times by the company for particular projects (though Malpaso's file of such preferred players appears to include few women except Locke).

The core of this kind of extended family was drawn together in the early years of Malpaso from among people whom Eastwood had known and respected from earlier moments in his career. Irving Leonard, who had been Eastwood's business manager when he was starting out in Hollywood, was made president of Malpaso. An old friend of Eastwood's from the early 1950s when he was still a contract player with Universal, Robert Daley, joined Malpaso in 1970 as executive producer. Daley's arrival marks the turn of Malpaso from Eastwood's tax-saving device toward production proper, and his name appears in the production credits for every Eastwood movie from *Play Misty for Me* (1971) to *Bronco Billy* (1980), after which he started up his own production company. After that time, his place as executive producer was taken by Fritz Manes, who is one of Eastwood's oldest friends; the position of executive producer has recently been taken over by David Valdes. Other people involved at the heart of Malpaso include Sonia Chernus, who works as story developer and has written a couple of screenplays for Eastwood, including the rescue of the script of *Outlaw Josey Wales* after the departure of its original director, Phil Kaufman.[7] A former secretary of Eastwood's, Jo Heims, was also part of the core personnel and is credited with the screenplays for two of Eastwood's earliest directorial efforts, *Play Misty* and *Breezy*; Heims died in 1973. And perhaps the most influential member of the group was Don Siegel, the director from whom, Eastwood says, he has learned the most about directing and who died in 1991.

About Siegel more will be said later; for now it is impressive to note the relative consistency of the Malpaso group—and of its extended family of (mostly) journeymen—across the years. The closeness of the small number of people involved, their reliance upon known associates, the determination to nurture new creative talents and develop inexpensive properties, the work ethic and the parsimonious sense of expenses that are needed to bring films in on time and within budget—all these factors and others that I shall discuss later constitute an image of Malpaso as a quintessential small business in terms of the structuration of capitalism in America. Indeed, Malpaso could almost be defined as a family business, with its core workers united in their distrust of and disdain for the excess of big business; Eastwood says, "I always believed that if all the industries in this country were run like the movie industry, they'd all be in the tank" (*Esquire*, 14 March 1978, 44). The Hollywood industry's difference resides, however, not just in its size and its concomitant excesses, but also in its ethics. The industry's exaggerated budgets are an indication of its lack of morality, and the ostentatious concern for money is another in Eastwood's view—for him, "talking about money is grotesque. . . . I don't check out other people's accounts and they don't check out mine—because I own the whole operation" (43).[8]

This kind of "family business," then, runs on the conviction that the best work can be done by a small and tightly knit group of people with similar values and with a collaborative commitment to the owner—in this case Eastwood himself. The private status of the company is an essential part of its ethos: lock, stock, and barrel it is owned by the proprietor, whose relationship to the other individuals is thus patronal, and their relations to each other are mediated by the fact that it is their relation to the patron that has brought them together. (One might note in passing that this is almost exactly the situation that is represented in *Bronco Billy*, which is at pains to emphasize the importance of the "head ramrod.") Within such a structure the central unit of people develops a commitment to basic essentials of craft and artisanry. The industry that exists around and beyond such a company—here the corporate world of Hollywood—is threatening in certain ways ("frightening," to use Daley's word), and the small company's survival depends upon producing a product that is at least equal to the corporate product but cheaper to make and thus relatively more profitable. The quality of that product in turn depends upon the signature of the patron, Clint Eastwood the box-office star.

The structural functioning of Malpaso itself in the industry is akin to that of, say, a small independent producer of fashion jewelry that sells its product to large department stores for distribution. It is, in a sense, a sophisticated cottage industry. But what is perhaps most interesting about it is the way that its material place and its own imaginary of itself are constructed as both subservient to and yet superior to the larger industry. The subservience—perhaps emblematized by the location of Malpaso's offices among the Warner Brothers offices in Burbank, just as they had previously been located in a bungalow on the property of Universal—is in fact a dependence: in the current situation of the American film industry, Malpaso's products could not be widely distributed and exhibited without the power of a Warner Brothers or a Universal. The superiority, on the other hand, derives from the imaginary sense of being able to produce a commodity that maintains a ratio of quality to profitability that the larger corporation cannot match.

To note such a dialectic of dependence and superiority is, of course, to suggest an analogous dialectic of complicity with and resistance to the corporate structures of Hollywood. For Eastwood personally the dialectic is played out in his displacement from Hollywood to his home in Carmel: "Here I see things a little bit differently than I would in L.A.," he says (*Esquire*, 14 March 1978, 44). But at other levels it is tempting to see the Malpaso situation as effectively an embodiment of one of the central contradictions of the Hollywood industry. That is, Hollywood's massive corporate mechanisms have chronically turned out products in which populist ideological values seem to be promoted. The anticorporate narratives of the standard westerns, or of classic movies like, say, *It's a Wonderful Life*, have always bespoken an ideology ostensibly at odds with the corporate capitalist ideology of the institution that produces them.

This contradiction has perhaps never been particularly bothersome for Hollywood, and indeed its perennial success in sustaining it is a measure of its power. Despite the fact that, as Douglas Gomery points out, the total of Hollywood's annual domestic revenues are smaller than even just the *profits* of a single industrial corporation like IBM,[9] it still stands as a paragon of the American capitalist system: always veering toward monopoly, concentrated ownership, and vertical organization, it at the same time produces a cheap commodity for popular consumption along with a set of ideological interpellations which belie and contradict those elements of organization and capitalization. Malpaso is in a sense a perfect alibi for the Hollywood industry: as a company it embodies the very values that the Hollywood commodity promulgates, living out the role that the small community of homesteaders plays in a western.

Misogyny

As I suggested earlier, the most important member of the Malpaso "family business"—in its early days, certainly—was Don Siegel, the man who directed Eastwood in his second major American film, *Coogan's Bluff* (1968), and in several other of his post-spaghetti movies, including his perhaps best-known film, *Dirty Harry* (1971). Of the eight movies with which Eastwood was associated in the years 1968-71, four were directed by Siegel: *Coogan's Bluff*, *Two Mules for Sister Sara* (1970), *The Beguiled* (1971), and *Dirty Harry*. A fifth Siegel-Eastwood collaboration appeared in 1979 with *Escape from Alcatraz*. While *Dirty Harry* is, even two decades after its release, probably Eastwood's most popularly significant film, it is by no means his only formative collaboration with Don Siegel. Together these movies have certainly played a large part in the shaping both of Malpaso's success and of Eastwood's career and in the making of his popular-cultural image—not least because these are the movies that consolidated his presence in the public eye most immediately after the unexpected successes of the spaghetti westerns. But at another level their importance resides in their embodiment of a practice of filmmaking that is, by and large, unusual in relation to Hollywood's standard methods; this practice becomes the model for Eastwood's in his later career and becomes, too, the origin in a sense of the style of his later movies.

Of course, the same years, between 1968 and 1971, also saw the release of *Hang 'em High* (1968), *Where Eagles Dare* (1969), *Paint Your Wagon* (1969), and *Kelly's Heroes* (1970), all movies that attempted to assert or exploit Eastwood's growing reputation in the international film market. I have suggested earlier how Eastwood's signifying presence is manipulated in *Hang 'em* and how that movie is implicated in the narrative of Eastwood's relation to the template of the western; and in a later section ("Servicemen") I shall look at the two war movies in this group. *Paint Your Wagon* is, as I have said, remarkable mostly for the way it figures in Eastwood's imaginary as the film which underscores the need for a filmmaking practice different from the Hollywood mode which it seemed to represent. Otherwise *Wagon*'s attempt to cast Eastwood and Lee Marvin as the singing gold prospectors in Alan Jay Lerner's adaptation of his Broadway musical, and the story of their ménage à trois with Jean Seberg, is mostly disastrous. The reviewer Rex Reed perhaps summed it up best when he said that it is "a monument to unparalleled incompetence. . . . [T]hey bought an expensive musical property and hired actors who can't dance or sing" (quoted in Zmijewsky, 100). The film's total domestic receipts by 1988 still fell far short of its $17 million production budget.

The Siegel collaborations stand in quite sharp contrast to the kind of big studio production that Eastwood undertook in these years. Whereas the big production movies represent all that Eastwood dislikes about and complains about Hollywood, the Siegel movies partake of the "family business" ethos almost completely. Before joining up with Malpaso, Siegel had been known in Hollywood as something of a maverick. He has a long history of doing battle with the interests of the big studios and of asserting his independence and his right to make movies in his own way. Simultaneously he had developed a style of filmmaking which, drawing on and deriving from his experiences making B movies in the 1940s with Warner Brothers, was relatively quick and cheap to carry out. Thus his reputation as a maverick was always offset by the fact that he brought in movies on time and quite cheaply.

Siegel's first box-office hit was *Riot in Cell Block 11* for Allied Artists in 1954, but he became more in demand after the celebrated *Invasion of the Body Snatchers* in 1956. That movie remains one of the most important science fiction movies in American film history, and it will probably secure Siegel's place as an important filmmaker. This is certainly the movie which first occasioned the enthusiasm of French critics for Siegel's work. The foreign adulation of his movies led him once to comment that he is "without honor like a prophet in his own land" (P. Douglas 1974, 105), even though a number of Anglophone critics have by now dealt extensively with his work.[1] The critical consensus is that his work up to the 1970s brings action movies to a degree of formulaic precision and effectiveness that few other directors have been able to match; for example, one of these, *Baby Face Nelson* (1957), is cited by Lovell as "an exemplary action film, superbly economic and consistently inventive" (68), and others remain important within the genres of crime and war movies: *The Lineup* (1958), *Edge of Eternity* (1959), *Hell Is for Heroes* (1962), *The Killers* (1964), and *Madigan* (1968).

Siegel's sense of what is principally wrong with standard Hollywood practice is "the stupidity of producers in general" (Lovell, 48), a view that appeared not to change very much until the late 1960s, when he worked with Jennings Lang at Universal and, simultaneously, with Eastwood and Malpaso. His published interviews suggest that he was especially concerned about the lack of freedom that most producers give directors. This antagonism toward the industry is, of course, largely what ensures his place in the Malpaso "family business." But his views about the way to make a movie cheaply, on time, and in the way that he wants would also have endeared him to Eastwood's company. In other words, his fundamental insistence was that he should have control over most of the stages of filmmaking, and it is upon this insistence that his effective manner of making action movies in particular relied.

That control began with the script—upon which, he says, "I spend a great deal of time, in fact most of my time" (46)—and ended with the editing process, which he oversaw absolutely. His handling of the stages between script and final cut was marked by two things: his efficiency and speed, and his noninterventional approach with his crew and actors. In terms of the rapidity of his filmmaking, he often shot films in sequence; or if not in sequence, then "I'll complete shooting in one direction before I turn around and shoot the other way, which saves an enormous amount of time in moves and lighting" (47)—and of course also saves money. Also his habit was to rehearse whole scenes, partly so that this way of shooting would not be confusing for the actors, but also to reduce the number of takes that would be necessary. With an actor, Siegel says, "I leave him alone," and similarly with his photographer, "I never encroach on his domain or undermine him with his crew" (47).

The advantages of these habits and practices are clear: the director, who is also as often as not the producer, has the maximum control over the final product, while at the same time he promotes independence on the part of his crew. The procedures entail shooting with an eye to the cost of the project, so that rationalized processes of setting up shots and shooting in sequence and on location help prevent excessive time and money being spent on takes and retakes. As Eastwood has said, in relation to the egregious cost overruns of Michael Cimino's *Heaven's Gate*, "All those takes are almost always the director's fault" (*Stills*, June/July 1985).

On the other hand, these kinds of processes have their possible demerits. The quality of a film produced under those conditions is not always going to be of the highest. That is, as Siegel himself admitted while describing his procedures, "I am not talking about the qualitative aspect of what I do. I am talking about time and expense, factors important in determining if the picture will make or lose money. A good picture that loses money is not what any director wants" (Lovell, 47).

Even though Siegel was capable of making highly formalized and structurally sophisticated movies (such as my own favorite, 1964's *The Hanged Man*), many of them have a rough-and-ready quality to their images and editing. But on the other hand again, this quality often lends itself well to the action movie genre where, for instance, inconsistencies of editing and diegetic placing can actually be exploited to enhance the action movie effect. This is, indeed, a necessity that Siegel turns into a virtue: some of the immediacy of the action sequences in *Dirty Harry*, for instance, is clearly the result of one-take set-ups and of the habit of editing all available shots together into fast sequences. This effect is enhanced by the frequent use of a hand-held camera to help promote a blurring of the image in the action sequences. The point to be made here is that what we can call the economical manners of filmmaking that Siegel adopts can sometimes enhance the core action sequences, while perhaps other parts—expository scenes, for instance—might as a result look rough and unpolished.

Siegel's procedures also produced a particular set of stylistic tics or signs that crop up again and again in his movies, some of which Eastwood as director inherits. For instance, he will deploy exceptionally high-contrast lighting to heighten the effect of action movement (as in a film like *Baby Face Nelson*), and he often uses a style of backlighting—which Eastwood and one of his frequently employed cinematographers, Bruce Surtees, will later deploy regularly—that loses figures in the image foreground. His preference for punctuating scenes with pull-away shots instead of unadorned cuts or dissolves is used especially frequently in *Dirty Harry*, though it appears in many of his movies. Perhaps it cannot be said that these stylistic markers in a Siegel film are directly caused by his urge for economy and speed, but they are signs of a particular kind of aesthetic in which the verisimilitude of the image is what is primarily at stake and which is no doubt promoted by the mode of shooting that he adopts.

At any rate, all of the procedures and stylistic marks that I have mentioned are ones that reemerge in movies Eastwood directs. As a director Eastwood has internalized both the production procedures and the aesthetic values with which Siegel operated. The production ideology is explained by Eastwood as a matter of planning and organizing the production and shooting of a movie, in much the same vein as Siegel explains his movies (*Film Comment* 5/6 [1984], 68). In terms of style and aesthetic, Eastwood claims that "there isn't as much a style to my films—an individualistic style—as there is to those of Don Siegel. Mine vary" (69), although it is in fact the case that similar stylistic marks emerge over and over again. But the fundamental lesson that Eastwood seems to have learned from Siegel is that to properly organize a film's production schedule, and to expedite it with the help of a cooperative and nurtured group of workers, is a fundamentally aesthetic decision with economic effects, or an economic decision with aesthetic effects. This approach to filmmaking—which Eastwood thinks of as "the new approach to moviemaking" to which Hollywood is beginning to pay attention—effectively "boils down to editing while shooting" (P. Douglas, 116). The process of shooting in sequence is the extreme of this approach, and Eastwood even prefers to do his editing on location, thereby cutting down postproduction time drastically.[2]

The film in which the imbrication of this production ideology and aesthetic style is first put into effect is the Eastwood-Siegel collaboration, *Coogan's Bluff*. The negotiations that led to Siegel's agreeing to be the director for this movie appear to have been a kind of courtship (with letters from Siegel cloyingly addressing Eastwood as "Dear Clintus"). Siegel had to be made satisfied by the script and also assured that he could film it as he wanted; and Eastwood needed this movie—his first with a contemporary setting—to allow him to assert and develop his control over his star persona. The urge for control and independence in both men led to arguments and discussions about the script over which Siegel almost quit; they agreed on the tenth version of the script, which was settled when they "decided to string together all the scenes they liked from all the preceding versions" (Guérif, 62). Eastwood describes their final agreements as "a meeting of the minds" (*Focus on Film* 25 [1976]).

In *Coogan's Bluff* Eastwood plays an Arizona sheriff sent to New York to extradite a prisoner. For the purposes of the diegesis, New York consists of two main elements: first, a bureaucracy that includes the police, who disdain Coogan for his western dress and manners, and the probation officer, played by Susan Clark, who tries to understand him; and second, the community to which the prisoner, Ringerman, belongs—urban criminals and dropouts who are characterized primarily by their drug-taking and their hippy lifestyles. The structure of the narrative is simple. The movie's action begins when the first element can no longer control the other—Ringerman escapes from a police hospital—and Coogan effectively does the bureaucracy's job for it, capturing Ringerman after an extended motorcycle chase scene in Fort Tryon Park.

The action sequences in *Coogan's Bluff* can be taken both as instances of how the Siegel ethos turns out on film, but also as precursors to the action sequences in later Eastwood movies and as early indicators of the kind of style Eastwood himself uses. There are two main set pieces in the movie, the first when Coogan enters a bar and gets into a fight, and the second, which I just mentioned, the final sequence in the park. The former sequence is a good instance of how Siegel works in action sequences. The barroom situation is established in one shot, which is held for some while, with Eastwood threatened by a semicircle of antagonists. The ensuing scene appears to have been shot in sequence with probably two cameras plus a hand-held one. Every shot takes a different line on the action, breaking down the space that had been established until it is all but incoherent. The cameras follow the action of fists, bodies, and pool cues, almost always blurring the image. The stability of the scene is maintained in an unusual way: as the horizontal space of the scene is broken into movement and blur, a set of shots from along the floor and crane shots from above the action impose a different axis.

Even though *Coogan's Bluff* is a very basic movie, both in terms of its narrative and its mise-en-scène, it is an effective movie at the box-office. It predates *Dirty Harry* as an American exploitation and modulation of Eastwood's spaghetti performances, while it also works with the same kind of thematic and generic elements as will be found in *Dirty Harry*. Specifically, the conflict in this movie between Coogan and the forces of the establishment over the proper way to get the job done will be laid out in extreme form in the later movie, whereas here there is a final reconciliation between Coogan and the institution—a reconciliation that is narratively made possible by his relationship with Julie. In *Coogan*, Julie's attempt to comprehend and accommodate Coogan's western ways makes her what we might call a commutational figure in the relation between him and the establishment. Her role is, of course, to allow a reworking of the effort in westerns to obtain the consent and assent of women for the world of male action. Later in *Dirty Harry* any similar figure is absent, and, as we shall see, that absence gives license to the film in what critics came to call its fascism (see the sections "Just Entertainment" and "The Opposite of Fascism").

The Eastwood-Siegel collaborations continue, after *Coogan's Bluff* and its "Dirty Harry" themes and action-movie efficiency, with two very different kinds of film: *Two Mules for Sister Sara* (1970) and *The Beguiled* (1971). The first of these is what we might call a picaresque western, starring Eastwood alongside Shirley MacLaine. The origin of *Two Mules* is a story by the well-known director Bud Boetticher, and the screenplay for it was written by Albert Maltz, one of the Hollywood Ten, whose rehabilitation comes with this film after twenty-two years of forced unemployment in the industry.[3] The story, set in Mexico, involves Eastwood as Hogan, an American mercenary, encountering and rescuing a nun (Shirley MacLaine as Sara) from a band of rapists. The subsequent picaresque narrative reveals that Sara is actually not a nun, but a prostitute who is collaborating with the revolutionary Juaristas. She persuades Hogan to assist her and the Juaristas, first in a guerrilla attack on a French convoy, then in an attack on a French fort that provides the movie's climactic action sequence.

Maltz's screenplay takes advantage of some of the discourses that, as I suggested earlier, the spaghettis had opened up for the western by the late 1960s: the Hispanic presence and the political struggle of the Juaristas constitute the movie's diegetic background. Although the film seems to be mostly a comedy, it does contain moments of what passes for serious political commentary, such as a scene of the firing-squad execution of a Juarista. However, it is far too hasty to say, as Guérif does, that "it would have been obvious that this is a leftist film, if only Eastwood had not been blindly considered a reactionary" by his critics (74). While the diegetic sympathies are with the Juarista cause against the French imperialists, nonetheless the narrative revolves around the heroism of two Yanquis intervening on behalf of the Mexican revolutionaries and saving the day for them. Equally to the point, the narrative stresses the developing love story between Hogan and Sara in a standard Hollywood format: the love story transcends the political theme, which is only incidental at best or merely the occasion for the climactic action sequence of the attack on the French fort. As Siegel himself points out (deploying a somewhat strange logic), "I worked very hard at making that battle sequence work because there was really nothing in the story that justified it" (Kaminsky 1974b, 232).

Guérif's remark is, of course, as much as anything a signal of the vapidity of the habitual ways of thinking about the relation of popular culture to politics. To think of this as a leftist film is to do no more than register the fact that its diegesis represents a revolution. But the mere presence of such a historical moment—even if it is unusual in a Hollywood film (and as I suggested, at this point it is becoming less unusual)—does not automatically constitute the film as leftist in any sense. The relation of the main narrative line to the politics of the Juarista revolution is much akin to the reaction of Josey Wales to the words of Lone Watie in *Outlaw* that I commented upon earlier: silence and indifference.

The putative political character of *Two Mules* is compromised somewhat further by the function of the lead female character and by the somewhat bizarre gender politics installed at the movie's real center (as opposed to its Juarista background). MacLaine's character, Sister Sara, is set into a relationship with Hogan's masculinity that becomes almost allegorical. She begins the movie as a woman who has been rescued from rape, and immediately after the encounter emerges dressed in a nun's habit: thus her virginal state is twice established. As the pair conduct their little picaresque journey and become attracted to each other, the nun gradually exhibits more and more signs of exceeding, as it were, her virginal role: Hogan is surprised, for instance, to hear her language become crude and sexual, to see her drinking heavily, and to watch her become an agent in the action scenes. When the two of them take refuge in a whorehouse Hogan realizes that Sister Sara is actually a prostitute.

The movie's gradual revelation of her as a whore corresponds to its revelation of her as a Juarista sympathizer, and it is difficult to not read this parallelism as a measure of the movie's political intendment—she becomes a political whore. This negative intendment is perhaps confirmed by the picture's short final sequence, after the successful battle over the fort. There Sara and Hogan are riding away from their adventure in the usual hypostasis. Sara, having gone from nun to prostitute and revolutionary, is now proposed as an entirely ambiguous figure: she is dressed as a "lady" in a bright scarlet dress. This further transformation to "lady" is not a comfortable one—her clothes are coded as those of a pretentious whore. The signs of impatience and disdain that Hogan shows for her in this final shot leave little doubt about the gender positions that are being proposed here: that the woman's whorish nature peeps through whatever masquerade, and that it is this which defines her beyond any of the elements of their adventure together.

Most of the narrative of *Two Mules* depends upon the almost perpetual use of highly regulated shot/reverse shots of Hogan and Sara, almost effecting a kind of equalization of the male and female leads, but actually presenting them in a kind of symbiotic struggle for the lead. The movie's final depiction of Sara becomes in that light an all the more trenchant suggestion of the woman's inferiority. That is, the female lead—the usually powerful presence of Shirley MacLaine—is ultimately dismissed and negated. Strangely enough—or perhaps not strangely at all—this gesture is replicated elsewhere. The shooting of *Two Mules* was reportedly quite difficult, not least because of a consistent struggle between MacLaine and Siegel. Siegel's conclusions about MacLaine after that struggle perhaps can be read as his commentary on the kind of politicized whore that the film constructs and finally dismisses: "It's hard to feel any great warmth for her. She's too . . . unfeminine. She has too much balls. She's very hard" (Kaminsky 1974b, 229).

The offscreen difficulties between Siegel and MacLaine were exacerbated by the unusually lengthy time spent shooting in Mexico—sixty-five days. Many of the personnel, including both Siegel and MacLaine themselves, became sick at some point in the schedule. On the face of it, this would legislate against the Siegel-Eastwood filmmaking ideology, as would the way that Siegel chose to shoot the climactic action sequence at the fort with "over seventy camera set-ups from which we took about 120 shots, none of them on screen for more than five seconds" (Kaminsky 1974b, 231). However, the movie was still brought in under its budget of about $4 million, and also brought in on time. In that sense the movie fulfills the Malpaso guidelines, as does the fact that Siegel and the film's producer, Martin Rackin of Universal, did not get along, in part because Siegel did not have final cut. However, as Siegel pointed out, underlining some of the points I have made earlier, "If you cut the picture in the camera, shoot the minimum, and get to do the first cut . . . then there isn't much leeway in [the producer's] editing the picture" (233).

The kind of misogynist gesture that *Two Mules* constitutes becomes the driving force in the next Eastwood-Siegel collaboration, *The Beguiled* (1971). This film is the story of Eastwood as a Union soldier, McBurney, wounded in the war and finding refuge in a girls' school. As the girls and women there tend him back to health, he flirts with all of them—from the twelve-year-old who had first found him wounded to the black housekeeper, the young women students, and the director and her assistant teacher. The flirtations lead to seductions and the seductions lead to tensions among the women. After being discovered in bed with one woman, McBurney is pushed down a flight of stairs by another. The injuries he receives cause the women to amputate his leg. His fury at the amputation—specifically referred to in the movie as a castration—leads him to try to lay down the law to these women by suggesting, in effect, that they are to become his harem; they respond by poisoning his food, and the movie ends with McBurney's burial.

Siegel has talked about *The Beguiled* as "the best film I have done, and possibly the best I will ever do" (Lovell, 59). This judgment was not shared by audiences, and *Beguiled* is one of only a handful of Eastwood movies that have not reached *Variety*'s list of all-time box-office winners.[4] Siegel and Eastwood both speculate that the problem for audiences is the death of the Eastwood character at the end, and one might speculate that the castration/amputation might not have helped the movie's word-of-mouth. On the other hand, it could be that audiences found less than convincing Siegel's attempt to make what aspires to the condition of an art movie. One might like to imagine too that the misogyny of the movie would have been offensive to viewers. But at any rate, Siegel's judgment about this film seems to point primarily to his pride in some of the structural devices that are deployed within it. In interviews he makes much, for instance, of his use of images of a crow to symbolize and to echo the narrative fate of McBurney. The crow is shown tied down and trying to break free, and after McBurney's death is also shown dead. At other moments McBurney is turned into a Christ figure—he is shown passing by various pictures of Christ's passion on the walls of the school, and the scene in which his leg is amputated is shot from above in such a way as to suggest the crucifixion. But these kinds of device are in fact extraordinarily heavy-handed and effectively only add to the misogyny implicit in the film. That is, the elevation of McBurney to an object of sympathy, as in the crow metaphors (of which Siegel has said, "I wanted to show that these women and girls are like a little covey of sparrows keeping a man captured as they keep a magnificent crow captured" [Kaminsky 1974b, 239]), and to the status of a Christ implicitly endorses a judgment against the movie's women, who are to be read as hysterically and viciously overreacting to the sexual presence of a man in their midst.

In this film, then, McBurney is offered as suffering hero whose only crime appears to have been his sexual philandering, and the real crime in the movie is what is taken to be the condition of femininity. The females are hysterical, whatever their age, race, or status, and their revenge on McBurney is a result of the sexual disorders and frustrations that, in the movie's intendment, an all-female community will necessarily produce or provoke. Siegel's comments on the film suggest an even broader misogyny than the film itself might be capable of: "Women," he says, "are capable of deceit, larceny, murder, anything. Behind that mask of innocence lurks just as much evil as you'll find in members of the Mafia. Any young girl who looks perfectly harmless is capable of murder" (237). These extraordinary remarks move from a perhaps feasible proposition (of course women are *capable* of deceit, murder, and so on) to what amounts to a damning statement about the essential nature of femininity ("*Any* young girl . . ."). As often happens—at least in my narrative of the film industry—the logic of a scenario is here deployed as a logic about life, and vice versa.

The story so far, then, with Malpaso and with the Eastwood-Siegel connection is a threefold one, which addresses first, the area of production ideology; second, filmmaking practice and style; and finally, the intendments of the movies that are made. In regard to the last of these factors, it is of course dubious to try to say that Eastwood's role as actor in movies that Siegel directs renders him responsible for those intendments. Indeed, the same holds true for Siegel himself: I am not suggesting that the meanings of these films can be traced back to their origin in Siegel the man. Rather, it is a question of a coincidence between discourses: that is, the social and cultural discourses that produce misogyny of the sort that Siegel replicates in his own comments are also those that make possible—and indeed make intelligible—movies like *The Beguiled* and *Two Mules*. One might go further and say that one function of such movies, which are produced as entertainment, is to act as guarantors and reinforcements of discourses that in their turn guarantee and reinforce the discourse of Hollywood cinema. Thus, what is at stake here and what is mostly of interest is not so much the individual utterances or the possible complicities of the director or star, but the dialectical situation wherein their understandings of their own work conflate the available discourses and values of the culture in which they find themselves with the discourses it is possible to utter and the values it is possible to profer within the arena of American filmmaking.

The story continues, of course, with the most significant of the Eastwood-Siegel collaborations, *Dirty Harry*, and with the multifarious cultural issues and, indeed, the controversy that that film brings up—issues that I will deal with in upcoming sections. But here I am interested in showing how the third strand of this narrative—dealing with the issue of intendments—passes down what we can readily call a tradition from Siegel's work into Eastwood's, concentrating on his first directorial effort, *Play Misty for Me* (1971).

While Eastwood had had a small opportunity to try his hand at directing before (taking over from Siegel on one sequence of *Dirty Harry* while his mentor was ill), *Play Misty* is his first full-length operation. The narrative involves Eastwood as a radio DJ, Dave Garland, who unwillingly becomes involved with a woman, Evelyn (played by Jessica Walters), with whom he has slept. After what Garland takes to be that casual sexual encounter, Evelyn becomes more and more demanding of Garland's time and attention, and progressively more psychotic in her dealings with him: she attempts suicide in his apartment and later wrecks the apartment and tries to kill Garland's cleaning woman. She is put in a psychiatric hospital but returns to try to kill Garland. The movie's climax is a showdown between the two of them in which Evelyn is killed.

At the stylistic level the movie exhibits many of the hallmarks not just of Siegel's influence but also simply of its time. That is, the movie is not altogether free of the late-1960s cinematic mannerisms that are now usually signals of a made-for-television movie. The fact is not surprising, given that the ideology of production and the filmmaking manners that Malpaso promotes are designed, as I have said, for the kind of speed and efficiency that television production both requires and entails, and given, too, that Siegel himself worked extensively in television. The fundamental nature of *Play Misty* is dictated by the fact that it was shot in sequence and follows the most basic patterns of Hollywood film style: most sequences consist of establishing shots that map out spaces, followed by the breaking down of those spaces into lucid interiors; characters are established first in movement by way of pans that follow them through small spaces, then in stasis in standard shot/reverse shots. For the action sequences the style is basically that of Siegel, with violently quick cuts between mobile camera positions and hand-held shots. Over this simple structure Eastwood's directing and editing adds a layer of mannerisms: for example, the continual use of particular sounds—telephones, door bells, music, car engines—to mark the dissolves from one scene to another; or a number of cambered shots, which appear toward the movie's action climax.

The shooting and editing style give the movie a pace that soon exhausts its rather thin narrative, and so the movie is filled out with two lengthy but almost extraneous sequences. These are, in fact, joined together, and constitute a substantial lull before the final violent sequences where Eve returns to capture Toby and lure Garland to the showdown. The first of them is a long romantic sequence between Toby and Garland, set in the woods beside the Carmel beach, and the second is a set piece shot at the Monterey jazz festival. The romance scene is perhaps the place where the 1960s style of the film is most painfully evident. Toby and Garland have sex for the first time in the film in the woods, accompanied by a slow romantic ballad ("The First Time Ever I Saw Your Face," performed by Roberta Flack). The sequence consists mostly in a set of static studies of their naked bodies, intercut with close-ups of various natural sights in the woods (leaves with dew on them and the like). The sex scene culminates in the hackneyed shot of Toby's naked arm stretched out across the turf to signify her satisfaction, and then the scene ends with the couple walking off into a literal sunset and a long shot of their kissing for quite some time after the song has ended. The sequence is a long-winded way of providing the simple information that Garland and Toby are the narrative's "proper" couple, about to be assaulted by Eve's madness. The next sequence at the jazz festival is similarly lengthy and does little to advance the narrative, except at its very end to supply the information that Toby has a new roommate (who turns out to be Eve).

The least that can be said of the flavor of these sequences now is that it is dated and an instance of the industry's attempts to assimilate something of the style of late-1960s subcultures. Such efforts are by and large not to be repeated in Eastwood's later movies—only *Breezy* (1973), with its similar obsession with the ethos and flavor of the hippy subculture, comes close to the sentimentality of the romantic interlude in the woods. But in other respects *Play Misty* does give notice of some of the techniques that Eastwood will repeat over and over as director and that will come to constitute his style. Particularly, *Play Misty* adopts Siegel's so-called documentary lighting—that is, the backlit shot that silhouettes foreground figures—and emphasizes the colors produced by northern Californian sunlight.

Although it is visually hackneyed and more or less uninteresting, the sequence in the woods is significant for the way that it points to the assimilation process to which I just alluded. That is, *Play Misty* can be regarded as a reactionary movie insofar as it constitutes an attempt to come to terms with changes that have been rung in the culture by the social and political disturbances of the late 1960s. The scene is an attempt at rescuing from the hippy ethos its emphasis on sexual love and its way of linking the "naturalness" of sexual expression to nature itself. It is against what we might call this romantic organicism that the movie contrasts the figure of Eve.

Eve functions as the agent of another kind of cultural change that can be associated with the 1960s—she is the newly sexually liberated woman who can pick up men whom she fancies and sexually pursue them. Yet this film charges Eve with not being able to escape the older stereotypes of femininity. Thus, even as she emerges as a product of her time into sexual permissiveness, she retains the possessiveness, the jealousy, and of course the psychosis, of the Ur-woman (the choice of Eve for her name is interesting here, of course). What is to be served and saved by Garland's dispatching of Eve is his own right to respond to the now culturally acceptable sexual advances of a woman but without having to expect to deal with what he calls her "smothering" him. The movie's narrative thus produces something akin to a proposition: that if women expect sexual liberation, they cannot also try to tie men down into committed relationships; women's punishment for wanting both is madness and then death—as, of course, it has often been.

Just Entertainment

The film industry's need to construct the kind of fusion I have previously referred to—between cultural verisimilitudes and generic ones—is a situation often muddied by the theoretical and descriptive terms that tend to be used in relation to it, both in the discourses of the industry and in the discourses of critics, theorists, and workers in the tributary media. In terms of the discourses that, as it were, greet the film product's release, I have tried already to suggest some of the difficulties of two of the most common ways of conceiving of the relation between the product and the culture in which it is produced. Films are not, or not ever very simply, reflections of the culture. Nor is it the case that they unproblematically make that culture. Rather, there exists a dialectical relationship between these two kinds of effect that precludes our simply stating that, for instance, *Thelma and Louise* reflects a feminist backlash against the antifeminism of the Reagan years, or that some given studio-era movie reflects the socioeconomic ordering of capitalist America in the 1930s or 1940s. Equally, it is simplistic to suggest that a particular movie can simply or unmediatedly produce some cultural effect, or unproblematically instantiate and install some particular social meaning. This is an especially questionable move to make when such effects and meanings are attributed—as they so often are—to the putative controlling activity of "auteurs." Either of those ways of thinking about the relationship of film to culture will be found exemplified in all kinds of reviewing practices, in criticism, and even in theory. The relationship is not often enough understood as dialectical and overdetermined.

Partially in reaction to the obvious inadequacy of either of these formulations, some critics and theorists have begun to think in terms of what (at least, in television studies) is called the "uses and gratifications" approach.[1] This is effectively a theoretical, and sometimes empirical, way of thinking about audience reception, and in its best light can be said to have the virtue of being able to conceive of audiences as heterogeneous and not as the merely passive recipients or dupes of a set of meanings proferred by the text. This approach often derives from a sense of dissatisfaction with the kind of cultural theory and criticism that has internalized the line of the Frankfurt School in thinking that capitalist control of the culture industry necessarily entails a monolithic and overpowering ideological control.

Perhaps because this approach has its origins in a reaction to such a view (which is, I would suggest, an unconscionably reductive and often uninformed view) of the supposedly politically pessimistic approach of Theodor Adorno, the "uses and gratifications" approach often becomes extremist (a) in its unwillingness to recognize that there can indeed be meanings proferred by texts as intendments, and (b) in its reluctance to consider in any sustained way the industrial production of such meanings. Some forms of this approach tend to exacerbate even this extremism by merely and confidently averring that spectators are involved in the production of uncircumscribable uses and self-gratifications, which are "resistant" in relation to the texts they consume and thus (so the logic often goes) are also resistant to the capitalist culture from which the text arises. There is little attempt, for the most part, to make any kind of empirical check of audiences as they supposedly resist not only texts but also the texts' ideological proferrings. Rather there is here a tendency for the critic to take just him- or herself as ethnographic subject—the critic's own "resistant" readings are posed as being generalizable for mass audiences. This is often, in my view, a solipsistic form of criticism, which has and can produce little knowledge of the cultural significance of texts.[2]

If these rather common ways of theorizing the media from outside the industry are unsatisfying, that is not to suggest that the industry itself offers any particularly lucid or useful alternative. It is more or less a shibboleth both within and without the industry that it has no efficient way of predicting, to any tolerable degree of accuracy, audience reception—or indeed of knowing much about its audiences at all. What goes by the name of "market research" in Hollywood is notoriously unreliable and even aleatory, consisting largely in trial screenings and the use of audience samplings for particular films in a small number of locations. Thus, on this level, the industry itself is incapable of generating a discourse that would describe in any generality—let alone in any complexity—the relation of its product and the cultural formations into which it sends that product.

The industry does, of course, operate on the assumption of some notion of consumer satisfaction, measured in box-office receipts. Yet this is a notion that is inappropriate from the start, if only because individual consumers do not necessarily have to be "satisfied" in the same way as they would by other kinds of commodity. That is, it is of variable importance—and often of completely minor importance—that any consumer should enjoy a particular product, so long as he or she has paid the price of admission. A consumer who is "not satisfied" with a particular product will not necessarily boycott all future products that are proferred. Indeed, part of the uniqueness of the Hollywood industry is the degree to which all of its products are in a sense trial products. The relative inefficiency and the more or less ad hoc nature of the industry's approach to its audience allow for no particular view of the relation between cultural verisimilitudes and industrial codes. The lack of a sophisticated vocabulary in this regard perhaps constitutes at least a partial explanation for the relative stolidity of the industry's products, and for their propensity to keep returning to tried and tested formulae. And yet the demand for difference and variation seems to entail some attempt—as in the case of *Pale Rider*'s adoption of a discourse of liberal ecology—to draw contemporaneous discourses, current events, and topical issues into films; an attempt, that is, to tap currents of discourse that the culture has generated elsewhere and then to accommodate them within the framework of industry formulae.

To do this is to immediately risk what we might call a mistaking of cultural formations. As we have seen, there are cultural elements that Hollywood's narrative frames and the professional values that inform them cannot unproblematically include. To attempt to include them is to risk producing an incoherent text, or a too controversial one, or one that audiences simply cannot grasp in the context of their own frames of cultural verisimilitude. The industry's risks in this respect are actually not awfully large, since there is a de facto embargo in

Hollywood on scripts that can be thought of as too controversial or as too immediate in their address of current events and topical issues. Rather, culturally contested issues tend to be dealt with, for safety's sake, at some remove. That safety is ensured in two ways: temporally, in the sense that a certain degree of cultural consensus must have been reached before a film dares address particular issues (as I write in 1992 there has still been no major Hollywood film in which AIDS has been a primary topic, for instance); and then narratively, in that the conventional structures of Hollywood narrative can be deployed to defuse and distance any controversy that might attend a particular issue.

There are many possible examples of Hollywood's operation in this latter respect; an almost random instance, however, might be the movie *Country*, directed by Richard Pearce and released in 1984. That film ostensibly addresses the plight of American farmers in the period of the early 1980s when their farms and property were being repossessed by banks for nonpayment of loans and mortgages. The farmers' difficulties were caused in part by government subsidy policies and inflation, leading to lower grain prices and heavy losses for many of them. The crisis led, notably, to increased corporate ownership of American agriculture. *Country* appeared several years after the farming crisis began, and long after the reporting media had sanctified its importance and established its interest (along with evoking a certain degree of sympathy for the small farmer). For Hollywood to address this issue at all, the crisis had to be well advanced and the parameters of public discussion already set.

Equally important, the nature of this particular crisis could be made to resonate with certain long-standing themes and structures of movie narrative, notably the populist strand of movies where the small, hard-working family is threatened in its livelihood by government and big business. *Country* deals with this crisis on those terms, stressing the familial drama that occurs around the collapse of a family business and the attempted repossession of its property. The film's suggestion is that the political issue of American agriculture in the 1980s is important first of all in terms of its emotional impact on families and more particularly on the love relationship of, in this case, a husband and wife played by Sam Shepard and Jessica Lange. In other words, from the starting point of a serious political issue the film structures a populist melodrama of family life and love.

Country stands here, then, simply as an instance of how what I am calling the fusion of cultural and industry significations works to produce a product whose reception can be expected to be, quite simply, untroublesome. That is, the way in which a film should optimally (or satisfyingly) be received is through a consumer's untroubled acceptance of the fact that it has managed to forge a coincidence of two verisimilitudes—the film should be adequate both to cinematic conventions and to the paradigms of a consumer's social and political understandings and contexts. That this particular film was made because of the political concern of its star, Jessica Lange, and because of her determination to speak on behalf of debt-ridden farmers makes it somewhat unusual in Hollywood, but the blunting of that political edge and the subsuming of the political drama beneath an affective one, in both the production and the narrative, makes it fairly typical.

What is at stake here is the function of Hollywood cinema as a political entity, that is, as an institution and an industry. I am stressing the obvious point that any particular film that Hollywood makes will of necessity be bound up in a system of cultural and political formations; a film intervenes in those formations even as it emerges from a relation with and among them. I feel that the point needs stressing for a number of reasons. Not least of the reasons is that both the tributary media and some of the most current critical or theoretical productions are concerned to downplay those relations. Either in its own way will elide or slight much of what I still think of as the crucial substance of the cinematic institution and its products today: namely, their implication in a historical logic of commodities and in the circulation of meanings that are inescapably ideological and political.

Hollywood as an industry and an institution has a vital interest in maintaining the political fiction that its products and their provenance are apolitical. The simplest formulation of this interest arrives in the expression "it's just entertainment," and variations thereupon. And the dialectical extension of this ideological notion that would always have the word "just" attached to the word "entertainment" is the notion that if it is not just entertainment then it must be art. As a term in the discourses of cinema, art—traditionally and chronically a depoliticized arena, even if it is an arena that American culture feels must be defended from politics on a regular basis—has the function of transcending politics in the same way as "just entertainment" does. The interplay of the two terms is a crucial symptom, then, in that one or the other of them can be taken to justify and vindicate any particular product. Together these two terms or categories map out the terrain on which Hollywood prefers to operate, and separately they provide alternative poles, to one of which every cinematic product must aspire.

One point in Clint Eastwood's career where these kinds of issues are highlighted is after the 1971 release of *Dirty Harry*, directed by Don Siegel. That movie was widely understood to be making a particular political intervention. The issue at stake was, at one level, simply the depicted behavior of Harry Callahan, the maverick police detective who hunts down a killer; at other levels it was the implicit ideological positions of the character Callahan, of the film itself as text, and of Eastwood and Siegel, the film's principal makers and defenders.

Callahan's obsessive and violently ruthless hunting down of Scorpio exceeds by some margin the limits of offscreen police legality. Specifically, Callahan is shown as an officer for whom respecting the rules of engagement, as it were, and following the orders of his superiors are secondary to getting accomplished whatever he sees as his job. A good part of the film's beginning exposition is devoted to demonstrating these characteristics, while the rest shows Callahan putting them to work against Scorpio. For example, at one point Callahan beats Scorpio and tortures him by stepping on a knife wound that he had already inflicted upon the killer's leg; in the same sequence he also illegally searches Scorpio's lodgings. When Scorpio is released by a judge because of these actions, Callahan ignores orders from his superiors and from the mayor in order to finish off Scorpio in a showdown; the final shot of the movie shows him jettisoning his police badge in a rather ambiguous gesture.

Callahan's on-screen activities, then, are evidently beyond the pale of legal police activity, and the violence that attends them was deemed unusual for the time; even Siegel himself described the movie as "a wall to wall carpet of violence" (quoted in Kaminsky 1974b, 273), and the way in which the film seems to promote Callahan's excesses brought down upon it the charge that it condones a violent right-wing ideology. Various reviewers thought the film to be an out-and-out apologia for fascism. Even bearing in mind that the word *fascist* enjoyed a peculiar and even excessive usage of its own in the sixties and early seventies (being used popularly not so much to describe social phenomena that were the same as Germany's National Socialism, but rather as shorthand for excoriating the everyday workings of the repressive state apparatuses of capitalist America), it is hard not to sympathize with various critics who recognized in the movie an encouragement for reactionary politics in this country. These critics include Eastwood's perennial antagonist, Pauline Kael: "*Dirty Harry* is obviously just a genre movie, but this action genre has always had a fascist potential, and it has finally surfaced."[3] Even one of the more sympathetic writers about Eastwood's films, Stuart Kaminsky, recognizes the dangers produced by the film's rhetoric: "Don Siegel knew what he was doing. Each scene is carefully constructed to inflame lower middle-class phobias and to toy with its most sacred symbols, like the Constitution and the gun. It is an immoral picture, cracking a reactionary whip whose sting can only intensify mistrust and suspicion at various levels of society" (1974a, 125).

The context into which the film intervened is important here, of course. American culture in the early 1970s was riven with the strife caused by the Vietnam War; the police's lack of credibility and dubious reputation in those years was in part a result of thousands of incidents of police brutality against antiwar demonstrators. At the same time, citizens' rights in relation to the police had been strengthened by, among other things, the Supreme Court's Miranda decision in 1968 and the Escobedo ruling: these rulings had produced shrieks of outrage from the right wing, whose complaints about the "ultraliberal" Warren court have continued ever since. In that context it is not difficult to see *Dirty Harry* as a determined vindication of extremist police methods. Certainly some police personnel read it that way, inviting both Siegel and Eastwood to speak at police gatherings.

In other words, it is clear that in some sense the film was understood to be making a particular argument—an inflammatory one in the context where exactly the kind of action that it depicts was not only being condemned in much public discourse but also being constrained by law. The institutions of that law clearly come under attack in the movie's rhetoric. In contrast to the forthrightness and determination in the activities of the central character, the movie portrays a generalized weakness and softness in Callahan's superiors that increases the higher they are positioned within the bureaucracy. Indeed, the mayor, the judges, the district attorney, the law professors, and even the police chief are all posed in this film as in various ways complicit with the killer, unable to see their obligation to the community that Callahan thinks himself to be serving. Between that community and those agents of a mistaken bureaucracy there stand Callahan and a minority of his police colleagues; Harry's two partners and his immediate superior, a lieutenant, are the only public servants who are portrayed as having any understanding at all of what has to be done, and who admire and condone the resolve with which Callahan does it.

In some ways the repulsively portrayed Scorpio is diegetically not so central as he is narratively. That is to say, while the action narrative obviously requires his presence and enforces the relationship and showdown between Callahan and him, the discursive target of the movie is this bureaucracy. Scorpio becomes, as it were, nothing more than the occasion for the movie's point of contention, which is the critique of the established authority that has implicitly caused a whole range of social problems against which Callahan fights. At least one writer, Eric Patterson, has seen this critique of authority as "surprisingly radical" and developed in the movie to a "surprising degree" (Patterson, 93 and 103). The argument on which such a position is based is that Callahan stands up against the frustrations that bureaucracies and legal institutions can cause in contemporary life when their rules, checks, and balances inhibit obvious (or what seem obvious to many people) forms of action and remedy: when, in other words, civic justice obstructs natural justice. In interviews concerning *Dirty Harry* Eastwood himself has pointed to the existence of this proposition in the movie in a couple of ways. First he suggests that "Harry is a fantasy character. Nobody does what Harry does. He cuts right down through the bull, tells his boss to shove it, does all the things people would like to do in real life but can't" (*New York Times*, 17 Dec. 1976, C10). More explicitly, he claims that "Harry wasn't saying that the community as a whole had crapped on him, just the political elements of the city" (quoted in Kaminsky 1974a, 126).

However, this "critique of authority" is not such an unfamiliar element in Hollywood pictures as it might appear. The figure of the white male hero pitched into opposition with the forces of established authority is a frequent one in crime movies and, of course, in westerns. In relation to the latter, for example, *Hang 'em* sets up the opposition between Cooper and Judge Fenton that I spoke of before, as it picks up on the lengthy tradition of posing civic against natural justice and the outlaw hero against the official hero. Similarly, in crime movies a frequent figure is the independent private detective whose relation to the police is always strained and antagonistic. In other words, it is by no means a new development to see the protagonist in a diegetic relation to the forces of officialdom where the latter are too unintelligent, too timid, or too corrupt to get the job done.

This apparent critique in *Dirty Harry* is, then, no more than an extension—albeit in an intensified form—of a populist line in Hollywood movies among whose main effects is to underscore an ideology of individual power and rectitude and to promote a distrust of institutions. In that sense it is at least ambivalent to promote it, as Patterson does, as a radical gesture. Importantly, it is a critique that, as an element of familiar narrative and generic structures, necessarily participates in a certain kind of logic. That is to say, to make such a critique of bumbling, inefficient, and even corrupt bureaucracy or legitimated authority is also to promise a narrative solution to it. That narrative solution is always entrusted to the white male hero, whose actions, as serviceman to the community, pose private power as more effective and as more justifiable and morally empowered than corporate, official, or institutional power.

This is, of course, an ideology of vigilantism, albeit a vigilantism embodied in a single man. Vigilantism, as many commentators have pointed out, is a social phenomenon indigenous to America, having little prehistory in Britain, Europe, or elsewhere—even if one of the thinkers used most often to justify it is John Locke.[4] Historically speaking, the agent of vigilantism proper is generally understood to be collective; popular literary and filmic versions of vigilantism that locate the agent as an individual perhaps do so as a response to ideological requirements that are more extensive than the more strictly political aims of historical vigilantism. That is, whereas collective violence against institutions, laws, and social groups in American history might have had strictly defined political goals, the individual vigilante of the movies becomes as it were the ideal father who will protect and serve the community. In that paternal, not to say patronizing role, the individual vigilante in fact suggests that any need for collective agitation can be obviated.

It is in that regard that it perhaps makes sense to cautiously use the word *fascist* in describing such movies as *Dirty Harry* insofar as this fantasized ideal of the white male father who ruthlessly ensures security and carries out the right kind of vengeance on behalf of the community, on "our" behalf, directly addresses the kinds of psychological structures that have been associated with the fascist subject.[5] This is not to say, by any manner of means, that the viewer who goes along with the movie, who enjoys it, or who willingly or unwillingly submits his or her experience to its rhetoric and power becomes thereby fascistic. Equally, I do not wish to suggest that there is anything "wrong" with viewers taking enjoyment from, making resistant use of, or supporting such productions. Rather it is simply a matter of pointing out that particular significations are put into social and cultural circulation by this kind of utterance—they are proferred, as I put it, as intendments. Such intendments do not guarantee their audience, of course; they cannot ensure a nonresistant reader, but they do legitimate certain positions and formations for readers by either incrementing or inspissating a specific range of culturally available meanings.

That project is not specific to *Dirty Harry* by any means. I have wanted to stress that *Dirty Harry*'s effect, and the cultural controversy that the film caused, are to a large extent a function of the movie's belonging to a long history of generic and formulaic production in which the narrative structures bear the same or a similar ideological weight. *Dirty Harry*'s unusually spectacular resonance has to do with its intervention on that level: the politics of the film itself is unusually elaborated and exhibited, and the representations of violence that it includes are ones that exceed by far the conventions of cinematic verisimilitude at the time. Equally, the resonance is increased by the film's unusual propinquity to issues that were currently controversial and unsettled in the realm of public or civic discourse; in other words, the film's reception is also very closely dependent upon the particular historical moment to which it attaches itself.

Audience response to *Dirty Harry* was, on the face of it, much more favorable than the critical reception and the ensuing cultural controversy might suggest. The film was the tenth highest domestic money-maker in 1972, and by 1988 had grossed over $18 million in North America. Various reports suggest that audience reaction was quite vocal and even rowdy in support of Eastwood's character. It might well have been that kind of response that spawned some of the concern of the critics in their roles as guardians and surveillants of the integrity of the Hollywood product. But the absence of real information about audience response is a problem here as elsewhere with Hollywood production. It is easy enough on the one hand, to count box-office receipts or give anecdotal detail about audience reaction, but on the other hand those things say little about what the movie's effects on consumers might actually have been. The contrast between the big crowds at the movie theaters and the massively offended reviews (of all the major reviewing organs, only *Rolling Stone* praised the film) perhaps tells us little, then, except to underscore once again the cultural role of the critics and journalists in trying to regulate response and forge ideologically acceptable reading formations.

At the same time the tributary media are in a sense working on behalf of Hollywood, effectively as promoters and advertisers of the product. Part of the discursive role of reviews and journalistic criticism (as opposed to the popular discourse that the industry describes as "word of mouth") is to set parameters for cultural discussion, and one of the centrally important strategies in that task is the attempt to construct intentions for any given film—that is, the attempt to affirm or confirm that the film's meaning is not accidentally produced. It is in such a context that directors and/or stars come to act as important resources for the other media.[6] *Dirty Harry* was in this sense an important point in both Siegel's and Eastwood's careers: both became culturally more important the more the media tried to get the meaning of the film straight.

Since, as I have suggested, *Dirty Harry*'s proferred meanings need to be seen as a function of the film's belonging to a generic and formulaic history, it strikes me that it is a little ambitious to expect Siegel and Eastwood to account for the meaning of "their" film. The film is already caught up in the double vision—the political history—of Hollywood films without which it could not have existed: the bringing together of cinematic with cultural verisimilitudes. The work of Siegel and Eastwood does indeed ring changes on the genres they deploy. Those changes are perceived as extreme, or as too much of an increment in one go; thence the film is perceived as not being apolitical enough—in other words, it has exposed the usually covert political affiliation of the genre (as Pauline Kael underlines in the quotation given earlier) and even of Hollywood production itself. As a result the intentions of the filmmakers are sought.

Siegel's answers to questions about the politics of the film are quite sophisticated in some ways. Siegel shows an awareness of the difficulties of imputing the politics of representation to some assumed authorial intent, and thus he immediately (and explicitly) challenges the project of the tributary media:

> I show a hard-nosed cop who believes that the work he is doing is correct. That doesn't mean that I agree with the character 100 per cent or that Clint does. Harry, in the picture, is a racist, a reactionary. Those are things I loathe, but I'm bothered by the fact that so few pictures give credit to the police for what they accomplish. Policemen lose their lives protecting us. Now I'm not just talking about policemen who lose their lives in situations that have political connotations, but in robberies, assaults and dozens of other crimes. Some of these people are like Harry, genuine heroes whose attitudes I abhor. For me to have changed those attitudes to conform to a more acceptable political philosophy for the critics would have been a distortion of what we were trying to show. It would be nice if all heroic cops agreed with me politically; but they don't. It would also be nice if there were no violence in the world; but there is. (Quoted in Kaminsky 1974b, 282)

What allows Siegel to avoid the charge that he himself holds the political position expounded by the rhetoric of his film is his appeal to what is here a necessarily not much elaborated but nonetheless foundational notion of realism. Implicit in his remarks is the claim that there is a world out there that can be realistically represented and that such a representation can become a "distortion" if it is tainted by his own opinions or views as author. His own position may or may not coincide with the meanings that the film profers. The only concession he really makes in these remarks to the fact that he might have had some agenda in making this particular film comes when he claims to regret that "so few pictures give credit to the police." These kinds of views—assuming that they are not just factitious utterances designed to distance Siegel from the film's critical reception—help explain Siegel's status for much of his career as a somewhat marginal and eccentric figure in Hollywood. That is, his undermining of the authorial stance, his concomitant refusal to stand up for the politics of "his" film, and his stated determination to present a chunk of reality almost as a documentarist are all positions that work against the norms and conventions of the industry.

Siegel's remarks, moreover, stand somewhat in contrast to the way in which Clint Eastwood has responded to similar questions. While Siegel effectively distances himself from what is troublesome about the film, Eastwood is drawn into the process of defending the film and its politics. In fact, in the quotation that follows, he defends it on overtly political grounds, suggesting that Callahan's actions are justified and correct. Interestingly enough, he specifically refers to a real "general public"—rather than to the abstract community of the film's fiction, and the implication seems to be that his own position in relation to that "general public" is analogous to that of Callahan to the film's community. In that sense he can be understood to be turning his own position as entertainer into a political position in which he has a responsibility similar to Callahan's to be their serviceman:

> The general public isn't worried about the rights of the killer; they're just saying get him off the streets, don't let him kidnap my child, don't let him kill my daughter. There's a reason for the rights of the accused, and I think it's very important and one of the things that makes our system great. But there's also the rights of the victim. Most people who talk about the rights of the accused have never been victimized; most of them probably never got accosted in an alley. The symbol of justice is the scale, and yet the scale is never balanced; it falls to the left and then it swings too far back to the right. (Quoted in Kaminsky 1974a, 125-26)

Eastwood's comments clearly refer to a political situation in civic life itself, rather than strictly to the fiction of the film. Yet at the same time they act as a defense of the film, which is presumably a kind of illustration of the principle of victims' rights. Signally, even though he might be suggesting that Callahan's actions go "too far back to the right" after the 1960s vindications of the rights of the accused, Eastwood is apparently criticizing the justice system for its disequilibrium. In that way he speaks as a vigilante—implicitly approving the extralegal methods that Callahan uses to ameliorate a system that cannot properly protect its citizens—in line with the fact that vigilantism is seen by its proponents as "a constant struggle to contain victimization" (Culberson, 8). Equally, the ambivalence of all vigilantism in relation to the system with which it struggles is also present in

Eastwood's words. That is, vigilantism sees itself as "at once a vigilant protection of the status quo and a vigilant challenge" (6); for Eastwood the system is "great," but its nonetheless existent flaws demand violent action from vigilant citizens like Callahan.

If I seem to be belaboring this point, it is to underscore the fact that, even as he denies the fascism of the picture, Eastwood engages a political discourse and takes up a political position in relation to the film. That position, it appears, bespeaks a kind of identification that he makes with Callahan on two levels: first, at the level of the correctness of his political stance, and second, at the level of an analogy, as I mentioned, between himself as entertainer and Callahan as vigilante (both are servicemen to the "general public" or the community).

Eastwood's comments, then, can be taken to respond to at least some part of the tributary media's seeking out of the truth of the filmmakers' intentions—in ways that Siegel's comments do not.[7] At the same time, Eastwood avoids presenting himself as in any way responsible for the content of the film—he does not take on the role of "auteur" any more than Siegel does. Rather, he seems to offer himself as the mouthpiece for a whole set of values and positions that he somehow assumes are "out there" in the minds of "the general public." What I want to suggest is that, far from speaking for or on behalf of the general public, or indeed on behalf of himself, Eastwood is here unwittingly speaking as nothing more than a kind of functionary for the Hollywood system in the sense that he has perfectly replicated what I will call the vigilante position that underpins many Hollywood narratives. This relates to a point that I will want to bring up again in various ways in this book—that point being that Eastwood's relation to the industry is not exactly the maverick and independent one that it is often taken to be, and that he has in fact become the ideal worker in that industry, having internalized and acted out its values and ideologies in such a complete way that he can stand apart from it only as its paragon.

I will explain more of what I mean by this at different points in the book, but for now I mean only to point to an instance where there is a coincidence of—or identification between—Eastwood himself and the discursive structures of Hollywood itself. Another example can be had through some of Eastwood's other comments about *Dirty Harry*, where he speaks the political logic behind another of Hollywood's stock narrative formulae, namely, the principle of the preeminence of "natural" law over civic law. Interestingly, in the following remarks he again speaks in relation to a real world in which these principles and that logic supposedly pertain:

> We, as Americans, went to Nuremberg and convicted people who committed certain crimes because they didn't adhere to a higher morality. We convicted them on that basis—that they shouldn't have listened to the law of the land or their leaders at that time. They should have listened to their true morality. We sent them to jail on that basis. This is how it is with this man. Somebody told him this is the way it is, too bad, and he said: "Well that's wrong, I can't adhere to that." That isn't fascist; it's the opposite of fascism. (Quoted in Downing and Herman, 92)

The thrust of these pronouncements is an old story, familiar from hundreds of Hollywood movies: the execution of "true morality" is supposedly the citizen's duty, it is beyond law and politics, and "we, as Americans," are the guardians of this true morality. Leaving aside some of the contradictions of Eastwood's amateur political philosophizing—he seems, for instance, not to be bothered by the contradiction of Americans prosecuting the Nuremberg trials and putting people in prison in order to uphold this extralegal morality—we see here the simplistic repetition of the simplistic philosophy of vigilantism. Such a view proposes itself as a vindication of American democracy—democracy presumably being "the opposite of fascism," in Eastwood's terms.

The Opposite of Fascism

Eastwood's defense of *Dirty Harry* in the context of the critical controversy that the film provoked really makes matters worse rather than better. I do not mean by that to simply reject the political options that Eastwood takes here, but to point out one way in which his self-presentation is coincident with that of the industry in which he works; coincident, too, with the narrative structures of Hollywood. That is, he is apparently willing to espouse the politics represented in the fantasized narratives of American cinema and speak of them as if they were applicable to the politics of everyday life. One way of saying this is that in those comments the fantasy becomes the equivalent of reality. His responses are thus importantly different from Siegel's "realist" position, which is able to distinguish sharply between the task of representing reality and the gesture of endorsing the politics implied or depicted in the representation. Eastwood on the other hand acts, as I have suggested, more or less as a functionary, or as if he were a mouthpiece for the industry.

One of the more interesting aspects of Eastwood's comments is the fact that they all postdate the release in 1973 of the first "Dirty Harry" sequel, *Magnum Force*. This latter film is already a kind of response to the controversy provoked by *Dirty Harry* in that it engages both narratively and discursively with the kind of issues I have talked about: the role of vigilantism in a democracy, the nature of fascism, the social role of inefficient and corrupt officialdoms, and so on. Its reworking of those topics in relation to the previous movie pits Callahan against a group of young policemen who effectively form a death squad on a mission to execute known killers and criminals whom "the system" has not managed to deal with. As their spokesman puts it, in words that the earlier version of Callahan could himself have uttered, "We're simply ridding society of killers that would be caught and sentenced anyway—if our courts worked properly." Callahan finds himself upholding "the system" against this death squad and against the police lieutenant, Briggs, who turns out to be their leader: "I hate the goddamn system, but until someone comes up with some changes that make sense, I'll stick with it," he says.

The movie's point seems to be, then, that it is not Callahan who is the fascist. "Real" fascism in this context in fact looks very different from Callahan—literally, in the sense that Callahan runs around in his usual cheap jacket and slacks, driving his usual beaten-up car, while the members of the death squad are all dressed in shiny leather and metal uniforms astride gleaming motorcycles. On this and other levels, then, *Magnum Force* tries to make a distinction between the motorcycle killers and Harry, operating finally as a quite self-conscious repudiation of the vigilante group. There are numerous occasions in the film where the script allows Harry to assert his difference from the killers during verbal showdowns that take place before the inevitable physical ones. When invited to join the vigilante group with the appeal that "you of all people should understand," Callahan responds by simply saying, "I'm afraid you've misjudged me." Later, in the same kind of conversation with Briggs, the following exchange takes place:

> BRIGGS: A hundred years ago in this city people did the same thing. History justified the vigilantes. We're no different. Anyone who threatens the security of the people will be executed. Evil for evil, Harry. Retribution.
>
> CALLAHAN: That's just fine, but where does murder fit in? You know, when police start becoming their own executioners, where's it gonna end? Pretty soon you start executing people for jaywalking; then for traffic violations. Then you end up executing your neighbor because his dog pisses on your lawn.

Yet the differences that Callahan is trying to point to do not finally quite amount to a convincing riposte to the critics of *Dirty Harry*. Perhaps it is more a question simply of defining limits for his own reactionary activity, or more nearly, a question of distinguishing the out-

and-out "fascism" of the motorcycle executioners from some more acceptable imaginary of American democratic vigilance. Once again the worrying aspect of this—perhaps fascist at some deeper level—is the way it poses the individual hero as the all-powerful overseer of the system. But again this is a generic problem, and it is interesting to consider that Eastwood (insofar as he has a hand in forging *Magnum Force* as a kind of riposte) again appears to assume that the generic possibilities can in some way be used as an argument for a particular kind of political correctness.

In terms of its relation to the cinematic history from which it derives, this movie would appear, then, to be an effort to deploy the flexibility of the genre toward a redefinition of the political enemy. That is, the vigilante group becomes just another instance of villains working within a corrupt system, with the at first supposedly liberal police lieutenant turning out to be the worst of the lot. Here, then, the target is the same as it was before in the most general terms: a corrupt officialdom against which Harry, the individual cop who is full of integrity, has to fight for the sake of the greater good. One of the problems for the vigilantes is that they have no communitarian shared goals to fight for—they say they "began with the criminals that people know, so that our actions would be understood"; the film implies that, exactly, the people will *not* understand because their true and individual defender does not approve. Callahan is the guardian of the civic conscience as well as of citizens' lives and properties. This time he is "let loose" directly on the agents of officialdom itself, instead of displacing his attack on them onto an external force like Scorpio.

In this context, as Kaminsky remarks, "Harry becomes, by default, the most liberal guy around" (1974b, 148). Accordingly, the movie's script allows him the opportunity to demonstrate this in several different ways. Harry's liberalism is produced in relation to the nonprofessional parts of his life, seen for the first time. Where the early film had left a connotative gap for Harry's personal existence (the shadow of the death of his wife acting as a kind of mysterious cause for his obsessive rectitude), *Magnum Force* shows him in an eroticized relationship with the former wife of a colleague, in a friendship with that colleague, and most spectacularly in bed with an Asian woman who has more than a hint of the hippy about her. On the professional level his obligatory new partner at the beginning of the film is an

African-American man whom he treats with respect and even care. There is even a moment when he can be read as tolerant in relation to homosexuality: when the close-knit camaraderie of the leather-clad motorcyclists becomes the subject of a squad-room joke, Callahan says, "If the rest of you could shoot like them, I wouldn't care if the whole damned department was queer."

All of these elements are carefully, even calculatedly, set within the film's discourse as ways of answering the previous "Harry" movie, and it is easy to imagine that this is their primary function. At the same time some of them work to underscore once again the heroic masculinity of Callahan. Quite aside from that part of the masculine ethos that is vindicated in both the verbal and the action showdowns, some of these elements contribute to a different, though intertwined, kind of masculine power: that is, the power to gain consent. As we saw earlier in relation to *Pale Rider*, this consent is often the boon that women give—one way or another, reluctantly or freely—to the white male hero. Here it is given by the Asian woman whose consent to Harry's sexuality has overdetermined meanings: she stands for the consent of women, Asians, the young, and, to a degree, the marginal. In that latter respect she represents the spirit of the counterculture that Scorpio had dishonestly appropriated with his hippy looks and the famous peace sign on his belt.

These discursive and narrative elements, then, reinforce the sense that the filmmakers here are attempting to "liberalize" Callahan and present an image of "real" fascism against which another political imaginary could be set. That political imaginary is, by definition, not very different from the one for which *Dirty Harry* was attacked: an all-American version of the community's being protected and saved by the single serviceman whose use of violence and whose willingness to go beyond the strict limits of the law remain unquestioned.

So, then, the interesting thing about this supposed defense is the way it sets up what is ultimately a quite small space of difference between what it proposes as "real" fascism and the ideologies that it seems to be willing to support. In that this movie is determinedly discursive in this sense—it attempts to explicate a position in relation to other cultural discourses and in relation to another film and its genres—it is a highly unusual product.[1] This is also an unusual situation in the sense that *Magnum Force* represents the willingness of the filmmakers to attend to the role that the tributary media always ask of them—to supply an intentionalist commentary on particular films (in this case *Dirty Harry*). This commentary is rarely supplied in Hollywood by means of another film; more normally it is a function of the director or star speaking about or commenting upon the film in interviews and the like.

It is probably not irrelevant in the light of this unusual intervention to note the writing credits on this movie: John Milius and Michael Cimino are credited with the screenplay, and Milius is given a further credit for a story based on the characters created by Julian and Rita Fink. It seems that Milius had also done some of the writing on *Dirty Harry*, but without being credited. According to Carlos Clarens (307), it is Milius who wrote one of the more well-known lines in *Dirty Harry*: "This being a .44 Magnum, the most powerful handgun in the world, and it could blow your head clean off, you gotta ask yourself a question: do I feel lucky?"

Those lines, in slightly different form, become the voice-over for the opening sequence of *Magnum Force*. As the movie's opening credits and music play, the screen is filled with a side view of a .44 Magnum against an all-red background. As the written credits are ending the camera moves slowly into the gun to watch the thumb cock the hammer and the finger move to the trigger. The gun turns toward the camera so that the viewer is looking down the barrel and Eastwood's voice delivers the lines; the gun fires into the camera with scarcely a pause after Eastwood has asked, "Do you feel lucky?" Of course, one point of this introduction is to make a formal connection with *Dirty Harry*. Another is the rather gratuitous one of inviting the viewer to guess whether the gun will fire or not after Eastwood has spoken—in *Dirty Harry* the same lines had been uttered twice, once early in the film when it does not fire, and once at the climax when Callahan's sixth bullet kills Scorpio. But another point here is to fetishize the gun and its violent shot in an almost pornographic way.

This contemplation of the gun is consistent with Milius's already well-known fascination with firearms and is even an effective distillation of it. Milius, who would later direct Eastwood's *Thunderbolt and Lightfoot*, had already released the infamous *Dillinger* (1973), controversial for its excessive violence, and had become something of a media presence by spouting extreme right-wing views and by broadcasting his fascination with—nay, his fetishization of—firearms.

Since the early seventies, he has done nothing particularly to soften or liberalize the image of himself as a hard-line conservative.[2] Perhaps his most pathetic contribution to Hollywood history is the paranoid vision of *Red Dawn* (1984), a movie akin to *Magnum Force* in that it deploys the underlying conventions of Hollywood narratives to argumentative effect—the argument being, of course, that only the masculine tradition of vigilance can protect America against Communism and its expansionist ambition.

To note the presence of some of Milius's political extremism at the heart of *Magnum Force* is not to suggest that he is in any sense the "auteur" for this film. But it is evident that the project of repudiating the criticisms made of *Dirty Harry* can only be helped by Milius's willingness and ability to locate the necessary argument. To distinguish between the illegitimate vigilantism of the death squad and the legitimated overseeing role that Eastwood/Callahan plays is perhaps not quite to offer the viewer a distinction between fascism and "the opposite of fascism," but it is to involve a Hollywood film in the kind of explicit argumentation that is rarely seen.

The general shape of this argumentation is one that depends, as I have hinted, on a binary of fake and real. That is, the argument against the death squad is that they do not embody the *true* American tradition of vigilantism, whereas Callahan does. They are a distortion or a misrepresentation of the truth of America. This binary is one that crops up as a kind of obsession throughout the "Harry" movies. It is, for instance, a motif applied to Scorpio in *Dirty Harry*: his affecting of the peace badge and his adoption of hippy clothing and hairstyles mark him as a fake. The same obsession appears later in *The Enforcer*, as we will see, in that there Callahan's antagonists appear as a group of politically motivated terrorists, but are in reality merely posturing. They are contrasted in the movie to the black activists with whom Callahan can establish a rapport and for whose community, he implies, he is working.

The effect of this obsession with the counterfeit is to generally undermine the integrity of particular social formations. This is underscored in *Magnum Force* again by the use of images and ideals of masculinity. That the death-squad policemen are mistaken, distorted, and ultimately fake versions of the American male avenger tradition is reinforced by their questionable sexual orientation. Harry's partner has alluded to this, and Harry has at first suggested his tolerance of it so long as they are good at their jobs. But this comes at a point in the movie when he has still not worked out their part in the executions. Later, their fakery is discovered, and the movie's showdown re-presents their leather-clad camaraderie and casts a suspicious light upon it. The counterfeit or distorted nature of these men is signaled in other ways, too, as in a shot of Davis on the firing range, where the camera shoots him from below; what I call the "under-the-chin" shot, usually marking male heroism, is in this instance off kilter, a visual cue that Davis is "bent," a distorted hero.

The imputation that these men imperfectly and inappropriately mimic some real and honest American tradition is the central rhetorical device of *Magnum Force*—and it appears elsewhere in the "Harry" movies, as we shall see. This is a rhetorical device that is a combination of two familiar kinds of rhetoric: on the one hand, the infighting technique of constructing a narcissism of small differences, and on the other hand, the demonizing that is carried out in reaction to enemies of an altogether different stripe. But the most important point to be made about this rhetoric is that it belongs properly to a discursive world that is different from the discursive world of Hollywood cinema. The importation of it here by Milius and the other filmmakers sits uneasily with their concomitant championing of a tradition that has been bred precisely within film—the tradition of the narrative in which the individual white killer male is offered as our protector.

This admixture of the rhetoric constituted by Hollywood narrative and the more strictly political rhetoric of *Magnum Force*'s argumentative assertions can certainly be considered a fusion akin to the kind of fusion that I have suggested Hollywood always tries to bring about. But in this case the fictional is taken for the real, and the strategy becomes thus at some deep level a *con*fusion of discursive realms. It is that confusion that makes *Magnum Force* a remarkable film. But it would be a further distortion and a confusion to suggest that it is a film that champions "the opposite of fascism."

Pauline's Knee, Harry's War

Eastwood does not go with the herd.
—Richard Grenier

Let us venture, then to correct Trotter's pronouncement that man is a herd animal and assert that he is rather a horde animal, an individual creature in a horde led by a chief.
—Sigmund Freud

Eastwood's critical nemesis, the critic Pauline Kael, says that movies such as *Magnum Force* have replaced the old-style John Wayne hero with "a man who essentially stands for nothing but violence" (*New Yorker*, 14 Jan. 1974, 86). She goes on to point out how the Callahan character "lives and kills as affectlessly as a psychopathic personality." It is the numbing and distancing effect of such movies that she objects to, claiming that they routinize violence to the point of alienation, and that they give no encouragement to the audience to think about the social issues—which may well directly affect them—embedded in the film. For instance, in her review of *Dirty Harry* she indicts the film for not pausing to consider—or to allow the audience to consider—the social conditions under which Scorpio could actually get his high-powered rifles and machine guns. Still on *Dirty Harry*, she notes with some distress that

> the movie was cheered and applauded by Puerto Ricans in the audience, and they jeered—as they were meant to—when the maniac whined and pleaded for his legal rights. Puerto Ricans could applaud Harry because in the movie laws protecting the rights of the accused are seen not as remedies for the mistreatment of the poor by the police and the courts but as protection for evil abstracted from all social conditions—metaphysical evil, classless criminality. (1973, 387)

With similar issues in mind, she concludes her ruminations on *Magnum Force* by noting the obvious fact that audiences flock to see films like this, and by suggesting that in the mid-1970s the audience "rather likes its fantasies to be uninvolving."

The implicit view here of an audience's relation to these movies is that it is constituted in what is commonly called escapism. Audiences, we are often told, in fact do not go to the cinema to be reminded of the frustrations and inequities of their everyday existence, but exactly to escape them, or even to produce some fantasized solution to them. Kael's objection to this phenomenon, sustained throughout the 1970s, is effectively to the kind of violence and amoralism in which such escapes and solutions seem to consist. Her position is, of course, an awkward one in that her exhortation that audiences—especially minority audiences—should recognize more clearly their own oppression cannot quite deal with the fact that such audiences have their own reasons for cheering and applauding. That is, the pleasure that audiences take in the products of the culture industry is difficult to reconcile with ideological monstrosities, like *Magnum Force*, that seem to be capable of procuring such pleasures for them.

Accounts of this phenomenon often make appeal to a notion of ressentiment. That is, the escapism is seen not simply as some passive consumption of the movie's proferred meanings, but just as much a registration or a recognition of the movie's radical anger or antiestablishment tendentiousness. This is a line that is pursued by Robert Mazzocco, in an insightful article on Eastwood and America (*New York Review of Books*, 1 April 1982) where he talks about how African-American and other ethnic minority audiences might find in the "Harry" movies and Eastwood's westerns "a glamorized version of [their] own reveries of omnipotence, [their] own amorphous sense of distrust." This kind of ressentiment is something that *Magnum Force* actually endeavors to represent and that it tries to play upon: there is a quite overblown and, indeed, almost comic example at the beginning of *Magnum Force* where the camera rests for a moment on a citizen (looking rather like Archie Bunker) who, as part of a mass demonstration, is yelling angrily about the court's having just released, "on a technicality," a known crime boss.

The affects that are supposedly evoked in an audience by the kind of overt and exaggerated fiction of civic anger in which *Magnum Force* delights are not quite "classless," as Kael has hinted. Rather—and if the idea that such films operate to provide imaginary (and/or escapist) narratives and images for the channeling of audiences' ressentiment has any seeming—they are affects that might be expected to be all the more easily invoked in audiences whose everyday experience of oppression is great. In that sense what has seemed to white liberal critics as a kind of mystery about the enthusiasm of minority audiences for Eastwood's films can be explained rather simply. But given the ambivalent way in which minorities are represented on the Eastwood screen, there is nonetheless still some kind of contradiction in minority audience reactions. That contradiction would point to the notion that the prime point of interest for such audiences is not so much the representations of minority characters, or their at best ambivalent treatment within the narrative frame, but rather more the Eastwood figure and the central narrative account of his upholding of a "natural" justice.

In this process an admiring identification with the white male hero would become the mode of defusion of the aggressive energies of ressentiment, permitting a "general character of harshness and cruelty [to be] exhibited by the ideal—its dictatorial 'Thou shalt' " (Freud [1923] 1962, 45). That this kind of identification is at play in the cinema is almost a commonplace assumption in much liberal criticism of Eastwood and his films, as well as of a whole history of Hollywood movies; it has become, in other words, a shibboleth, a reflex to explain the pull that such movies exert on their viewers. It is also and at the same time a guiding assumption in the discourse of the industry. Indeed, Eastwood himself has subscribed to this view. While filming *Joe Kidd* in 1971, he made the following comments for an article in *Time* (6 Dec. 1971): "A guy sits in the audience; he's 25 and scared stiff about what he's going to do with his life. He wants to be that self-sufficient thing he sees up there on screen in my pictures. A superhuman character who has all the answers, is doubly cool, exists on his own without society or the help of society's police forces."

Later in this book I shall be trying to interrogate this notion of identification more closely. But for now I want simply to say that the kinds of assumptions about films and audiences that have been enshrined in this thesis of identification at least have the virtue of recognizing that the activity of audiences in front of the screen is not a simple consumption of the movie in a way that directly and unproblematically turns the viewer into the film's subject. Eastwood and Kael could probably come to some agreement on that issue, even if for divergent reasons. Eastwood's view of this identification process appears to suggest that its most important factor is its promoting in the viewer a vicarious sense of power that is, as he makes explicit, individualized. Kael and Mazzocco, on the other hand, want to suggest that the imaginary construction of such an individualized sense of power is also alienating at some level. The difference between them is perhaps best stated by saying that for the white liberal critics a movie's proferred meanings are as important as the process of identification, since the proferred meanings simultaneously derive from and interact with other kinds of social signification and ideology. For Eastwood, on the other hand, those other discourses are supposed to coincide with the movie's proferred meanings in a way that cuts down the space between the movie theater and the social life in which it is rooted.

Eastwood's view is a misrecognition that is consonant with the problem I pointed out earlier in relation to the confusion of the meanings of the narrative conventions of the cinema with discourses of civic life. The liberal critical view is often taken to be a misrecognition of an opposite but related kind: it is often accused of assuming that viewers are the dupes of the movie's proferred meanings, which are inculcated by means of the identificatory system. That is, the liberal critics are understood to be worrying that audiences will become as it were infected by nefarious ideologies and moralities from the cinema, and are thereby taken to imagine that the proferred meanings translate directly to beliefs that are acted upon or which inform real subjects in the real world. If that were true, they could certainly be accused of a misrecognition akin to Eastwood's. However, as I think Kael's writings often show, these are not the assumptions upon which such criticism usually works. The anxiety that, for instance, Kael has about cinema is that its pleasures—which she is happy to acknowledge, both for herself and other viewers—inhibit political and social empowerment and participation.

One of the reasons I am spending so much time trying to draw out the similarities and the distinctions between these views is that in their way they echo in the popular register some of the claims and arguments made by various academic and theoretical discourses on film and popular culture. In a context where the theoretical *dernier cri* is for the canonization of the spectator's pleasure—the "uses and gratifications" model—the kind of intervention that Kael makes would appear hopelessly moralistic and even elitist. However, I think that in contrast to the current critical rush to disembarrass criticism of its supposed surveillant role over the consumerist pleasures of the popular, Kael's perceptions of what we might call the disinvolvement of those pleasures are viable and useful.

Equally, on a more topical level, I am interested in what I will call the "reception practices"[1] by which Eastwood and his films are constructed and into which they necessarily intervene. Pauline Kael herself, as one of the leading journalistic critics in the country for over thirty years, has been influential in those reception practices, as has another woman critic, Judith Crist. Both women in their ways have been significant antagonists to Eastwood and his films, both specifically objecting on numerous occasions to the gender politics of his films and more generally exhibiting concern over the ideological production in which he engages. Eastwood has said throughout his career that he pays little attention to critics—although the debate around *Dirty Harry*, and *Magnum Force* itself might be enough evidence to suggest that his disclaimers are disingenuous.[2] At any rate, these two have been the epitome of the liberal establishment critic for Eastwood, and it is perhaps not irrelevant that they are women. As I have pointed out, within the diegetic world of the genre movies that Eastwood most often makes, one of the most frequent functions of the women characters is to represent a resistance to the masculinist ethos, politics, and violence of the hero. In those narratives, however, the women's role is also to finally alter their relation to that ethos and give their consent to its heroics—something that Crist and Kael have not yet done.

It would be impossible, of course, to guess at the degree of threat that Eastwood might experience from such a refusal, but it is perhaps these women's obstinacy in not giving consent that produced the rather unsavory symptomatic event on national television where Eastwood, having been asked by his host, Burt Reynolds, who he would choose to be if he could be a woman, replied twice: first, that he would be a mixture of an old prostitute and Judith Crist, and second, a combination of Margaret Rutherford and Pauline Kael (see Kaminsky 1974a, 161-62). At any rate, it is at least consonant with the Hollywood narratives that, as I am beginning to suggest, Eastwood lives that in the realm of criticism it is two women to whom he has most frequently to attend.

The kind of power struggle that the "Harry" movies enter into with the liberal establishment is in fact sustained in the next such movie, *The Enforcer*, a movie that has a kind of double articulation around the question of gender: first, it responds directly (i.e., in the direct, argumentative way that *Magnum Force* responds to criticism of *Dirty Harry*) to the criticisms that are made about Callahan's sexism, and second, it constitutes a general demonstration against the "womanliness" of liberal criticism. I propose in the next section to look at that movie and other subsequent movies that pick up on the Harry tradition, most of which inflect that tradition through the issue of gender. But for the moment, I want to look at another kind of defense of the Callahan-Eastwood ethos.

It is unusual to find in the tributary media much real support for the kind of position I am sketching out and imputing to Eastwood. That is, the assumption that the logic laid out by the history of cinematic and narrative conventions is equivalent to or unproblematically transferable to a logic of the civic realm is not exactly omnipresent in those other media. Indeed, despite the strong presence of writers like Crist and Kael, it is not within the discursive purview of most popular reviews, article journalism, or television shows to see movies as anything but "just entertainment"; in those spheres movies are generally considered to be as distant from the realities of politics as they can be made to be. Yet from time to time one can come across writings that will replicate exactly, and defend, the positions that Eastwood's movies take up. I have in mind one such article in particular—by Richard Grenier (in *Commentary*, April 1984, 61-67)—though there are others.[3]

Grenier's article, "The World's Favorite Movie Star," in this right-wing journal is written roughly ten years after the release of the films I have been discussing, but in some way this is hardly apparent; in other ways, it is exactly the point, as I shall explain. Grenier is writing during the first term of Ronald Reagan's presidency, at a time when, as he himself remarks, many of the social and civic gains that had been made in the 1960s were being rolled back under the avuncular eye of the movie President. Grenier's central point is to show how Eastwood—and in his phrasing he conflates almost absolutely Eastwood and any of the characters he plays—has consistently articulated those values and beliefs of the right wing that only in the 1980s are coming to be reinstalled in American life.

It seems that what is important about Eastwood for Grenier—and implicitly the reason he is *the world's* favorite movie star—is that he has tapped into a vein of American culture that is definable by its class, race, and region. In his attempt to define these areas of appeal, Grenier reconstructs the familiar divisions that help inform the ideological profferings of westerns: the split between the sophisticated East (epitomized by New York, "where the critical community is centered") and the workaday West. Overlaid onto the regional distinction is a class distinction: Eastwood attracts "skilled industrial workers, farmers," and the like, as against the "young, affluent, and educated, centering roughly on the university, pre-university, and post-university sectors of the population" who will go to watch Woody Allen or Meryl Streep. He also points out that a large part of Eastwood's audience is made up of "blacks [who] are the first to suffer from increased inner-city crime, and they (if not all their leaders) tend to have extremely severe law-and-order attitudes."

Although Grenier is careful not to overtly construct at the same time a gender division (like so many right-wing ideologues of the Reagan and Bush years, he speaks as if there is no sexism while recognizing other social divisions as his problematic), he nonetheless betrays his position in relation to gender in several places in the article. First of all and with no apparent self-consciousness, he adopts the movie discourse that has always suggested that the sophisticated and liberal East, home of book learning, is irredeemably effeminate, whereas the West is the proper locus of American masculinity. Thus, the audiences in the West and the South who go to Eastwood movies are in his account "men who if they no longer work with their hands come from a different America from the Vassar that produced Jane Fonda and Meryl Streep." Elsewhere, describing Eastwood's first directorial effort, *Play Misty for Me*, he delights in the movie's climax, where Jessica Walters, playing "a very forward woman who gradually reveals herself to be hysterically jealous, psychotic, and, ultimately, murderous," is delivered "a bone-crushing punch to her face, knocking her through the windows, over the balcony, and down into the ocean below." Having thus enthusiastically described the woman's apparently deserved death, he lightly adds that the Eastwood character's actions here are "all in justifiable self-defense" and adds the gratuitous remark that "one doubts that [this] is Gloria Steinem's favorite movie."

So, there is a gender division in Grenier's discourse, and it is evident in the way in which gender is not directly addressed as a social division but is left to operate as it were symptomatically. The other divisions (between the East and the rest of the United States, between educated liberals and down-to-earth workers, between soft African-American leadership and their more clear-sighted constituency, between Jane Fonda and Clint Eastwood, and so on) help Grenier establish the existence of "virtually two nations, each easily recognizable by manners and speech." Here he replicates the ideological work of the right wing in the Reagan years, which attempted to both construct and exacerbate populist, anti-Eastern, and antiliberal-intellectual sentiment in the American population. The effort of this particular article is to construct Eastwood as both the epitome of the targeted populist class and also its transcendent hero.

The way in which Grenier treats the biographical data of Eastwood's life is indicative of this. He begins his account of Eastwood's life by praising Eastwood's genealogy: "English, Scottish, Irish, Dutch, a close approximation of this country's original stock." That somewhat astounding view of America's ethnic origins (presumably if Welsh were substituted for Dutch, Eastwood would be less an approximation and even more the real thing) becomes the foundation for a narrative of Eastwood's pre-Hollywood life that endows Eastwood with all the necessary elements of the twentieth-century version of the white male settler. He is a "child of the Depression," and the economic travails of his family led to his attending "ten different schools, making him something of a loner, a wanderer, another throwback to an older America when the country was filled with men roaming the land, looking for work and a place to build a new life." This twentieth-century pioneer's upbringing nurtured in Eastwood the right moral stuff. He learned, according to Grenier, that "you don't get something for nothing"; his "self-sufficient" grandmother, who "lived by herself on a mountaintop, probably had more to do with my turning out the way I am than any educational process"; he learned the virtues of honest work in a series of laboring jobs; he went to a community college at nights to better himself; and so on. The only possible flaw in Eastwood's background is quickly covered over in Grenier's account. That is, although he was drafted into the army at the time of the Korean war, Eastwood never actually saw combat in the service of his country; but Grenier is quick to point out that this was just "a fluke" and that, in any case, Eastwood "escap[ed] death narrowly" in the crash of a navy bomber.

Grenier's mention of this incident implies that what he calls this "routine mission" was an official one, but in fact Eastwood was on a weekend pass and unofficially accompanying a pilot friend on a flight to San Francisco.[4] But the passage is an important moment in Grenier's text because, in the context of his main argument, Eastwood's almost nonexistent military career has to be not only explained away, but also made to look tolerably spectacular. That is because the article's prime agenda is to appropriate Eastwood and his image in support of the double-headed ideological program of the Reagan presidency: severe law and order at home, American military adventurism abroad. As he himself says, soon after the beginning of his article, "There is a link between the extraordinary reluctance of many on the Left to use U.S. military power anywhere in the world, even in self-defense, and the efforts of many liberals at home to inhibit the application of harsh penalties against even confessed criminals."

Although Eastwood is no more than a kind of honorable noncombatant in America's real wars, he can be enlisted into the ideological war that the right wing has perceived itself to be fighting during the last twenty or so years: after all, Eastwood's "ethic," says Grenier, "is not different from that of a soldier. Volunteer or conscript, the infantryman answers his country's call. His life is placed in peril . . . he kills the enemy, feeling no qualms. . . . It is the law of war, and also common sense." One way of describing the war to which serviceman Eastwood is here being called is to say that it is the war to win the Vietnam War. It is sometimes difficult to grasp the degree to which the perceived loss of the Vietnam War—both to the Vietcong and to the liberals at home—has entered and affected the psyche of the American right wing, but Grenier's article is a bundle of telling symptoms that is almost desperate in its desire and determination to reverse that imaginary history.

The symptoms include continual carping and critical remarks about the domestic battles of the 1960s and 1970s. Predictably, in relation to the "Dirty Harry" movies, Grenier complains about the 1966 Miranda ruling, "the ultra-liberal" Warren court, and the nefarious effects of the exclusionary rules. He rails against the ACLU—"when you try to do justice and pursue criminals in a great, modern U.S. city you come up against the American Civil Liberties Union." He blames the victims of the National Guard at Kent State University, implying, just as Eastwood does in relation to Scorpio in *Dirty Harry* and the radicals in *The Enforcer*, that they were only "fake" peace demonstrators. And for good measure he takes a swing or two at liberal critics led by Pauline Kael and feminists led by Gloria Steinem.

These were all part of the list of abiding targets of the right wing during the 1980s. But the most obsessively present issue is that of war, and the Vietnam War in particular. Grenier reminds us that it was in the year of the Tet offensive in Vietnam that *The Good, the Bad, and the Ugly* drew vast crowds in America, allowing that movie's presentation of Eastwood to suggest that American conduct of the war had more public support than the "elite" and the liberals allowed people to believe. The whole article sets this kind of hypothesized popular support against the liberal hold on the media. Eastwood himself is then implicated into this version of "the silent majority," not only by dint of his films but also because of his helping to finance the much-publicized adventurism of Bo Gritz, a Vietnam veteran who in 1982 set out armed to rescue American MIAs from Laos.[5]

Certainly there are some good reasons to think that this war is Eastwood's war—his defense of *Dirty Harry*, his importing of Milius's overtly right-wing perspective into *Magnum Force*, his subsidizing of Gritz, and so on. Equally, his vigilante sympathies are expressed when, asked about the hijacking of a TWA jet in 1985, he says, "Someone should be able to find those guys who killed that sailor in cold blood . . . and I don't think they should have to come to trial" (*Newsweek*, 22 July 1985, 54). But my point here, and in commentating on Grenier's article at such length, is most of all to sketch out some of the context in which Eastwood and his films intervene, how they can be used or appropriated within larger cultural narratives. I have also been trying to suggest that the ease with which Eastwood can be assimilated into and appropriated for the right-wing narrative and ideology that Grenier exemplifies is in part a product of his immersion in the already prepared narratives and ideologies of the Hollywood industry. That is, the industry's conventions, both narrative and discursive, already contain the materials necessary for the promulgation of a right-wing version of America and its politics.

That those materials are already there is in a way confirmed by the parting shot of Grenier's article. Having shown that most of Eastwood's movies up to 1984 are entirely consistent with the most savage and cynical right-wing ideology, he proceeds to suggest that this coincidence is an almost natural one—certainly an endemic one—which points to the innate correctness of that ideology. In a telling instance of how American cultural discourses can be used to protect against the necessity of politics, Grenier has the following to say: "Perhaps Eastwood's patriotism, his belief in the legitimacy of force when necessary, and his determination to see predators punished are so deeply ingrained that he doesn't even think of them as political. Perhaps he thinks such fundamental assumptions should be beyond the realm of political debate. And the man might have a point." Thus, it would seem, the ultimate defense against the threat of competing political positions is to move the goalposts and to claim that some assumptions are so "fundamental," so much a matter of "common sense," that there is nothing to be said around them or in opposition to them. In the miasma of such rhetoric as Grenier's—or indeed in such rhetoric as that of *Magnum Force*—it is all too easy to lose sight of what is being held up as essential: the right of the chief of the horde to exceed or ignore established laws and rights both at home and overseas and to employ ruthless force wherever he thinks it appropriate.

Amongst Men

Scorpio's first victim in *Dirty Harry* is an attractive young woman whom he shoots while she is swimming. The movie's opening sequence shows the killer's gun barrel close up and his view of her in the sights of his high-velocity rifle, before a single bullet enters her neck and she sinks beneath the water. The scene is replayed in *Magnum Force* when the assassins throw a bomb and fire machine gun bullets into a crowded private pool party. The camera picks on several of the victims, but particularly on another young woman, swimming topless, who receives a bullet between her naked breasts. Each of these killings is eroticized in its own way—the first combines the spectacle of the woman with the crude close-up of the gun barrel, and the second emphasizes the woman's naked breasts. The eroticization is presumably for or on behalf of heterosexual male viewers whose gaze is presumed in much film criticism to coincide both physically and metaphysically with that of the camera as it first objectifies, then records the sexually charged murders of these women.

The fact that these murders are committed by the people upon whom Callahan is then turned loose in search of the community's revenge is little mitigation of the fact that the movies offer them as titillating moments. Indeed, this contradictory construction can only be described as cynical. That is, the erotic impulse of the murderers and of the mise-en-scène itself—even while demanding a correction and inducing a process in the films that is concerned with the righting of sexuality—bespeaks a recognition that this urge to erotic murder is at least of interest to and probably essential to the heterosexual male subject. At the same time, what I shall take as crucial here about that contradiction is the way in which it introduces—or even entails—an element of uncertainty in Eastwood's action movies, and the way in which it can be said to begin a narrative of Eastwood's dealings with sexuality and violence, or with masculinity and its vicissitudes, that carries across many of his subsequent films, especially the cop movies.

The recognition of the appeal of eroticized violence and the need to correct it (to displace it, keep it in check, or repress it) becomes, as I shall argue, an increasingly uneasy one in Eastwood's cop movies. Indeed, it eventually becomes a central problematic, reaching a kind of apotheosis with the Eastwood figure in *Tightrope* (1984). In that picture the detective Wes Block is almost disabled by his recognition that the erotic and murderous desires of the nameless killer whom he stalks are also his own; the process of narrative correction thus becomes a highly difficult and self-reflective one, which is finally and ironically facilitated by the intervention of a feminist rape counselor with whom Block becomes involved. The narrative that I am referring to, then, starts here in these symptomatic scenes of the slaughter of women, and it appears to come to some sort of at least provisional conclusion with *Tightrope*.

In a book about the sociology of fatal violence committed by men against women, Deborah Cameron and Elizabeth Frazer describe the phenomenon as "the lust to kill" (1987). Their argument places sexual murder on a continuum with other paradigmatic forms of masculinity. That is, what they propose is no longer just the familiar linkages among rape, masculinist representational systems, and everyday male sexuality and behavior; they go a step further and propose that sexual murder should be seen as intrinsically a part of that nexus. The erotic aspect of killing is, in their view, an epiphenomenal function of the subjectivity to which men aspire in masculinist society and culture. The gender power relations that subvent a masculinist culture produce male subjects who are misogynist and sexually violent in their urge to accede to the transcendent power of ideal masculine subjectivity: as Cameron and Frazer put it, "misogyny, transcendence, sadistic sexuality [are] the basic ingredients of the lust to kill" (167), but also of a more generally constructed masculinity in masculinist society. Thus in their view, to study the sexual murderer is to "learn from their very excesses what is usually hidden in male sexuality" (119).[1]

For many people the distance between the horrific "excesses" of male sexual murder and those two images from Eastwood movies that I have cited may seem hopelessly great. But Cameron and Frazer have, I think, a good explanation about how this distance comes to be installed: they suggest that what prevents a general recognition of the continuum they try to establish is the tendency to think of the male sexual murderer as an individual "sex beast who is seriously mentally disturbed, a sufferer from some individual pathological condition" (118). In other words, there is an ideology of individualism and pathology that separates understandings of the egregious from recognitions of the everyday. This ideology, it could be claimed, is sustained especially by the kinds of narratives whose point it is to punish such pathology. To rid the diegetic world of sexual terror is to rid it of the one beastly man, and the individualism is again stressed by the fact that it is nearly always one other man who does the job.

One of the modes in which this construction of a murderous masculinity is corrected in the narratives of Eastwood's movies is through the rhetoric of fakery or counterfeit that I spoke of earlier. The function of this rhetoric is to establish control over exactly the titillation I have described, but also over the threat to ideal masculine subjectivity that that titillation entails. A narrative image of the activity and shape of a properly constituted masculinity is established, against which particular forms of activity are judged and found dangerous: thus, for example, the narcissism of small differences that arises in *Magnum Force* between the supposedly homosexual bikers and the determinedly heterosexual Harry. Harry's function in relation to Scorpio is a related case: even though Scorpio is explicitly a sexual murderer only in the opening scene that I mentioned, his representation is highly sexualized and his relation to children in particular is suggestively eroticized. Harry's "true" male sexuality, then, recognizes its antagonists, and the films themselves deploy and specifically exploit the elements of masculinity that are to be excluded.

This, then, is the beginning of my narrative about the relation of Eastwood's films to this kind of issue. The beginning is an entirely conventionalized setting up of certain elements of masculine desire as fake or perverse and their narrative counterpositioning against the wholeness and integrity of Callahan's sexuality. This is a positional drama of demonizing, of course, which is consistent with Eastwood's defense of the "Dirty Harry" movies, as well as with Grenier's extension of those movies into the logic of the American military imaginary and foreign policy. My suggestion will be that this begins to change quite radically in later Eastwood cop movies. I do not especially much want to suggest that the ensuing narrative represents an expulsion or a negation of the demonizing dramas of pathology and punishment, of an ideal masculinity and its projected "others." But I will suggest that in this narrative there is at least the rather uncanny spectacle of a populist, right-wing masculinity interrogating itself.

The first—though I think, finally, not very large—step on this narrative of interrogation is the third in the "Dirty Harry" series, *The Enforcer* (1976), directed by James Fargo. Just as *Magnum Force* is an unusual movie for its responsiveness, as it were, so *Enforcer* has to be seen as a riposte. This time the answer is being made to Eastwood's feminist critics. The form of the answer was perhaps worked for from the beginning of the project when Malpaso engaged Stirling Silliphant to write the screenplay. Silliphant, although he was beginning to put his energy into movies like *The Towering Inferno*, had earned strong liberal credentials within Hollywood by virtue of scripts such as *In the Heat of the Night* (for which he won an Oscar in 1967). The script of *Enforcer* offers several occasions, as did *Magnum Force*, for Callahan to dress once more as the liberal and to argue explicitly for a point of view that is supposed to stand against the charges of sexism made against Eastwood and his movies.

One instance of this is in an early sequence where Callahan sits on a panel to interview a prospective inspector, Kate Moore (played by Tyne Daley). The scene becomes the occasion for a diatribe against the dangers of putting inexperienced women in a position that is perilous for them and for their (male) partners simply in order to satisfy affirmative action guidelines—guidelines that themselves are part of a cynical mayoral publicity plan to ensure reelection. Callahan delivers himself of the view that the possible street deaths of police officers is "a hell of a price to pay for being stylish." The argument placed in Callahan's mouth is a familiar one in American civic discourse: that affirmative action in relation to women can potentially do more harm than good in the execution of the job, and that therefore objections to it are not an expression of sexism but simply of an objective concern for proper efficiency on the job and for the safety of personnel. The argument fits almost exactly what Hirschman describes as the "jeopardy thesis" that runs through a whole history of "the rhetoric of reaction" (1991, chap. 4), wherein it is assumed that a forceful argument for politically reactionary positions is to construct a self-evidently horrifying—though not necessarily accurate—answer to the implied question, "Can you imagine what would happen if . . . ?"

Callahan's position is that he would find a properly qualified and efficient woman inspector quite acceptable, and in fact the picture goes on to confirm and illustrate this. Moore begins her demonstration of her abilities by quoting her knowledge of legal statutes. After she has been made, predictably enough, Harry's partner, the rest of the movie shows her quickly becoming better and better at the job, earning his respect and allowing him to demonstrate that he is not essentially sexist. Of course, the film's argument assumes that Callahan's male ways of doing and perceiving the job are the criteria that Moore must live up to, but nonetheless the movie clearly offers itself as a demonstration of Callahan's—and by extension Eastwood's—reasonableness and lack of sexism and as an argument against feminist charges. The movie is thus the first instance in the Eastwood cop sequence where there is some kind of alliance struck up between the male protagonist and a female one, and where the alliance has an argumentative purpose.

But around that alliance the rhetoric of the movie is otherwise familiar enough. Callahan's and Moore's antagonists are a gang led by a Vietnam veteran, Bobby Maxwell, posing as political terrorists, but their real interest—or at least, the real interest of their leader—is in extorting money from the city of San Francisco for solely personal profit. Their fake radicalism is set against that of a group of black activists—the epitome of one of white America's worst nightmares in the late 1960s—who become involved in Callahan's detection work. The leader of the Uhuru group, Mustapha, forges a working relationship with Callahan based on mutual respect. Although the motives for this are only skimmed across in the movie's exposition, what is suggested is that Mustapha and his men are resisting the culture and politics of white America in a way that makes them Harry's kin; they are, then, the real activist group against which the fake one is defined.

The counterfeit nature of the terrorists is given almost from the beginning but is underscored heavily in a scene where one of them is killed by Moore. A woman terrorist is dressed as a nun who attempts to shoot Harry while he is roughly interrogating a radical worker-priest (himself another perversion of what is acceptable).

Moore's tip-off that this is no real nun comes when she sees her brightly painted red fingernails—presumably these are the marks of a sexuality that nuns cannot really exhibit. By this time the narrative has already specifically linked the terrorists with the pimp and prostitute culture of the city, and so here the linkage between perverse sexuality and fake politics is made explicit. In searching for leads, at one point Harry explicitly enters the world of this fake and perverse sexuality. He visits a massage parlor and, in what is supposed to be a comic scene, watches a group of old women performing the labor of writing sex letters to male clients who will never see the real origin of these counterfeited sexual fantasies. Here the point of view of Harry's real and reasonable sexuality is posed against the fakery of another part of the culture. As if this series of linkages between fake politics and perverse and counterfeit sexuality were not strong enough, Callahan reaffirms the point in the movie's showdown sequence. As he is about to blow Maxwell away with the aptly and phallically named Law's rocket, he mutters, "You fucking fruit," thereby affirming the less than true masculinity of his antagonist.

There are many other ways in this movie that this rhetorical binary is applied, forming a nexus of signification around the central concepts of sexuality and politics. To elaborate further upon them here would be to consign the movie entirely to its generic description. This is indeed what the movie does to itself in the final sequence when Moore is predictably shot and killed by the terrorists: the woman who has proved herself "real" dies so that Callahan can finish off the job. Although Moore has filled her male partner's criteria, still as she dies she thinks she has "messed up." Despite the movie's double movement of arguing its antisexism and demonstrating that it can accept a qualified woman, the generic conventions of the "Harry" movies demand the death of Callahan's partner: Moore becomes, then, a generic sacrifice.

Enforcer is perhaps not an especially remarkable movie on levels other than its determination to be, as I put it, argumentative, and its retreat into the formulaic shape of the other "Harry" movies is almost entirely dull.[2] Yet the picture does mark a first stage in Eastwood movies of the development of a discourse that confronts the relation of the ideal policier image to the femininity upon which it dialectically has always depended, and also the relation of that image to the fantasies in which it is constituted. It will, in fact, be more than half a dozen years before Eastwood makes another movie that actually deploys the Callahan figure by name (*Sudden Impact*, released in 1983, and the only one of the "Harry" movies that Eastwood himself directs), and it is not until *Tightrope* in 1984 that the content of those fantasies is extensively laid out.

In the meantime Eastwood makes a rather strange and almost unclassifiable film that subjects the policier image to a series of revisions, especially around its representation of the savior male. This film is *The Gauntlet* (1976), in which Eastwood plays a cop, Ben Shockley, who is ordered to bring a prostitute, Gus Mally (played by Sondra Locke), from Las Vegas to Phoenix, where she will be a witness at a gang boss's trial. Mally can identify the key figure for the prosecution because in a professional encounter she has been abused by him—or rather, she has been sexually abused with his gun. This figure turns out to be Shockley's chief, Blakelock. Both Shockley and Mally become Blakelock's target, since he would be ruined if she were allowed to testify. From rocky beginnings with each other, the two form an alliance and decide to overcome the various efforts to stop them from arriving. The gauntlet of the title refers to the movie's final sequence, where, in a hastily revamped bus, they ride into the city streets, which are lined with armed policemen.

Gauntlet was highly touted on its release, if only because of the way the tributary media focused on the making of the film and particularly on some of the action effects (like the spectacular collapse of a house under an equally spectacular rain of police bullets, and an extensive helicopter chase in the southwestern desert hills)—effects that helped make this Malpaso's most expensive film to that date.[3] Popular critics have responded in no consistent manner to the movie, however. It earned the catchall, noncommittal adjective from *Variety*: "offbeat." On the other hand, Guérif thinks it Eastwood's "most serene film, the most accomplished in its control, blending extreme violence and a distancing brand of humor" (125). Simsolo, as is unfortunately his wont, is almost rhapsodical: "the very model of a film that is both falsely naive and terribly complex, built from a leaden script full of stereotypes that then explode one after the other, leaving fantasy to have free rein" (1990, 102; my translation).

On the other hand, Vincent Canby in the *New York Times* suggests that *Gauntlet* is "a movie without a single thought in its head" (22 Dec. 1977, C11), but this seems a harsh judgment on a couple of scores. First of all, most of the commentary, either pro or con, will manage to see the way in which the Callahan figure is transformed in this quasi-comic movie. Shockley is a down-at-the-heels version of Callahan, a drinker and a depressive, and someone who is chosen to do the movie's central task not because he gets a job done, but because his boss sees him as expendable. It seems clear that part of the movie's deliberate effort is thus to offer a kind of obverse of Harry, a Harry manqué. But second, few of the commentaries have much to say about what I think is the principal means of that transformation and what gives this film its central interest: that is, the alliance between the cop and the prostitute and the issues around sexuality that it—at least in a gingerly way—begins to explore.

This alliance is narratively quite unexceptional in many ways. Shockley and Mally are thrown together, bicker, learn to like and even love each other, and finally reach their destination together: this is the standard format of the road movie, even if it rings some changes on that format—for instance, this particular road movie appends an excessively violent set of action sequences to the usual romantic comedy. But most importantly, Mally is a prostitute, with a "B.A. from Finch College," whose sexual presence is as verbal as it is physical, and whose general level of street knowledge and intuition is much higher than that of her male companion. She is, in short, a powerful and independent woman—from the other side of a social spectrum to Inspector Moore, but nonetheless a strong figure, especially when set in contrast to Shockley's initially rather depressive and run-down character.

Mally starts out with a clear critique of men, demonstrated in her simple abuse of Shockley as "you big prick," her asides on the "macho mentality" and the "tin-star egomaniacal" behavior of her companion and other men, and her responding to Shockley's slapping her by kicking him in the groin with the words, "Sorry. I just had to jog your thinking." Her general tone toward all the men in the movie is disdainful, sardonic, and insulting, and at one point the script gives her the floor to deliver a diatribe against, first, cops, and then men in general.

That moment occurs as she and Shockley are protecting themselves by hijacking a police patrol car and its driver. The latter takes the opportunity to ask Mally a set of prurient questions about her profession and, indeed, her gender; these questions get more and more personalized and, when she does not answer, are followed by his recounting a quite lurid fantasy about watching her at work. At various moments Shockley tries to stop this monologue, but Mally lets it continue before delivering herself of a diatribe in response. The sequence in which this diatribe takes place is for me the heart of the film, and perhaps its only real point of interest. Mally's speech works, in its first part, to give the underside of precisely the wholly honest and full-of-integrity image of the police that the Callahan figure had tried to deliver. She runs through a list of exemplary and everyday police crimes—including being on the take at bars, covering up for politicians, strong-arming Chicanos at the barrio on Saturday nights, skimming the haul from captured drug pushers to feed dope addicts on the force, and so on—and thence compares the work of a prostitute favorably to all this because after work a prostitute can clean herself up with a hot bath. In the second part, Mally goes after the patrolman's sexual imaginary, suggesting to him that "you don't like women like me; we're a bit aggressive and you're frightened. But that's because you've got filth in your brains. And I'm afraid that the only way you'll clean it out is to put a bullet through it." She finishes by asking the astonished patrolman whether his wife knows that he masturbates.

My point about this scene is not that it turns the movie into a feminist movie or anything of that sort. Rather, and much less ambitiously, it constitutes a particular moment in which and through which the hegemony of the fantasized male of most of Eastwood's movies to this point is broken by a woman's voice. Equally, at that moment Shockley shows his general assent to Mally's diatribe: they pass conspiratorial looks when she has finished. Shockley gives a small but definite smile, and gently nods his head (and this is almost exactly the same suite of gestures that greeted Moore in *Enforcer* at the point where she began to earn Callahan's respect). More to the point, it is the underpinnings of the male imaginary that are laid open for attack in this sequence. Mally is not going to be perceived in the audience's terms as aggressive simply because she is a prostitute, but rather because she exposes masculine prurience and turns it back on itself with a moral condemnation. The harshness of her critique and Shockley's connivance in it mark a peculiar moment in the adventures of Eastwood's cop figures.

It probably goes without saying—given my stress in this book on the way in which the political and rhetorical arguments that emerge from Eastwood's movies are always regulated by a relation to the cinematic genres and conventions in which they work—that Mally's irruption into the male imaginary will ultimately be compromised in some way. And certainly the demands of the road movie turn her from the role of "wild nag" into which Shockley early casts her, to the role of perhaps still nag, but at least now complicit nag, by the time she has fallen in love with Shockley and they have reached Phoenix. But their alliance is cemented and even epitomized when Mally becomes the one who shoots Blakelock, almost as revenge for the abuse she had suffered at the end of his gun.

The moment at which Mally shoots down Blakelock is perhaps not an altogether startling one in the history of film, but it does accrue to itself a certain amount of power by pointing back toward another central rhetorical moment in the movie—the moment when Mally describes the sexual details of her previous encounter with Blakelock and reminds the viewer that "he told me that if I screamed, he'd pull the trigger." It is true that, in accord with both cultural and generic conventions, the movie has had to tame the shrewish whore that Mally is at the beginning and turn her into a woman about to marry and settle down. At the same time, what is allowed in this moment is the knowledge that even the hard-nosed whore gets revenge for the abuse she suffers from men. While the first of these moves is conventional, the second is not, and while they may not be logically contradictory, the latter is hardly a regular matter of cultural verisimilitude.

These gestures in *Gauntlet*—its setting of a woman's voice against the idealized serviceman that Eastwood had become by the mid-1970s and its depicting a woman's revenge against masculinity—never enable the film to transcend the limits of its generic ambition, but they certainly help establish, as it were, a line of inquiry for Eastwood's cop movies. The line is picked up explicitly in *Sudden Impact*, which pitches Eastwood and Locke into the same kind of alliance as they have in *Gauntlet*—an alliance against, on the one hand, corrupt or ineffectual officialdom and the legal system, and, on the other, against a particular version of "fake" or perverse masculinity.

Once again the Locke character, Jennifer Spencer, comes armed with a kind of critique of masculinity. This is hinted at in an early scene where her car is stopped by a group of leering and sexually aggressive male youths. Jennifer's response is to summon them to her window, and ask one of them if he needs a lift; that he does of course provokes her to tell him in that case to "shove a jack up your ass." Her no-nonsense response to men and their aggression is by no means confined to this sort of exchange, but in fact produces her as the killer whom Callahan is looking for during most of the movie: Jennifer is engaged in a killing vendetta against a gang that had raped both her and her younger sister (who is shown several times in a traumatic coma). Her preferred mode of execution is a bullet to the genitals and the head of each of the gang members whom she seeks out in turn—including one woman, Ray, described as a "dyke" in the movie and portrayed as a particularly abhorrent redneck by Audrie J. Neenan.

Significantly, the gang is made up of a class cross section of the men in a small California seaside town. In addition to the typical lower-class villains, they include a local businessman and even the local police chief's son (whom the chief protects, by means of his power, from Jennifer's spree and Callahan's investigation). The involvement of the businessman particularly allows the introduction of standard middle-class male pleadings against punishment for sexual violence: it was a long time ago, I was drunk, I didn't mean anything by it, I'm respectable now, and so on. The point is clear that the kind of male sexuality upon which Jennifer is avenging herself is a generalizable one, which crosses classes (and even genders in the case of Ray). Although the gang rape of the two young women is depicted, through Jennifer's flashbacks as she is about to commit her murders, as something extraordinary, the film suggests (partly through the incident with the youths on the street) that it is an epiphenomenal event.

The film is in most other respects a relatively straightforward rendering of the "Dirty Harry" genre. Its first part is filled with Callahan's familiar struggle against the liberal democratic establishment, which thinks of him as "a dinosaur" and of his violent methods as hopelessly out of date; there are the obligatory scenes of urban violence in which he can vindicate for the audience's benefit precisely those methods (with one of those scenes showcasing the immortal lines, "Go ahead. Make my day"). Callahan's and Spencer's relationship is formulaic too, beginning with a bickering meeting that leads them to bed together. There is also a conversation between them where they compare their very similar views of justice: Spencer reckons that this is an "age of lapsed responsibilities and defeated justice," and Harry remarks fondly that he doesn't hear that kind of thing enough. As the two of them intensify their similarities or agreements, the film's villains are thrown into the pot of the fake and the perverse. A notable scene depicts their leader Micky in a motel with a voluptuous blonde woman and indicates that he is unable to have sex without hurting her and without hearing her tell him how strong and beautiful he is.

The only real generic differences between this and other "Harry" films are at the level of locale (the second half of the film takes place in San Paolo on the California coast) and Callahan's arrangements with his partner (his black partner mostly stays in San Francisco but still manages to get himself killed on a visit to Harry; otherwise Harry has the help only of a young local cop). The other important shift in the Harry genre—which is easily seen as an extension of the genre's logic rather than a reversal of any kind—occurs at the end, where Harry, knowing that Jennifer is the killer he is looking for, helps her kill off the rapist gang and deliberately tampers with evidence to allow her to remain uncharged.

This last gesture is an important shift, in my reading of the film, and there is a complex negotiation going on here. Callahan has killed off Mick after they have both made explicit their recognition that they have to submit to the classic one-on-one combat: Mick succumbs to the "amongst men" logic of the showdown, and is killed by Callahan.[4] The movie thus puts a visual marker or a seal on this affair "amongst men" by having Mick finally die as he falls and is impaled upon the phallic horn of a carousel unicorn. Yet the moment of his death also "signs" the alliance between Spencer and Callahan in that the carousel is one that she is in San Paolo to restore. In other words, the movie thus complexly renders a moment where the "amongst men" issue must be finished in order for the male-female alliance to be consolidated. The upshot of this is the ending, where it is suggested that Callahan's own position in relation to the law has to change if he is to accommodate the woman's point of view, her voice, and indeed her safety. Thus he in a sense gives up on the law amongst men for a second time by effectively exonerating Spencer for her crimes and pinning them on the dead male antagonist.

Now, I am not trying to suggest here that his decision—which is in effect a generic one in that it is a decision for natural justice against the requirements of written law—is an unusual one for these kinds of movies or for Hollywood in general. Rather I want to point out how the alliance with the woman necessitates a particular kind of recognition: that the law that Callahan has been enforcing is indeed a matter "amongst men" and that it normally excludes women and their interests; the "amongst men" is sealed and the masculine law must change at the point where the presence and, in the movie's discourse, the "rights" of women are at stake and are to be respected.

This is, of course, a critical moment, and a radical one in that it marks a kind of problematic disjuncture between, on the one hand, the law and the man's heroic, serviceman relation to it and, on the other hand, a femininity that demands a satisfaction that cannot legally be given. The movie tries to make this disjuncture look less severe than it is by having Callahan and Spencer appear to be coincident in their views and aims and by having them leave the last scene of the movie arm in arm. But this alliance between a feminist claim about the law and a right-wing "law and order" agenda is finally unsteady in that the movie has suggested throughout that rapine and violent sexuality is endemic to the very culture that is founded on the law and that Callahan stands up for in an extreme way. In that sense, after he has dispensed the law to the rapists, his final gesture of dispensing *with* it can be understood as a peculiar kind of recognition about the relation of law and masculinity. And it is a recognition that obtains its closest scrutiny in *Tightrope*, the very next film that Eastwood makes.

It is perhaps not unlikely that the impulse or direction that the four "Harry" movies take has been significantly affected by Sondra Locke, Eastwood's companion for many years, who stars in the last one and also in its non-"Harry" predecessor, *Gauntlet*. But *Tightrope* stars Geneviève Bujold instead and is directed not by Eastwood himself but by Richard Tuggle, prompting the *Village Voice* reviewer, J. Hoberman, to say that he would "like to think *Tightrope* is so personal Eastwood couldn't sign it." Indeed, this movie, perhaps more than any other Eastwood movie until *Bird* in 1988, has been understood by the critics as "his." It is certainly both tempting and feasible to think of this movie as a deliberate exploration of at least the persona that Eastwood had inherited, as it were, from his previous films.

And it also makes sense, I think, to see the movie as part of an ongoing project to explore masculinity that begins as soon as *Dirty Harry* itself becomes the object of charges of sexism and misogyny. Equally, I want to suggest that those two perspectives must be linked, since the Eastwood persona, the whole basis of his stardom, depends upon a sense of masculinity and masculine power that can only be fissured by extensive repetition: its consistency will break down and its certainties dissolve.

To examine or perhaps encourage this process may or may not be part of Eastwood's deliberate aims in these movies. It would, at least, be precipitous to follow Ron Burnett's line and say outright that in *Tightrope* Eastwood is deliberately trying to "undermine the power of his own image" (1985, 80). Nonetheless it is the case that the movie takes as its central problematic the realization that I think is produced in *Sudden Impact*: that the male sexual imaginary that produces misogyny and violence against women is not confined to a few putatively pathological individual subjects but is in fact endemic. Thus in *Tightrope* the distinction between the sexual murderer whom Eastwood, as Wes Block, hunts down and Block himself is continually and in many ways quite explicitly blurred.

The movie begins with the most stereotypical representation of masculinity as an everyday threat to women: that is, the readily exploitable scene of a man's following a woman through deserted and unlit streets. The ensuing sexual murder of this woman is almost immediately linked visually to the possibility that it is Block who has done it. That is, the final shot of one scene shows the killer's feet clad in sneakers and is cut to the next sequence with Block's feet similarly attired. Narratively the movie is then constructed as a thickening out of this founding similarity. Block's investigations of the first murder lead him to a number of female prostitutes, some of whom he appears to know already and with all of whom he engages in sex. Each of these is killed after Block has visited them, and in ways that reflect Block's own sexual activities and proclivities back to him when the bodies are found: bondage with handcuffs, oral and anal penetration, and strangulation.

The narrative device of marking the similarities between the hunter and the hunted (which in her review Pauline Kael calls the doppelgänger device) is a common one, of course, even in Eastwood movies; it could be said to be at the center of *Magnum Force*, for instance. However, here Eastwood has made a movie in which those similarities are constantly marked as issues of male sexuality—male sexual violence and power. The stakes are raised by the fact that Block takes care of his two daughters from a broken marriage (the elder of whom is played by Eastwood's real daughter, Alison), and raised further by the introduction of a feminist discourse into the film in the person of Beryl Thibodeaux (Bujold's character), who is a rape counselor.

This heady and even lurid mixture of elements produces a discourse about masculine sexuality that I think is not negligible, even if it is finally consumed by the film's resolutory scenes. That is, the inevitable showdown with the real killer turns into an overlong and crude chase scene that threatens to outweigh the rest of the film and its explorations (and which includes a remarkable horror shot, which belongs in another film, of Block's baby-sitter stuffed into a clothes dryer). And Block's romantic reunion with the feminist rape counselor in the final sequence begs almost any interesting question that the film might have asked about gender politics or the male sexual imaginary.

And yet at the same time, the film's structure of thought sets up a proposition that many more ambitious or pretentious filmmakers (that is to say, less "popular" filmmakers) would be hard pressed to sustain: that is, the proposition that the "amongst men" within which both masculine imaginaries and male lives are caught cannot be so easily divided into a "good" and an "evil" camp, and that both camps play out their aggression across the bodies of women. This sort of insight often serves as a critical description of the narrative and symbolic character of the culture industry's products, but it is a proposition that is quite rarely generated self-consciously by those products.

"Who Knows? Maybe It Was You"

Concluding his article about *Tightrope*, Ron Burnett says that it "reveals the burden of male fantasy as simultaneously blind, unmoving, empty, yet, as it were, the geographic site where change must begin" (84). His point agrees with the one I have just been making insofar as he recognizes that the film profers itself as an investigation of heterosexual male fantasies, and yet at the same time can emerge with only the most superficial and generic—that is to say, "blind, unmoving, empty"—ways of closing the books on the investigation. While indeed the film may lay out the problematic of a particular masculine sexual construction—and even suggest the need for that to be changed—it can work that terrain at best partially (in abrogating the investigation as it does) or at worst cynically (in replicating the titillating exhibition of the contents of the investigation).

The problem here, of course, is a familiar one concerning the constraints and the very limits imposed upon popular cultural discourse. We are used to seeing those limits displayed everywhere and at once in contemporary life, and we often quite readily take up the positions that they thus profer us. At other moments as spectators at what Debord calls the society of the spectacle or as the subjects of what Touraine calls—perhaps even more appropriately—the programmed society, we will find ways of asserting our agency: we can critique the spectacle, deride it, or ignore it; we can take pleasure in it, laud it, or fetishize it. Or we can do all of these things at once. The spectacle-text cannot, that is to say, presignify or prelegislate our reactions, even though it can (and does) heavily and deliberately qualify itself so that only a certain delimited range of consumptive uses and gratifications is likely.

And it is important, in thinking the limits of popular culture itself, to remember too the nature of the product that any film ultimately is: it is a commodity intended for a very peculiar kind of momentary consumption, where issues of quality, satisfaction, and value are differently posed than they are with other commodities. Film is a commodity that can affect our imaginaries—our fantasies and our memories—in ways other commodities rarely or only intermittently do, and (thus) it is a commodity that enters the symbolic and ideological economies in which we live to a degree that is extreme, even if it is inherently circumscribed in its ability to legislate and fix those economies.

In that light a film like *Tightrope*, or films that perform similar or analogous rhetorical investigations, will always constitute a problem case. The effort of *Tightrope* is tendentious at one level in that it wants to offer a critique of one of the most crucial and unthought elements of its own and its audience's personal, cinematic, and, finally, cultural experiences—heterosexual masculine sexuality as it is constructed to be obstinate, violent, and unreflexively vapid in and by this culture. At another level, the qualities as commodity that it lives by and needs to reproduce in order to be successful are achieved only by a negation or an invalidation of exactly the critique that it allows itself to embark upon. In other words, the popular cultural codes and verisimilitudes to which the critique addresses itself finally stand guard over the critique and the investigation, folding them back into the generic confection of an ending where exactly the troublesome and troubled male fantasies with which the film has concerned itself are lost sight of. The last shot of the film—as Block and Thibodeaux walk away arm in arm—shows them disappearing into a moralistic syrup where Block has renounced his troubled fantasies and traded the contents of a pornographic imaginary for a new mother for his children. He can be all the more secure in his new moral future because she, as rape counselor and feminist, has the necessary feminist authority to absolve him and furthermore possesses the necessary womanly skills to maintain his cure and rehabilitate him.

The crucial moment of renunciation in this film has, of course, been prepared for throughout the movie. In particular, it is most

Renunciation: Block and Thibodeaux in *Tightrope*

overtly decided in the scene where Thibodeaux, having intuitively recognized Block's proclivities, decides to test him by attaching one ring of his handcuffs to her own wrist and silently inviting him to lock the other. Confronted by this woman who is to rescue him from his own fantasies and behaviors, he passes the test by refusing her invitation and unfettering her hand. Once again, the "fake/real" dichotomy of which I have spoken emerges to control the rhetoric of the scene and to ensure its place in the correct (verisimilitudinous) narrative development: instead of the "fake" and perverted desires that he acts out with prostitutes, Block chooses the straight love of a "real" woman. The film's proferred meaning here is clearly that there is something noble and resolute about his willingness to believe that he can abandon those of his desires and fantasies that live in the red-light district.

All kinds of viewers will have all kinds of reactions to this renunciation and to the moral lesson that is proferred through it. One possible reaction—my own—is a kind of annoyance that this film, which has outlined some of the conditions of an endemically problematic and even frightening heterosexual male sexuality, and has provoked a speculation and investigation about some of the construction of heterosexual desire and its manifestations, should finally see fit to fall back upon that moment of self-congratulatory and secure repression. That annoyance is, of course, the origin of a critique of the movie; at the same time, even this ending and the disappointment it occasions leave imaginary residues—memories of the film, its images, and its gestures that remain provocative, evocative, and problematical. For me one such element is a right-to-left pan of Eastwood's naked and oiled body as Block fucks from behind a young blonde prostitute (played by Rebecca Perle). The camera follows their joined bodies in medium close-up: from the feet, across the man's buttocks, and to the woman's face pressed by his into the sheets, pausing there for a moment before moving further to her hands, which are handcuffed together above her head.

This representation is literally pornographic—written across or on the body of a prostitute—but also highly affective. The power of the scene is enhanced by the gently smooth movement of the camera and the essential stillness of the bodies, as too by the almost lugubrious strings and synthesizers that play from Lennie Niehaus's sound track. The scene is finally a delicately poised representation of the condition of a particular heterosexual male imaginary. Such a fantasy is always based upon a loss, and its representation will always attempt to fill in the loss that has caused desire in the first place. Such fantasies live in the threat of their necessary ephemerality and in the forever unsatisfiable urge to come again. Their representations are also always unsatisfying and always a matter of the re-representation of loss. Thus this scene too connotes the regret and even the shame that attends such fantasy and its unfulfillable nature.

My point here is that the imaginary power of an image such as this cannot necessarily be eradicated by a purely narrative gesture of renunciation such as Block later performs and through which *Tightrope* pretends to be able to foreclose upon the fantasy it has tried to represent. The narrative of the film, that is, attempts to suggest that the fantasy can simply be forgotten. It works on an either/or logic, a good/evil, real/fake binarization. The movie works toward denying Block and its audience the possibility of maintaining one kind of fantasy in the context of another: Thibodeaux's offering of her wrists to be cuffed is precisely not an invitation to enjoy with her the kind of sexual activity that Block enjoys elsewhere. Her knowing smile as she offers her wrists indicates what the audience, too, already knows: that Block is destined to repress one set of desires for another (for her).

And yet the desire can survive, just as the image will, as a kind of residue even after the film has pronounced its moral judgment on that kind of masculine imaginary. To resist that pronouncement, and by way of rejecting the film's exhortation that I excise my pornographic desires, I recall this scene with the handcuffed prostitute and particularly the fact that here the film has invited me, as male spectator, to consider that it might be me in this scene, doing this with the woman: "Who knows? Maybe it was you," the young prostitute has said to Block while he questions her about a previous murder, his questions all turned by her into a coded solicitation. And to resist the notion that men's desires might inevitably murder women, I recall this scene and particularly the remarkable and almost rhyming frames in which I see oil drip slowly to the carpet from this woman's foot and in which the man's buttocks are shown to twitch as he gently comes into her body.

Gay Subtext

My descriptions of the representations of male sexuality in Eastwood's films, and my considerations of the meaning of such representations, have been predicated upon the notion that these representations and meanings derive from the power of what I have been calling the "amongst men." The "amongst men" operates as a foundational logic that has as its telos the almost contradictory goal of establishing the centrality of heterosexual relations in the culture—an end-point that is, of course, emblematized perfectly in *Tightrope*. Much of what gets represented in Eastwood's films in regard to masculinity registers the way in which this telos leaves the residues and marks of another kind of sexuality. But what that other kind of sexuality is not, is homosexuality. These films demonstrate, that is, an almost permanent disavowal of the homosexuality that the notion of the "amongst men" would almost automatically invoke. Homosexuality in these films is merely, as I have suggested, a matter of fake or dishonest sexuality, and constitutes—as in the ending of *Enforcer*—precisely that which needs to be blown away in order to keep the logic of the "amongst men" free of any perverse taint.

A distinction is made, then, between the way in which "another" male heterosexuality is marked in these texts and the way in which homosexuality is treated. The meaning of homosexuality is that of a perversion that is a little too close to the "amongst men" than is comfortable for cultural or cinematic verisimilitudes. As Robin Wood points out tirelessly, any film that allows what I call the "amongst men" to flirt, as it were, with the signifier of real homosexuality must always include what he names a "homophobic disclaimer" (293). But whereas the renunciatory and disclaiming gestures of *Tightrope*, for instance, cannot quite resolve the difficulties and complexities of heterosexual masculinity, the homophobic disclaimer (the very type of which, one might claim, is the obligatory heterosexual joining with which so many films end) is always effective: masculine homosexuality is always, so to speak, the enemy, and the way in which the gay subtext comes to an end is often the very same way in which the bad guys come to an end.

Something of what is at stake here is suggested in Tania Modleski's discussion of two recent movies, *Dead Poets Society* and *Lethal Weapon II* (1991, 137-45). Modleski claims that these two films "appear to represent the limits of mainstream culture's representation of male homosexuality" (145). For her those limits are, in the case of the first film, "repression," where any and all homosexual implication is simply glossed over, elided, or ignored; and in the second case, "expression," where what she finds is "an astonishingly open *expression* of male/male desire that nevertheless is accompanied by phobic denial of homosexuality per se." For some reason, Modleski seems shocked at "the public's seeming obliviousness to this dimension of much current popular culture," but in a context where there are only very limited codes of cultural verisimilitude to which a Hollywood film can appeal in representing the "amongst men" and where there are only the most crude and stereotypical cinematic verisimilitudes, this should perhaps not be so surprising. Indeed, it is precisely the point of the "amongst men" ideology that it should permit the expression of male affection, closeness, and of what Eve Sedgwick calls "homosociality," while at the same time excluding actual sexual connection from the field. In that sense one might suggest that spectators, far from being oblivious to the homosexual character of such representations, are proferred exactly the intendment that allows them to foreclose upon it in the end.

Things often go somewhat awry in Hollywood representations, of course, and the level of intendment of a particular film is sometimes left unclear. According to Robin Wood's readings, one such place is one of Eastwood's early Malpaso movies, *Thunderbolt and Lightfoot* (1974), which he understands as an "honorable exception" (293) to the rule that the gay subtext of the "amongst men" logic should be systematically disclaimed. Wood reckons, indeed, that this film displays an unusual "explicitness about the sexual nature of the male relationship (while still, of course, coding this rather than directly dramatizing it)" (230), and it would certainly seem to be the case that *Thunderbolt* is far more willing to remain with its gay subtext—far less hurried to end it—than one might normally expect. At the same time, I want to argue that even here the logic of renunciation finally works, and that as a result *Thunderbolt* attempts to become a movie quite different from what Wood makes of it.[1]

Thunderbolt is, as Wood points out, a kind of *Bonnie and Clyde* for men. Eastwood plays Thunderbolt, who teams up with the younger Lightfoot (Jeff Bridges), ostensibly in search of a cache of loot remaining hidden after a robbery that Thunderbolt had undertaken in his younger days. This couple, upon whom the movie concentrates, is at first hunted by and then joined by an older couple of men, Red and Goody (played by George Kennedy and Geoff Lewis, respectively). The second couple is the obverse of the first in that theirs is a relationship founded more upon disdain and antagonism than upon the respect and, indeed, the mutual dependency and understanding developed between Thunderbolt and Lightfoot. The tense and antagonistic relationship of Red and Goody (who are coded as dominant and effeminate, respectively) carries over into their joint relationship with the other two men: Red and Goody are the "bad" couple that finally falls apart when its dominant member, Red, dumps Goody's wounded body and leaves him to die after the four have tried to pull off a robbery—a repeat of Thunderbolt's earlier job—which has ended in disaster and an encounter with police. Thunderbolt and Lightfoot escape this encounter, while Red is arrested after having turned against them, and they themselves go on to discover the hidden loot for themselves. Lightfoot, however, has been badly beaten up by Red at an earlier point, and the end of the movie sees him painfully expire in the Cadillac that Thunderbolt has bought for him (a gift that Wood sees as amounting to a wedding present). Thunderbolt is left alone, then, contemplating the loss of his youthful companion while the sound track plays a lugubrious song by Paul Williams, "Where Do I Go From Here."

The "explicitness about the sexual nature of the male relationship," or the "male love story," that Wood sees in this film is largely construed around Lightfoot, whose very name, when juxtaposed to the more masculine connotations of the name Thunderbolt, locates

Gay subtext: Eastwood and Jeff Bridges on the set of *Thunderbolt and Lightfoot*

him as the "feminine" component of the couple. Even though the two men show interest in women (and in fact have sex with women in one of the few scenes of the movie to depict women at all), this is perhaps no more than what Wood sees as a "guarantee [of] the men's heterosexuality" for the benefit of the movie's audience. For the most part, the movie treats the two men and their deepening affection as if this were a heterosexual couple. Lightfoot, dressed in leather trousers in the movie's first scene, is a figure of display in the film, and his character is built mostly through intimations of his effeminacy or of what Wood sees as his "undefined and open" sexuality. This signification culminates during the robbery sequence toward the end of the movie where, as part of the plan, he has specifically to dress as a woman and lure a watchman. Wood comments on the moment of Lightfoot's "masquerade" as follows:

> Significantly, from the point where the disguise is adopted, the film keeps the two men apart for as long as possible, and the sexual overtones are restricted again to the implications of the editing. Lightfoot walking down the street in drag is intercut with Thunderbolt removing his clothes in preparation for the robbery; Lightfoot's masquerade is then juxtaposed with the 'erection' of Thunderbolt's enormous cannon [to be used in the robbery]. This culminates in the film's most outrageous moment: in a washroom Lightfoot, back to camera, bends over the watchman he has knocked out, his skirt raised to expose ass clad only in the briefest of briefs, from which he extracts a revolver; the film immediately cuts to Thunderbolt, fixing his cannon in its fully erect position. In its recent treatments of male homosexuality, the Hollywood cinema has never dared give us anything comparable to that.

This long quotation can perhaps stand as a synecdoche for the kind of argument that needs to be made in order to demonstrate the nature and extent—the explicitness—of the gay subtext in this movie. The important point, however, is not simply that such a subtext exists, but rather that the movie maintains it for so long and explores it in such depth, apparently without the usual impulse to renouncing it or denying it.

The virtue of Wood's reading is that it recognizes quite fully how the film is obsessed with the ways in which heroic masculinity is traversed by (and even, in the case of Red, traduced by) its own homosexual significance. Or, to put it another way, his reading shows how this movie draws out a homosexual subtext in the homosocial behavior of its four main characters. At the same time, I think it is still the case that this subtext is finally renounced in a way that Wood does not quite register, and that there is an effort to cover over the meaning of that subtext by another explanation of the behaviors of the central couple.

The most sweeping gesture in the renunciation of the subtext is, of course, Lightfoot's death itself. Although Wood sees this as "one of the most necessary deaths in Hollywood cinema," he does not acknowledge how this gesture—once again, the simple one of ending the gay subtext by "blowing away" its protagonist—is essentially the homophobic disclaimer that he says is absent from this film. As such a disclaimer it profers the occasion for the film to assume a different set of meanings. That is, the death scene picks up on a meaning that has been mooted in the course of the film but that has been only sporadically present: that is, the film has attempted to establish a father/son relationship between Thunderbolt and Lightfoot that, even if it does not "explain away" the homosexual subtext, nonetheless attempts to stand as the central definition of their relationship, and then also to draw the movie into a rather vague allegorical schema about America.

The paternal metaphor of Thunderbolt's name is present throughout the film, of course, and is reinforced at first by the film's opening sequence in which Thunderbolt is fraudulently assuming the role of a priest and delivering a sermon in church. But perhaps the moment at which the metaphor is fully realized is when Lightfoot, in the process of picking up a woman to take back to his and Thunderbolt's motel, engages in a discussion with her about their respective names. She has remarked on the strangeness of his name, and he counters by mocking her name, Melanie. He then laughingly suggests that "maybe we have the same father." At that point the movie cuts directly to a shot of Thunderbolt in the motel room.

In this same sequence the rudimentary seeds of an allegory about the state of America are planted when we learn that Thunderbolt's body has been badly scarred from his time fighting in the Korean war. The meaning of this apparently trivial information is taken up again in the final sequences of the movie, with Thunderbolt and Lightfoot rediscovering the loot and Lightfoot's subsequent death. It is of course entirely appropriate that this screenplay by Cimino should contain such an allegory—this has been his stock-in-trade in subsequent movies, notably *The Deer Hunter*—and perhaps equally apt that it should be a rather badly worked out allegory. But the signs are there in *Thunderbolt*. The cache of loot turns out to be hidden behind the blackboard of a schoolhouse that is fronted by a huge American flag and that has been turned into a museum. Here as elsewhere, the screenplay allows the characters to indulge in half-baked ruminations about America's history (Thunderbolt ruefully but reverently utters the word "History" when he sees the schoolhouse), and the suggestion is of the familiar post-Vietnam refrain that America, with its sanctified past, has lost its way. As Lightfoot is dying in the shiny new Cadillac, he pulls out two cigars "for a celebration. After all, we won, didn't we?" As he dies, his conviction that "I feel proud of myself. I feel like a hero" becomes nothing more than a pathetic irony. The death scene is followed by Thunderbolt's portentously breaking his cigar and driving on to nowhere in particular.

The film's ending on this note is clearly an attempt to put Thunderbolt, the rootless father who has survived the Korean war, into a position of responsibility in relation to the footloose youth who has been wasted as he followed the path of his father—and implicitly the path has passed through Vietnam. As I have suggested, the allegory here is not strong, even if it does take itself quite seriously as an observation on America's having lost its way. But the main point I have been wanting to make is that, however slight or even forced this allegorical discourse might be, it arrives in the movie as a sort of recuperative master code, renouncing the gay subtext that the film has dallied with for too long and attempting to pull the film's meanings back into a more acceptable discourse. Because of these operations *Thunderbolt* is perhaps among the more cynical and dishonest movies in the Eastwood corpus, but its specific interest is that it ultimately demonstrates in a quite unusual way the inevitable destiny of the gay subtext of the "amongst men."

Eastwood Bound

There is a quite well known photo portrait of Clint Eastwood, made by Annie Leibowitz, which figures the star in what have become his trademark street clothes—green T-shirt, brown corded trousers, and running shoes. He is standing erect against the backdrop of what looks like the film set of a western. The rebellious, maverick, sometimes Promethean hero that Eastwood is so frequently and fully taken to represent is here heavily tied by ropes around his body and legs. His hands, also heavily bound, are held out in front of the body at about waist height. His expression is perhaps not his most familiar one, but it certainly can be glimpsed occasionally in his movies: it is a look of vague bewilderment, with a slight crooking of the mouth into a mixture of amusement and annoyance as he looks back at the camera. His eyes are narrowed at the same time as his brows are arched slightly upwards. His straightened body seems to emerge from a billow of dust behind him.

This image was recently used as the cover to a Pluto Press collection of essays called *The Sexuality of Men* (Metcalf and Humphries). I do not know how it came to be selected for that cover, but it does seem an interesting and apt choice in certain ways. The several male British authors in the book are concerned with how, as they put it, "popular versions of what it is to be a 'real man' have become so outlandish as to prompt the idea that all is not as it should be for the male sex." Consequently these writers undertake the task of breaking the silence that seems to surround this "hidden subject, resistant to . . . first investigations," male sexuality (1). On the face of it, Eastwood's public and cinematic personae, among the most readily visi-

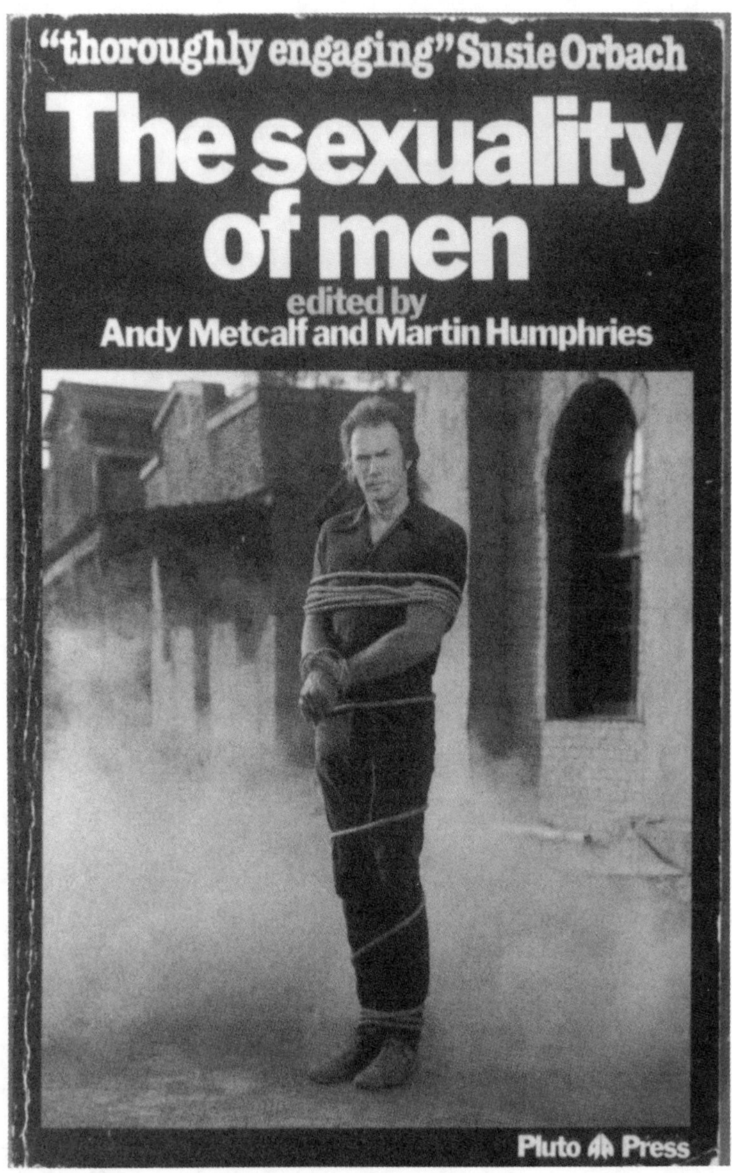

Eastwood bound. (Cover of Metcalf and Humphries, eds., *The Sexuality of Men*)

ble icons of masculinity in North American culture, can be readily taken not only as the epitome of the silence and the barriers to investigation that the authors are trying to break, but also as an obvious and symptomatic marker of the notion that "all is not as it should be" in regard to masculinity. The silence that many of his film performances appropriate as the sign par excellence of empowered masculinity, the erectness of his body, and the ubiquity of what the book's editors call his "oversized gun," the careless ordinariness of his J. C. Penney clothing, the limited but stark range of his facial and bodily gestures; all these contribute to Eastwood's presence within this culture as one of the more legitimated bearers of its masculinity, "real" or otherwise. At the same time, and as we have seen, many of the movies in which he stars and/or which he directs stand as somewhat troubled presentations or investigations of the kind of (or, of the image of) masculinity that they popularly stand for.

The trouble is perhaps hinted at in Leibowitz's picture, where this iconic male body emerges from the waves of dust around it to stand tall as the very type of a unique masculine beauty, but where it is simultaneously marked and immobilized by these ropes—signs of a certain helplessness or, at least, of difficulty. And yet the ropes in the photo (especially the five layers that encircle Eastwood's biceps, chest, and back and that are the focal point of the image) might also be indicative of a certain pleasure. That is, a pleasure in powerlessness—a pleasure that could certainly be grasped as an indication that "all is not as it should be" with this man, and that we might expect to be normally hidden from view in this culture and called "perverse"—is adumbrated across the ambivalent gestures of his face, and is, I would also claim, sketched across his films. Further on, I shall want to regard this pleasure in relation to the idea of masochism, and for now it can certainly be taken to provide an emblematic starting point for discussing male sexuality in that it presents an ambivalent moment whereby this male body, objectified and aestheticized by Liebowitz's photo portrait, comes to represent something a little "outlandish."

It has been possible for a long time now for discourses addressing North American notions of masculinity to actually rhapsodize on exactly the outlandish character of that special kind of man—the hero, often the westerner, who acts as the serviceman for the culture. There is little point in trying to demonstrate here once again the long history of that man, from Fenimore Cooper's pioneering heroes, through "classic" western protagonists such as Shane, to a plethora of action heroes in the 1980s, like Eastwood in *Heartbreak Ridge* or Mel Gibson in *Lethal Weapon*. But it is interesting to see how this brand of male protagonist in all such cultural productions is always in some way marked (and is made enjoyable or at any rate consumable for audiences) by precisely his inability to act as the ultimate solution to the narrative and social contradictions in which he is involved. Natty Bumppo's self-righteousness as he goes around killing and destroying as much or more of "the natural" as he claims to be conserving,[1] the desperate but ecstatic hypostasis of the cowboy faced with an ineluctable tide of westward expansion and modernization at the end of *Shane*, the ineptitude of Mel Gibson's character in *Lethal Weapon* in dealing with the family life that renders his own heroism possible; each of these in some way fails to transcend *fully* the contradictions of the narratives in which they figure.

Now, an orthodox critique of the male heroes in these kinds of popular cultural narratives would be to say that they actually present easy and transcendent solutions to contradictions. As in *Tightrope*'s overextended final action sequence and its cursory and self-satisfied ending between Block and Thibodeaux, the serviceman does his job by violently soldering together all loose narrative ends and entering a new and purer life. At the same time, as I suggested with *Tightrope*, such an apparently facile clinching together of contradictions and problems leaves marks and residues, and my claim is that in fact the resolutions and solutions are never fully realized despite the narrative's ending efforts. In this respect part of the interest of Eastwood's films is their tendency to remain, much longer than most other popular cultural narratives, in the rather special or peculiar state of gratification that comes of recognizing the factitious nature of the ultimate solution, and in doing so to exhibit the symptoms of what lies behind that gratification.

This at first sight might seem a peculiar opinion to be holding, and admittedly it is one that flies in the face of the overt narrative frames of popular movies such as Eastwood makes and stars in. However, I have something very particular in mind in that I want to propose that action and western movies like Eastwood's might actually exceed the familiar processes of narrative contradiction and closure and leave what I have called, in relation to both *Tightrope* and *Thunderbolt*, hysterical residues. Such hysterical residues I take to be the point of interference between the processes of narrative and the construction of diegetical worlds in film. My point is that action movies in particular (although I would like to say all Hollywood movies) throw up this kind of contradictory space, these elements that cannot be ultimately resolved and that remain as a kind of special emblem of the film's relation to the cultural world to which it attends.

Eastwood's movies in this regard quite routinely open out onto difficult and multivalent questions about the popular cultural representation of masculinity, beyond their always rather formulaic narrative frames; indeed, the narrative disposition of particular tropes of masculinity does not ultimately control or delimit them and leaves unmanaged and resistant representations of a male hysteria. Of course, I am far from discounting here the significance of narrative closure as a kind of punctual return to noncontradictory positions that satisfy both cultural and generic codes of verisimilitude. But I want to take the stress temporarily away from formulaic endings and ask to what extent they are but a lure beneath which particular kinds of representational and sexual-political questions can be left unresolved.

In Leibowitz's photo Eastwood appears to emerge, almost risibly classical, from his own peculiar waves to become an objectified spectacle. At the same time this spectacle is marked and bound. It is with the tension between (or rather, the pairing of) these two elements—the objectification and eroticization of the male body and the registration on this body of a masochistic mark—that I want to begin. I am interested in looking at the ways in which contemporary popular movies might effectively stand against some of the notions that writers in film studies deploy when talking about the interfaces of gender considerations with representation, but also I want to sketch out an argument for looking to see what happens when the purportedly "outlandish" nature of representations of masculinity in popular culture are apprehended, not as immediately and irredeemably contemptible, but as something by and through which some of the realities of male-sexed subjectivity are registered.

Paul Willemen, in a very short article about Anthony Mann's westerns, talks about the way in which the male heroes there are diegetically cast in two distinct ways, the one consequent on the other. First, they are offered simply as spectacle: "The viewer's experience is predicated," Willemen says, "on the pleasure of seeing the male 'exist' (that is walk, move, ride, fight) in or through cityscapes, landscapes, or more abstractly history." This pleasure can readily be turned to an eroticization of the male presence and the masculine body, and it is always followed up—in Mann's movies just as in most such Hollywood genre movies—by the destruction of that body. That is, the heroic man is always physically beaten, injured, and brought to breaking point. One needs to add to Willemen's formulation the obvious third stage, in which the hero is permitted to emerge triumphant within the movie's narrative line; this stage conventionally cannot occur before the first two. This third stage obviously provides the security and comfort of closure and is a crucial element in the production of spectatorial pleasure, but Willemen proposes that both of the first stages of representation are also in their way pleasurable for the spectator. The first "pleasure"—that of voyeuristic admiration of the hero's body and presence—is followed diegetically and graphically by the "unquiet pleasure of seeing the male mutilated . . . and restored through violent brutality" (16).

This intertwining in most action scenarios of what we might call on the one hand the solidity of masculine presence, and the demonstration of masculine destructibility and recuperability on the other, is readily apparent in most Eastwood movies, whether they be the westerns or the cop movies, or even the comedies in which his costar is an ape (*Every Which Way but Loose* [1978] and *Any Which Way You Can* [1981]). A first impulse would be to consider this as little more than the exigency of Hollywood habits and formulae, but of course it has its ideological ramifications, too. I would claim that this passage—from eroticization, through destruction, to reemergence and regeneration—is such a staple of action movies and westerns in general that it can readily be called the orthodox structuring code for those movies. There are, I think, several interesting characteristics to it that will bear commentary insofar as what is at stake here is a certain erotics of the male body that demands or entails peculiar diegetical and graphical representational strategies and processes of viewer identification.

Willemen implicitly proposes that the pleasure of the first two stages needs to be understood in terms of sadistic and masochistic frameworks, where objectification is pleasure yielded to the sadistic gaze, and where the destructibility of the male body is to be grasped as a masochistic trope. Since much film theory regularly deploys the frameworks of sadism and masochism as essential heuristic notions (the notion of sadism—especially in its relation to the gaze—almost chronically, and that of masochism more recently), it might be as well to briefly consider them here.

The cinematic erotics of the male body depends first of all upon that body's objectification. It is common, of course, to regard such objectification as the standard treatment for *female* bodies in the cinema; equally familiar are the many critiques, deriving so often from Laura Mulvey's seminal article, "Visual Pleasure and Narrative Cinema" (1989), that tie this objectification to the sadistic male gaze, to the structure of filmic diegesis, and to the supposedly irredeemably phallocentric nature of the cinematic apparatus itself. Male bodies, too, are subjected to cinematic objectification, but an objectification that is effected by specific cinematic means geared to the male body and perhaps to the female spectator's assumed gaze. The specific nature of male objectification has not been very fully dealt with by critics and theorists, but does receive some treatment from Steve Neale in his article, "Masculinity as Spectacle" (1983). Taking his cue from Mulvey's analysis of the way women's bodies are objectified and made the object of the gaze, Neale also tends to take for granted the sadistic/masochistic doublet. His thesis is that, because of the power of the ritualized structures and relays of the (a priori) sadistic gaze in cinema, a male body must effectively be "feminised" by the apparatus and spectator if it is to become objectified. Dealing with the masochistic stage, he suggests that what occurs there is a "testing" of the male hero, analogous to the investigation of female protagonists in standard dominant Hollywood cinema: "Where women are investigated, men are tested" (16).

Neale's contention, that in order for the male body to be thus objectified it has to be "feminised," is open to question, not least because it relies upon a sweeping generalization (increasingly often doubted in film studies) about the conventions and the apparatus of cinema—namely, upon the argument that they are oriented primarily and perhaps exclusively to the male spectator and his processes of identification. Neale's argument is in a sense self-fulfilling, or at least circular. If it is first assumed that the apparatus is male, geared to a male heterosexual gaze, then any instance of objectification will have to involve the "feminisation" of the object. However, instances of the erotic display of the male body are rife in contemporary film and media production, and can be shown to be geared to either male or female spectators (or both) in different contexts in ways that do not conform to the conventional treatment of the female body. There exists a whole cultural production around the exhibition of the male body in the media—not just in film, but in television, sports, advertising, and so on—and this objectification has even been evident throughout the history of Hollywood itself, while evidently having been intensified in recent years. Scarcely any of this plethora of images depend upon the feminization of the male; rather, the media and film deploy rather specific representational strategies to eroticize the male body.

In film, Eastwood's primary directorial mentor, Don Siegel, is perhaps one of the first Hollywood directors to have systematically foregrounded the display and the eroticization of the male body and to have turned that display into part of the meaning of his films. Siegel's films in this regard have developed a strong repertoire for dealing with the male body without deploying the particular formal strategies by which female bodies are offered to the male gaze in most Hollywood productions. That is, his work is often concerned with the activity and dynamics of all-male groups, and this concern has allowed the development of something like a cinematic obsession with the male body. Siegel's repertoire of shots and conventions, often duplicated in films that Eastwood directs, can be mined to produce a little semiotics of the heroized male body. Among his most frequently used devices are the following: what I call under-the-chin shots (where the heroized male figure, shot most often from the waist up, seems to loom above the spectator's eyeline); heavily backlit shots (in which either the details of hero's whole body or his face are more or less obscured while the general shape is given in silhouette); a preponderance of facial close-ups in which the actor's gaze is directed from right to left at a roughly forty-five-degree angle, used especially often to deliver Eastwood's characteristic snarls and slight facial movements; and traveling shots and pans that follow the male body's movement in a relatively unsmooth motion and usually avoid centering the body in the frame.

This is obviously a quite rough and schematic cataloging of the kinds of objectifying shots favored by Siegel, Eastwood, and later by other action movie directors. But the point here is that these kinds of representational strategy (developed, I think, into something like an industry standard in the last two or three decades) differ from those chronically used to objectify the female body. There is, in other words, a specific and even ritualized form of male objectification and eroticization in Hollywood cinema.

Another of Neale's assumptions—that looking at the male body is something of a taboo in our cultures—is also contradicted by the kinds of strategies that action/western movies typically make available to themselves. It might still be true, however, that eroticizing the male body ultimately produces a mixed pleasure. According to Willemen, "The look at the male produces [in the male spectator] just as much anxiety as the look at the female" (16). Certainly it is the case that such movies appear to take precautions against the possibility of such anxiety in particular ways. First and most important, the two-stage exhibitionist/masochistic process *must* always be followed by a narrative revindication of the phallic law and by the hero's accession to the paternal and patronizing function of the third stage of the orthodox action movie codes. Second (that is, less obligatory than the diegetic resolution), many of these movies accompany the pleasure/"unquiet pleasure" that they establish with a quite marked antihomosexual sentiment—which is to suggest that the masochistic moment is often crucially antihomosexual in its significance.

An example of this can be had from *Magnum Force*, with its band of extremely right-wing young policemen, part of whose "evil" in the movie's terms is their implied homosexuality and certainly their rather butch and leathery appearances and their close homo-bonding. In movies where homosexuality is not actually imputed to the antagonists (that is, to those characters who are to inflict physical damage on the hero's eroticized body), their sexuality is usually offered as perverse in some other fashion: this is the case, for example, with Scorpio, who is marked as effeminate and perverse in the different ways I have mentioned. In *Sudden Impact* there is an interesting melding of the two strategies: the leaders of the gang of rapists are, first, Mick, who in the motel scene is shown to be unable to conduct "normal" heterosexual relations, and second, Ray, the movie's "dyke," who procures Jennifer and her sister for the gang to rape and who also seems to have some heterosexual desires (for Mick), which the movie clearly presents as perverse.

Thus, even while these kinds of specifically masculinized representational strategy at the corporeal level are not a feminization of the male body, at the same time they do always carry with them a defense against possible disturbance in the field of sexuality. If it is actually allowed to show itself, this disturbance will always be ultimately annealed, covered over, sometimes literally blown away in and by the narrative frame. In what is perhaps the least well made of the "Dirty Harry" movies, *The Enforcer*, the first mention of homosexuality comes signally in the final scene as Callahan blows away Bobby Maxwell with the Law's rocket and the muttered words, "You fuckin' fruit." Clearly the function of such defenses is not confined to establishing the perversity and evil of the antagonist, but also to defend the picture from its having eroticized the male body in such consistent ways.

One particularly interesting text for the way it exhibits some of the strategies I am describing is the Siegel-Eastwood collaboration *Escape from Alcatraz* (1979). The first sequence of this movie, where Eastwood's character is brought as a prisoner into Alcatraz, is especially indicative of Siegel's concerns and his ways of working with the male body. In preparation for his incarceration at Alcatraz Eastwood's character, Frank Morris, is first stripped and searched in the prison's reception area. The camera then follows his naked body through a kind of gauntlet of objectifying looks from the prison guards as he goes toward his cell. Those looks are intercut by Siegel's typical low-angle, under-the-chin shots of Morris's striding body. These shots are remarkable in that they do not correspond at all nearly to the direction of any of the guards' looks; and similarly, the guards' looks are not used to construct the geography of the prison's space (this is done instead by means of a series of medium-length shots with Morris's body moving across the screen, but never exactly centered in it). Thus there is a disjuncture set up between the direction and function of the camera's look, and the direction and function of the guards' looks. In a more classical Hollywood mode, and in the objectifying passages where it is a question of a woman's body, these looks would normally reinforce each other. Here the purpose of the lack of coincidence is to deny or defuse the homoerotic charge of this sequence while still producing a voyeuristic look at Morris/Eastwood: to both look and not look at this male body, then, is to engage in a quintessential fetishistic process.

This sequence is mostly classic Siegel—framing the male body as an eroticized but simultaneously disavowed object in a sequence where the central concern is the movement through a space, but a space that does not need to be extremely logically defined. The sequence finishes with a slightly more unusual shot as Morris is deposited naked into his dark, barred cell. There, shooting from the guards' side of the cell, the camera picks out Morris's sidelit torso and lingers on it. A storm in the background lights up Morris's stern face for a millisecond, but otherwise all we see is the chest and its musculature. Morris is depicted thus as a kind of threatening Gothic beast as his shining body glistens in the darkness of its cage. The camera lingers over this final shot, both erotically regarding Morris's body and also clearly pointing out that body's larger-than-life potentialities, all the while prefiguring its inevitable "testing" later in the film.

This objectifying passage is quickly followed by the standard routine of destruction. Morris is variously assaulted by both inmates and authorities in the closed space of the prison. The moment of his worst torment comes at the hands of isolation block guards, and this acts as the catalyst to the acceleration of the movie's narrative line toward Morris's subsequent escape—and his escape will be from the masochistic moment as much as from the prison itself. The movie's final sequence has the prison governor wondering whether Morris and his fellow escapees could have survived the icy waters of San Francisco, while one of his officers muses that the men had vanished into air—the ultimate hypostasis of the heroic body.

As well as following the orthodox codes of the action narrative—objectification and eroticization, followed by near destruction and final hypostasization of the male body—*Escape from Alcatraz* defends against the apparent perversity and unquiet pleasure of the early stages by accompanying them with the standard antihomosexual component. After the opening sequence has suggestively turned the guards' policing looks into the dithering carriers of homoerotic objectification, the movie soon introduces a rather unpleasant homosexual inmate whose advances Morris rebuffs, setting himself up for a series of attacks and fights with this man who, predictably, ends up with a knife in his body before Morris escapes.

Further confirmation of the strength of these rather simple conventions is perhaps best given by way of the counterexample of Siegel's earlier picture, *The Beguiled*, in which Eastwood/McBurney is recuperating from serious battle wounds in a southern girls' school. The Eastwood character's lechery toward some of the school's inmates leads to their punishing him by rather hastily (and probably unnecessarily) cutting off his wounded leg—an amputation that is explicitly referred to as a castration. This corporeal removal is the culmination of Siegel's transgression of the standard rules for this kind of movie: the path of objectification, destruction, then transcendence is not followed here. At least, things are not in their proper order. The damage to McBurney's body has already been sustained before the start of the movie, thus depriving the camera of any opportunity to run the usual objectification routines. Furthermore, there is no triumphant transcendence in the end: after the rushed amputation, McBurney's anger and accusations provoke the women and girls to murder him with poison.

Audiences for *The Beguiled* have never been large, and it remains one of the least successful movies with which Eastwood has been associated, despite his and Siegel's satisfaction with it. Siegel explains the failure by suggesting, "Maybe a lot of people just don't want to see Clint Eastwood's leg cut off" (quoted in Kaminsky 1974b, 251). Whether that is the case or not, the lack of success of *The Beguiled* underlines in a negative way the fact that Hollywood dramas have induced certain expectations about the masculine corporeal, and cannot readily break them: the exhibitionist/masochistic stages must serve the end of the hero's triumph, and they are inextricably part of the diegetic necessity. Another way of saying this might be to suggest that the masochistic stage of such narratives cannot be presented as a complete castration and that the possibility of transcendence must always be kept available. The masochistic trope in this sense must be no more than a *temporary* test of the male body.

One familiar effect, of course, of the hero's more usual triumph over the deliquescence of his once objectified body is the promotion of various metonymically associated notions of regeneration, growth, rebirth, sacrifice, reward, and so on. In that sense one could talk of these various tropes as mythical; we have a tradition of such narrative ideologies to which to appeal, including the traditional story of Christ's ascent after the crucifixion. Indeed, in much occidental cultural production the Christ figure could be said to have operated chronically as a privileged figure of the pleasurable tension between the objectification and what I call the masochizing of the male body, and it is certainly no accident that so many of the films of the western or action hero take advantage of reference to that figure. Eastwood's movies—and especially his collaborations with Siegel—are rife with such references. Eastwood has starred in or directed several movies that make it an easily identifiable point of reference: *Pale Rider*, for instance, in which he plays a priest; *Thunderbolt and Lightfoot* (1974), in which he is a pretended priest and several shots allude to the crucifixion; or even *The Beguiled* itself, in which his role is explicitly linked to that of a long-suffering Christ, but in which there is no triumphant transcendence, only the death of his character.

Recent film scholarship has begun to investigate how the concept of masochism and its concomitant "unquiet pleasure" can be deployed in looking at the question of subjectivity (and especially male subjectivity) in filmic relations. One thinks immediately of Kaja Silverman's work—notably "Masochism and Male Subjectivity" (1988)—and that of Gaylyn Studlar (1988) or Leo Bersani (1986), the second of which is not concerned specifically with film but with the cultural production of "art" in general. Part of the point in each piece of work is to attempt to complexify and even undo to some degree the rather monolithic view of male subjectivity that film scholarship tends to propose.

In their different ways, and with certain disagreements, each of these three writers proposes the masochistic trope, the masochistic moment, as in some sense subversive of conventional or "normal" formations of subjectivity. Bersani, for instance, sees masochism as a formation that disturbs the fixities of literary and visual language to produce a designifying moment, or a denarrativizing moment; more specifically, he reckons that it produces what he calls an "interstitial sensuality" responding to a reader's pleasurable "interpretive suspension between narrative and non-narrative readings" (78). In a similar fashion, Silverman proposes masochism as a formation of suspension, though her preferred notion is that of "deferral"—masochism as a deferral of male submission beneath the Law of the Father and of the normative pressure of male sexuality. For her this is indeed a large part of the definition of perverse sexuality, that it be set against the aim-directed "normality" of the male subject. The fully consummated pleasure of the normal subject is associated with guilt, but the suspended, showy pleasure of the masochistic fantasy is a disavowal of the paternal function, a sort of escape from it and a way of punishing its imposition: "what is beaten in masochism is not so much the male subject as the father, or the father in the male subject" (56). Thus, in Silverman's account, the masochist "remakes the symbolic order, 'ruins' his own paternal heritage" (57).[2]

In these treatments of masochism as what I am calling a trope, there are considerable difficulties to be negotiated concerning the relation of theoretical schemas to textual matter, and equally to relations of reception. The assumption in what I have to say is that the filmic representations of masculinity act as a kind of demonstration of how masculinity is supposed to work (or, to put it another way, they profer particular meanings around the subject of masculinity and to the male subject). I want to stress here the process of narrativization in which a masochistic moment is but a part, a single element caught up in the machinery of the proferring of significance. I want to avoid the temptation of implying that this demonstration forms male subjectivity in and of itself, or that it produces some unavoidable male spectatorial position. Film does have its interpellative effect, of course, but that does not mean to say that it inevitably or indefeasibly determines forms of subjectivity. Cinema is not, that is, simply the symptom of the spectator elaborated as it were elsewhere. In other words, I see some kind of disjuncture between representation and subject positions that many film theorists still do not. While allowing for direct spectatorial identification and thus for the cinema's proferring of subject positions, I dare say that investigation of the representational strategies of film finally is capable of discovering more about the availability of cultural ideologies than about forms of subjectivity.

With such provisions in mind it becomes difficult to accept entirely the claims of Bersani and Silverman. Each of them exploits the notion of masochism as a perversion in order to suggest that it subverts, undermines, defers, or invalidates both the phallic law and the fixities in both subjectivities and meanings that depend upon phallic law. Silverman perhaps summarizes this position best in her claim that the male masochist

> acts out in an insistent and exaggerated way the basic conditions of cultural subjectivity. . . . [H]e loudly proclaims that his meaning comes from the Other, prostrates himself before the gaze even as

> he solicits it, exhibits his castration for all to see, and revels in the sacrificial basis of the social contract. The male masochist magnifies the losses and divisions upon which cultural identity is based, refusing to be sutured or recompensed. In short, he radiates a negativity inimical to the social order. (51)

Silverman theorizes, then, that male masochism is in itself an oppositional formation. But if, to paraphrase Judith Mayne, we submit the theory to the test of narrative[3] or investigate the function of the masochistic moment in representational practice, it might be seen that the "inimical" nature of masochism and the pleasurableness of its self-proclamation can be sustained only provisionally: that, in other words, popular cultural narratives in effect enclose and contain male masochism.

This proposition is not, I think, contradicted by Freud's discussion of masochism. In his paper "The Economic Problem in Masochism" ([1924] 1963), in which he ostensibly deals with the economic system of masochism, Freud is led to quite firmly narrativize the phenomenon. Its etiology is in what he calls erotogenic masochism, "found at bottom in the other forms": feminine masochism and moral masochism. Erotogenic masochism, the lust for pain, is for Freud the homeostatic result of a negotiation between the libido and the death drive, which he describes at length in "The Ego and the Id" ([1923] 1962). The relative stability of the outcome of this negotiation provokes exactly the narrative dramas of the feminine and moral forms of masochism. Strict distinctions between these two latter forms are not especially important for my purposes here. But what is common to Freud's explanation of both is the claim that they are exhibitionist and in a sense histrionic, the exhibitionism and the drama being designed to provoke punishment. The punishment most readily comes (particularly in moral masochism) in the shape of "sadistic conscience" or in an intensification of superego activity. Masochism for Freud, then, is characterized by the need of the subject to "do something inexpedient" in order to bring down upon itself the gratifying punishment of the superego. The point I mean to stress here is that masochism's "negativity" is largely a functional catalyst in a formulaic narrative of erotic gratification.

This narrativized context for masochism might need to be considered alongside Silverman's claim for the negativity of male masochism and for the subversive potential of "bringing the male subject face to face with his desire for the father" (59) through the masochistic moment. One would certainly not want to reject Silverman's particular project as a viable way of articulating radical moments of male subjectivity; but alongside it, one might also have to take account of how, in popular cultural texts, the place of the exhibitionist/masochistic is already accounted for and already pulled by narrativization into a plot, precisely designed to eventually explode the negativity of masochism.

Indeed, it might even be worthwhile to make the rather more wide claim that in fact (that is, in a narrativized frame) the male masochist importantly obeys and serves the phallic law. Masochism (to paraphrase Lacan) is primarily a neurosis of self-punishment, partly because of the way it has of entailing or invoking the superego's revenge, the return of "sadistic conscience." The masochistic moment certainly promotes deferral and suspense, but a suspense that can work only if it is in the end undone. Male masochism is at first a way of not having to submit to the law, but, equally important, it turns out to be a way of not breaking (with) the law, either. Masochism might well bespeak a desire to be both sexes at once, but it depends upon the definitional parameters of masculinity and femininity that undergird our current cultural contexts. Male masochism might, finally, be seen as another way for the male subject to temporarily challenge his desire for the father and to subvert the phallic law, and as ultimately another step in the way (might one even say the puerile way?) of guaranteeing the male subject to be the origin of the production of meanings.[4] Indeed, it might be said that male masochism is a kind of laboratory for experimenting with those meanings to which ultimately we accede. The rules of masochism are, then, primarily metaphorical, and the game is a game played out unquestioningly in the thrall of the symbolic; crucially, the lessons of masochism do not *last*, they come and are gone, forgotten as part of the subject's history of struggle in learning how to triumphantly reach symbolic empowerment. Masochism, grasped in this way, would be a closed space where masculinity sets the terms and expounds the conditions of a kind of struggle with itself—not a struggle necessarily for closure, but a struggle to maintain in a pleasurable tension the stages of a symbolic relation to the father—a struggle in which, ironically, the body becomes forgotten.

The pleasure proferred in action movies can be regarded, then, not so much as the perverse pleasure of transgressing given norms, but as at bottom the pleasure of reinforcing them.[5] This is where the narratives of such movies can be justifiably dubbed conservative: they marshal a certain identificatory pleasure into the service of a triumphalist masculinity by employing a process girded around and endlessly reproduced by the narrative conventions of Hollywood and its country's cultural heritage. But even in the most conservative and rigid kind of cultural production there is an underside, a double edge, or a residue. In this instance, something is continually being fended off in this procession. What is common to many of the action movies and westerns of the sort Eastwood makes is the way in which the exhibition/masochism trope and its pleasure/unquiet pleasure, along with their resolution into a triumphalist view of male activity, reside alongside a residual, barely avowed male hysteria.

That hysteria is often expressed narratively as the sensation of the dangers inherent in identification with women or with homosexuals (of both genders). Or else it is a hysterical formation that can be glimpsed in moments of incoherence or powerlessness in the male body and the male presence. Sometimes it is only barely visible in the joins of the text as it produces its apparently seamless cloth. The hysterical moment I am stressing marks the return of the male body out from under the narrative process that has produced what appears to be its transcendence, but that in fact is its elision and its forgetting. In other words, although there is in these movies a conservatively pleasurable narrative path which finishes by suppressing the masculine body and its imaginary, the body nonetheless returns from beneath the weight of the symbolic. What I mean to point to as this hysterical residue, then, is an unresolved or uncontained representation of the body of the male as it exceeds the narrative processes—such as in the momentary detail of the twitch of Block's body in the sex scene I described from *Tightrope*.

The meanings generally proferred by these movies concern the male body as that which has to be repressed. This of course sounds paradoxical to say, given the way these movies produce also an apotheosis of masculinity in the serviceman hero. But a simple instance of what I mean can be glimpsed at the climactic moments of any of these action movies, where the male protagonist's control of the narrative situation is never matched by control of his own body. The body here is always represented as de-eroticized, turned into a mass of mere reflexes. The male access to control is clearly marked as a symbolic or metaphorical matter, a process of forgetting the body, forgetting the previous stages of eroticizing and masochizing the body. And yet the body is still there, still in the field of representation, but no longer subject to the somatic meditation that the narrative has thus far constituted.

In warding off this hysterical residue, suffocating its somatic presence with the safe and deferrable pleasure of the symbolic, the male heroic text itself becomes hysterical. In the case of *Sudden Impact*, *Tightrope*, or *Gauntlet* there is an explicit alliance on the part of the male protagonist with what, as we have seen, is presented as the strength of femininity and women's voices and presence. Such alliances are always finally negated in the narrative in the sense that the women involved have finally to be pulled beneath the law (even when the law is the male hero's own version of justice) and have their independence replaced by a traditional, disempowered status in relation(ship) with the male protagonist. And yet they leave their marks on the experience of the movie.

Some of these marks can readily be seen in one of Eastwood's later movies, *Pink Cadillac* (1988), directed by Buddy Van Horn. The female protagonist, Lou Ann (played by Bernadette Peters), is the target not only of the Eastwood character, Tommy, a bail bondsman, but also of the neofascist "Birthright" gang, whose money she has inadvertently stolen. Before meeting her, Tommy has been a somewhat happy-go-lucky character, known for his histrionic modes of trapping his quarry. For instance, the film opens with him trapping one man by calling on the telephone and pretending to be a deejay for a country station giving away a date with Dolly Parton, later turning up in a limousine and livery to complete the act and capture the man. Or else, as the surprise ending to a rodeo scene, Tommy turns up as the rodeo clown to handcuff the winning rider. In terms of the narrative line, these early manifestations of Tommy's motile and protean body act as the scattered instances of his personal and somatic irresponsibility. It is precisely his changeable body that will be pulled into a different consistency by the end of the movie: he will have made his alliance with Lou Ann, rescued her baby held hostage by the Birthright, and driven off with her to make plans for a business alliance that will consolidate their personal one. Along the way, his protean abilities are displayed in at least a couple of other set pieces: one where he dresses up in a gold lamé jacket, puts on a mustache, and effects a Wayne Newton voice, getting into a chase scene where his aging body is made to look ridiculous; and another where he acts as a potential redneck conscript for the Birthright, gaining the confidence of the gang members by putting on a rictus grin and chewing and spitting tobacco, ending the scene with a comic forced swallowing of a rather too large wad of tobacco.

These hysterical manifestations of the Eastwood body here are, of course, the comic counterpart to the violent testing of the body that occurs in the action movies. Importantly, however, they are placed similarly into a direct relation with the man's alliance with the transgressive woman. At a crucial moment in the formation of this alliance, the Tommy role provides Eastwood with the opportunity to give one of his most egregious performances: for a number of lines he effects a woman's voice and flutters his eyelids in mimicry of some notion of femininity. Immediately after this their alliance is sealed at the point where Lou Ann says that she's going to take "no more shit from men," and he responds—in the context, gratuitously and even mysteriously—"That's one thing we have in common. I'm not gonna take no more shit from men." The alliance leads to his straightening up, as it were, on the way toward becoming the serviceman, the future father for her child, and future partner. Lou Ann's effect, then, in the movie is to provide the place where the body that is out of control can finally find repose. In the meantime, the memory of the Eastwood body remains untouched: the old panting body that runs around in a gold jacket with its mustache hanging off, the contorted face of the redneck as he almost chokes on his tobacco, the wildly fluttering eyelids of the man impersonating a woman.

It is perhaps to overread to suggest that all these moments are symptoms of the loss of control of the male body. They are, after all, at one level clearly just scripted opportunities for Eastwood to show off the supposed range of his acting abilities. At the same time, they are significant for the way in which the male body appears there as excessive—or, another way of reading it, as defective in relation to the image to which it aspires at the narrative's end. Equally, they are significant for their relation to the woman whose transgressive character is finally reined in along with the male body.

As I suggested, these symptomatic moments are a comic analogue to the action movie's masochistic moment, but they themselves remain masochistic in their histrionic and exhibitionistic qualities, which foreground the contortion, indignity, and even the aging of the Eastwood body. If the masochistic trope colludes with and finally reverts to narrative closure, such hysterical registrations remain as part of the history of the male body and are left floating, uncontained, and untranscended by the narrative. What the hysterical, in this sense, bespeaks or figures is something that in an article called "Vas" (1988b) I have called (paradoxically enough) "the unsymbolizable of male sexed experience." That article is an attempt to point out and begin to explore the male imaginary and its registration of both the body and the lived experience of male sexuality. It is generally understood in psychoanalytical theory that repression in the male subject seems to prohibit the speaking of the male body, to block its symbolization. The hypothesis entertained in "Vas" is that, in reality, repression is never complete and that some part of male somatic experience remains to be registered: this is the strictly unsymbolizable body, a body reduced to figuration outside the schemas of the phallic organization of the symbolic. This body is then left to be figured in ways that I call hysterical.

My most general claim here, then, is that in the cultural productions of this phallocentric society masculinity is represented first of all as a particular nexus of pleasure. That pleasure is produced in these films through a specific mode of objectifying and eroticizing the male body, and is fortified by a series of operations on that male body that, while they have the trappings of a resistance to the phallic law, are in fact designed to lead the male subject through a proving ground toward the empowered position that is represented in the Name of the Father. Masochism is in a sense a metonym for another frequently deployed masculinist trope—the fun of the chase, where the hunter momentarily puts aside his innate advantages in order to intensify and elongate the pleasure of the exercise.

Within such a representational framework something escapes or is left unmanaged. The hysterical is what always exceeds the phallic stakes, jumps off. The hysterical is marked by its lack of containment, by its bespeaking either the travails or the pratfalls of a body, and by its task of carrying what is strictly the unsayable of male experience. That is, what escapes the terrible simplicity of male heterosexual experience and the crude simplicity of homocentric narratives is always something that cannot or should not be represented or spoken. In that sense it is rather apt that Eastwood has become popularly known primarily for the silence of his acting performances and for the sheer presence of his body. And it is remarkable, too, that many of his films explicitly produce and locate that image of himself in a close alliance with femininity.

Eastwood's films tend to arrest themselves, as I suggested before, in the specific gratifications of that place for longer than most other movies would dare. The generous reading of this would be to say that, while they are in that sense predictably unsubtle popular responses (albeit rather belated ones) to the impact of feminism in this culture, they do concern themselves with the difficult task of representing masculinity at the hysterical moment of its potential deprivileging, and even at the moment of the deliquescence of masculinity's body (Eastwood is approaching sixty years old by the time he makes *Pink Cadillac*). These movies certainly do not represent an escape from the kind of masculinity that infuses the older ones, like the first "Harry" movies, but they can at least be said to attempt to play out that masculinity in relation to femininity. These are not, ultimately, movies that will encourage any radically new male subjectivities, but written across them in the shape of Eastwood's hysterical body are the silent signs of what might best be described as a coming out.

Those signs have the function, too, of pointing up the lure of the orthodox codes, where the pleasure of masculine representations is given as essentially and intrinsically bound up with the three-stage shift from objectification to masochism to empowerment. The central masochistic moment is thus a kind of necessity in the conservation of norms of male sexuality within the discourses of popular culture; it represents a way of structuring into the full subjectivity of the egoistic hero a resistance, a way of beating the father to within an inch of his life before replacing him or allowing him to be resurrected, and finally doing things just as well as he can. In this sense the masochistic moment, girded around by its moments of pleasurably perverse display and exhibition, serves a quite orthodox version of the masculine confrontation with the father. But this also means that the masochistic moment is *temporary*, a kind of trial, a rite of passage that we men know we have to go through but that will not take all our energy. What is crucial about it (to me, at any rate) is the way it so often seems here to be less a question of how we might negotiate our sexuality in lived experience, and more a question of how symbolic dramas are channeled and recuperated. Much more on the edge, more outlandish, than this masochistic nexus is the hysteria of being unable to be in control, the sheer excess of the body itself, and the hysterical symptoms we have written on our bodies—symptoms that no ironically masochistic regard for ourselves can completely erase.

Burlesque Body

The point that I have been wanting to make here is that action movie narratives, as those of Eastwood illustrate, tend to represent for the viewer a kind of masochistic trial of masculinity and its body—the kind of narrative that Nina Baym (1985) has described as "melodramas of beset masculinity." But this masochistic testing is perhaps most accurately seen as a kind of preening display attendant upon the narrative impulsion toward a different kind of state: a state where the body has in fact disappeared, and the masculine insolence of objectification and display in the masochistic scenario has been renounced. The renunciation is in the service of a conventional and verisimilitudinous morality. At the same time, the passage of the body through that process of eroticization, testing, and final hypostasis is not seamless; that is, at the edges, as it were, of this dialectic there remain hysterical residues—marks and memories of the intuition that this masculine process is in a sense out of control.

Those registrations of a still "outlandish"—as opposed, perhaps, to a domesticated—masculinity are perhaps more overt and obvious when the scenario attempts to meld the action movie genre with a comic element, as in *Pink Cadillac*. The comic body that Eastwood offers us in *Pink Cadillac*, as well as in such movies as *Every Which Way but Loose* (1978), *Any Which Way You Can* (1981), and even his self-satirizing movie, *City Heat* (1984), is a body whose function is to provide a certain kind of variation upon the pained and beaten masochistic body. This comic body is a bundle of symptoms that is cast into the obverse diegetical situation to that of the "erotogenic" masochism of the action movies—cast, that is, into a frame where the pleasure of contortion, complication, self-changing, and even burlesque is possible, but where at any rate the elements of the hysterical are always much more self-consciously present and therefore all the more open a reminder of the inevitable incompleteness of the transcendent project implied by the wholesome white hero.

The comic body in this sense might be considered much more obviously "feminized" (in Neale's sense) than I have been claiming the action body can be. It might even be considered the analogue of the body as it would present itself in what Freud calls the "female" kind of masochism, where "the subject is placed in a situation characteristic of womanhood." Freud's idea about what is characteristic of "woman" in a patriarchal order is, of course, an idea that the verisimilitudes to which Hollywood adheres and aspires have always given credence: the feminized subject is one that is "being castrated, is playing the passive part in coitus, or is giving birth" ([1924] 1963, 193). Yet even here it is clear that the male subject's taking on fantasies of femininity of that sort is usually beyond the grasp of Hollywood and its codes.[1] Instead of representing such fantasy directly, what Eastwood's movies often do is bring the male protagonist into a close relation with a woman. In other words, instead of overtly "feminizing" the male subject here, these movies substitute an alliance with the female, who is more "naturally" transgressive, rebellious, troublesome, or indeed herself simply hysterical.

In the comic vein, then, it is more easy to see a particular split or disjuncture, which is present elsewhere, too, but in less overt form. That disjuncture is between two modes of what we might call the usage or using up of the male body by the narrative. The first is a use of the body that is a literal, physical using up and the second, as the narrative frame brings its resolution and its tying together, a kind of disappearance of that body into rectitude. It is in or through this disjunction that we can glimpse the asperity of the moralism to which this kind of movie is given over as it transmutes the "wrong" body into a "right" one by making it disappear.

The male body before it is made to disappear into morality has much in common with what Jean Louis Schefer understands as the "burlesque body" of early Hollywood. He says that the burlesque body (epitomized in Laurel and Hardy) "neither carries nor guides the action: it absorbs it, and is the catastrophic and unbound place to which action returns" (1980, 73). In that sense the burlesque body could be the quintessential site of masochism—always the object and cipher of actions around it, although not appearing as their controlling source. Schefer is interested in how such bodies are *expérimentés*, which is to say both tested and tried out—similar, probably, to what Neale means when he says that the male hero must be tested. But for Schefer these bodies are also experienced; they are wise bodies, whose function is to act as if they never tire of repeating the same experiences and rehearsing the same experiments over again to show what Schefer calls the "permanence of the beginning of the world" (73), or the fact that the world must always be started over again with precisely the body as its stake, before the morality (and indeed, mortality) of the ending supersedes that body and makes it disappear.

This body that takes on the task of beginning the world over again before disappearing is, according to Schefer, a profound reminder of a kind of childishness that we have not forgotten, along with a reassurance that we can leave it behind. Schefer's descriptions of such a body focus upon "classic" burlesque film performers like Laurel and Hardy, but it is a body that often crops up in all kinds of comic performance, and my task here will be to show that Eastwood's two most successful films, *Every Which Way but Loose* and *Any Which Way You Can*, are both, indeed, particular versions of, or attempts at, the representation of such a burlesque body.

In these two movies Eastwood plays Philo Beddoe, an accomplished bare-knuckle fighter who subsists as a mechanic in the subculture of poor white America. Each movie follows him through that subculture toward a big fight, which will be the climax of the movie. This passage will include other preparatory fights organized, like the grand finale fights, largely for the purposes of betting and which become therefore sites of community interest and interaction despite their illegality. The narratives in each movie are fairly episodic, giving the occasion for many set-piece comic scenes, and both are loosely held together by one other narrative line—that of Beddoe's romantic relationship with Lynne Halsey-Taylor, a country-and-western singer played by Sondra Locke. The two movies are, indeed, linked by this narrative line, since romance is not resolved until the end of *Any Which Way*. Since the narratives of Beddoe's reaching—and, of course, winning—these big fights are in each case so rudimentary, the movies spend a long time dealing diegetically with various aspects of the subculture, and they profer a mostly sympathetic view of a poor, white, semirural or small-town life that centers around cars, trucks, and motorcycles, country music bars, run-down motels and houses, and so on.

None of this, of course, is what makes these two movies either remarkable or well known. The central signifier of each movie is the almost permanent presence at Beddoe's side of an orangutan, Clyde, which provides for a large number of the comical moments. Clyde's actual narrative role is small; that is, he is not an important agent in the narratives but rather their accompaniment. In many ways he functions simply as an extension of Beddoe, or as part of the diegetic presence of Beddoe himself. Among its various effects, the peculiar pairing of Clyde and Beddoe gives rise to a running discourse about the likeness of man and animal; this appears in both movies, but particularly in *Any Which Way*, which includes a lengthy sequence in a motel where shots of Beddoe and Lynne having sex are intercut with the prospect of Clyde in another room engaging with a female orangutan, and in another room again, shots of a long-married couple rediscovering their animalistic urges.

The interesting thing about this pairing is the way in which it inflects the heroic presence of Beddoe himself. The role that Eastwood plays as the bare-knuckle fighter is open immediately to the construction of yet another white male hero reaching his goal, and indeed any comic possibilities of this role in itself are not exploited for the most part in these movies. The fight scenes and Beddoe's character are played relatively straight, and the fight scenes themselves are quite brutal and bloody. The presence of Clyde is used to offset some of that brutality. As a spectator at the fights, for instance, he sets a comic tone with his mock-human gestures: he exaggeratedly covers his eyes and sets his huge mouth into a grimace when Beddoe gets hurt, or he defecates in the front seat of a police squad car while its occupants watch Beddoe fight.

Clyde's role in these and other instances is primarily to mollify the violence of the movies' main narrative events, and a large part of his effectiveness in this role is exactly in his significance as a kind of alternative human. He is an animal who, while mimicking and exaggerating the gestures of the human, is also liberated from some of the constraints under which human characters live. This liberation and its comic attributes are set against Beddoe's worries and difficulties, the pain of his romance, the violence of his life, and the power-

Man and animal

lessness of the subculture in which he lives. Clyde stands for a side or an aspect of Beddoe that is not allowed representation in the usual modes of the heroic figure. In that sense he can be understood as the very embodiment of what is normally elided from the heroic figure that Eastwood most often plays.

Clyde, then, is the figure of the appearance of that hysterical body whose destiny it normally is to go unremarked and renounced within the enactment and performance of the heroic narrative. In all of his antics and mimicries, Clyde plays out that which it is the function of most of Eastwood's narratives to recuperate, renounce, or transcend. But this is a comic movie, and in that context Clyde is permitted to demonstrate a proximity between the heroic body and the hysterical body, where the salient features of the latter are ultimately burlesque and childlike, in contrast to the serious bloodiness and brutality of the adult male. The trick of these two films, then, is to profer the underside, as it were, of the heroic figure. This secondary, burlesque body is played for laughs without foreclosing upon or detracting from the power of the white fighting hero, who still emerges as he is supposed to from the test of combat.

In relation to this hero, Clyde is like a child at the side of a powerful father, learning to be like him. During the course of the two movies, Clyde does in some ways grow up. In *Every Which Way* he is at first simply the infant, confined to making faces and gestures that are merely comic spectacle; yet those undirected and uncoordinated gestures become trained, and he grows into the creature who makes turn signals with his hands when riding in Beddoe's truck. At the start, too, his inability to control his excretory functions is the occasion of several jokes on the part of Beddoe. Before taking Clyde to meet Lynne for the first time in *Every Which Way*, Beddoe has to instruct him to control himself in this regard, but by the beginning of the second movie he has learned to control himself well enough that when he shits in the police car, he does so deliberately. He grows, too, in that his sexual urges, appearing first in *Every Which Way*, are finally satisfied in a ritualistic courtship display and its fulfillment in the second film. Indeed, Clyde grows up to the point that at the end of *Any Which Way* Beddoe refers to him as "a free person." Clyde's demonstration that he might have achieved this status comes as he makes his hand signal from the truck, just as he has learned to do, but this time the signal functions as a punch to the face of a policeman—he has been trained literally into the way of his father.

Yet Clyde cannot actually become his father, and so this course of development does not have the effect of abstracting him from the burlesque. On the contrary, he remains the burlesque or hysterical body, but is separated from its full significance by the fact that he does not take the continual beating for which the fully burlesque body would be destined and which here his father takes for him.

These two films, then, Eastwood's most successful, display the hysterical obverse of the heroic body that appears elsewhere. That obverse is the comic and burlesque body—here figured through an orangutan, man's avatar—that takes up a position that does not in any way negate the body of the white male hero, but simply comments upon it. But it also has another function, which it achieves by dint of its acting as a commentary in that way. That is, the hysterical body casts a light on the powerlessness that the heroic body lives with—indeed it *is* that powerlessness; but more importantly here, it casts a light on the powerlessness that such a body lives *within*. That is, these two films overtly celebrate the poor white subculture in which Beddoe lives. As I have suggested, the films concentrate on the diegetic representation of this culture to a large degree, in part because the narratives are otherwise thin, but also because there seems to have been on Eastwood's part a desire to celebrate it (he says that he made these films for this reason [see Zmijewsky and Pfeiffer, 206]). As the central signifier of the burlesque in these two movies, Clyde plays an important role in adducing the meaning of this subcultural representation.

It is one part of the function of burlesque to profer what Kristeva calls "the earthy laugh" that is related to "a subject liberating himself from the transcendental dominion of One Meaning" (1980, 224). Kristeva is talking about a context very different from these Eastwood movies—she is using the term burlesque to adjudge the effect of the painter Giotto's deployment of color as a way of resisting the authorized aesthetic of the Catholic church in his age. The burlesque in these movies produces a similar meaning in that Clyde stands as a symbol of the resistance of this subculture to the norms and behaviors of the wider culture. In the simplest way, this means that he stands as a literal embodiment of the supposed animality of the subaltern class, but endowing that animality with the positive value denied to it by the wider culture. He stands, that is, as a kind of proposition of the underlying, atavistic crudity of any culture, and the proposition is given force by his proximity to Beddoe the hero.

In such a proposition there is a registration of the resistance of the subculture to the ideologies and to the classes that scorn it. The movies are full of discursive marks of the same resistance and ressentiment. For instance, one of the comedy scenes in *Every Which Way* involves Beddoe in a bar trying to pick up a woman who turns out to be of a different class—she is a sociology major at USC who has come to study the macho ethos of such bars. Beddoe shows up the demerits of her class position by putting a set of false teeth in her drink in order to drive her away. In the same film, class ressentiment shows itself again when Beddoe churns up a golf course during a chase scene—a disrespectful gesture, at least, toward the golf-playing bourgeoisie. The many resentful expressions of this sort help define the nature of the class to which Beddoe belongs, and often these expressions are directed toward a sense of class solidarity, as in the moment when we are told that "hand-outs are what you get from the government. A hand-up is what you get from a friend." *Any Which*

Way is in fact structured to confirm such class solidarity. There Beddoe is forced into the movie's climactic fight by big betting interests in New York. Simply by winning he strikes a blow for his semirural community, but the result also brings together the factions within that community: specifically, the pathetic Black Widow motorcycle gang, who have been feuding with Beddoe throughout the two movies, end up in solidarity with him.

The burlesque functions within such double expression of class ressentiment and solidarity as an element of ironic self-depreciation that is modulated into self-celebration, and as such can be seen as a crucial element in the carnivalesque. However, in these movies it is not burlesque that we see at the carnival, but rather the brutality of Beddoe's fights. This is the central contradiction of these movies that want to celebrate the subcultural carnival but do not seem to be willing to compromise the secure spectacle of Eastwood as the guardian hero. It is as a counterweight in this contradiction that the body of the burlesque ape operates; Clyde is the hysterical body that resides with the heroic body as its other, continually reminding the heroic body of the powerlessness with which and within which *it* must operate.

Lethal Weapons

He [Sergeant Highway in Heartbreak Ridge*] is trying to understand all the things he never understood about women. He's had a lot to do with them but only superficially. He's never really tried to understand.*

—Clint Eastwood

In *Pink Cadillac* Tommy marks the inception of his alliance with Lou Ann by vainly reminding himself, "This is so wrong." He continues regardless, and finds himself pulled into the narrative lines of force that I have described. This reminder to himself is interesting in that it indicates how for the male protagonist to enter such an alliance he must drop or at least loosen some kind of moral code. This in its turn entails a confrontation with or a turning away from the forces in the diegesis that define the cultural stakes of what it is supposed to mean to be masculine. It may be that this ignoring of the phallic stakes of such codes is necessary for the appearance of the hysterical residues that I have been adumbrating. That is, these hysterical residues can be understood as the tics and gestures dependent upon a kind of negligence and even guilt in relation to the phallic regime. To posit such a guilt would not, of course, contradict Freud's understanding of the hysterical symptom, which is for him a certain kind of debilitation occasioned by guilt about childhood pleasures and sexual awakenings. The alliance with the woman, then, produces hysterical symptoms that bespeak guilt over the remaking of pleasure.

But there are also perhaps other kinds of guilt attached to these symptoms. One is suggested in what Eastwood says in the epigraph I have used above, and is particularly apparent in the movie about which Eastwood is speaking, *Heartbreak Ridge* (1987). That guilt derives from the recognition of having ignored the claims of women (and of feminism) to what we might call, for want of a better term, equal emotional rights. As I have been suggesting, that concern is one that has operated as an increasingly important thematic element in many of Eastwood's films since *The Enforcer*. It is in *Heartbreak Ridge*, however, that the concern reaches a kind of climactic point. But, as I shall attempt to say, it is a climactic point that tries to leave the earlier explorations behind, that tries, in other words, to tie up loose ends in the narrative of this concern and turn the explorations to their proper and righteous conclusions.

The sense that the movie offers—of men's having ignored women and of the need to rectify this, the need for men now to "understand" them—coincides with a popular cultural agenda that appeared in various magazines and journals in the mid to late 1980s: that is, the phenomenon of what was sometimes, almost laughably, called the "new man." This new man was presented at the time, mostly in women's magazines,[1] as the outcome of a male reaction to the demands and claims of a popular form of feminist discourse. There is perhaps no need here to stress how his emergence was to be articulated not so much with the political and civic demands of feminism, but rather with discourses about personal relationships, which may or may not have much to do with feminist analysis, but which certainly are easily assimilable to the cultural codes of bourgeois life.

This emergent male subjectivity was, at any rate, variously named as "the new man," "the sensitive male," or "the man of the eighties"—all expressions that are somewhat surprisingly deployed verbatim in what turn out to be two major box-office action movies in the mid-1980s, Eastwood's *Heartbreak Ridge* and *Lethal Weapon* (1987; starring Mel Gibson and Danny Glover and directed by Richard Donner). With these movies the discourse on masculinity that action movies generally constitute begins to find space for explicit consideration of a quality that at first blush would seem alien to it: "sensitivity" in the male.

Lethal Weapon is about a partnership between two policemen, Riggs (Gibson) and Murtaugh (Glover), and both characters contribute in different ways to one of the movie's central problematics: the contradictory impulses—between utter macho on the one hand and relative "sensitivity" on the other—that a male in the eighties is considered to have to cope with. *Heartbreak Ridge* deals with the training of a group of reluctant and improperly masculinized marine cadets by Highway; the extremities and exigencies of their training and their ultimate deployment in the invasion of Grenada are set against the backdrop of Highway's personal life, in which he is trying to reconstitute his broken marriage by sensitizing himself to his former wife's demands and desires. In both these movies the new "sensitivity" motive is clearly, as I suggested, a kind of response to the pop feminism of the women's magazines, or at least is a response to an area of popular culture that is trying to recuperate and popularize the concept of "strong" womanhood.

In *Lethal Weapon*, Murtaugh, the older, black half of the central male partnership, is shown trying to be the "sensitive" male when, for instance, he is dealing with his wife at breakfast. He is a traditional Hollywood male in many ways: that is, he'll do things like peremptorily ask his wife what the spot is on his tie or make a snide comment when she accidentally breaks an egg on the floor. But greeted by her patient but sarcastic responses he accepts her implicit rebuke of his manner and seems to express any further annoyances only with very deliberate and clumsy good humor. His sense of his family's integrity and importance is there acted out in such a way as to express his need not to alienate a basically strong and supportive wife. Indeed, with his family generally his demeanor is one of good humor and tolerance, to the point that he will act childishly and join in with his children's antics without any apparent self-consciousness. Although he acts "young" in this sense with his family, at work he is often depicted as harassed and confused, continually complaining that he is "too old for this shit." The family is thus offered as the fulcrum of his sanity, as the calm center around which the dangers of his job and the apparently psychopathic behavior of his partner, Riggs, circulate. Indeed, it is through this sense of family that the villains of the movie attack him when they kidnap his teenaged daughter.

However, after the establishment of his concessions to, and his implied need of, his wife and family, Murtaugh is shown worrying about precisely his "sensitivity." In a sequence at the police station, he anxiously reflects upon the term "an eighties man." In the context of his work he is clearly not sure that he *should* be an eighties man, since such a man can be easily confused with a nonmacho man, bending to women's will, allowing his "sensitivity" to become weakness, and generally being what he would call "a pussy." His anxiety is played upon by a colleague who, taking the anxiety rather lightly, tells him, "You know, I cried in bed last night." Murtaugh asks with some alarm, "Were you alone?" and the colleague replies, "That's why I was crying, because I was on my own." In that short set-piece exchange, the movie undermines the style of Murtaugh's dealing with family life, interrogates the whole notion of the new male's "sensitivity", turns it into a joke, and suggests that it is all some kind of sham.

The movie's plot itself also undercuts Murtaugh's clinging to the uxorious and childish ethos of the home. Riggs, on the other hand, is all the things that Murtaugh is not (young, single, unsettled, living a rough bachelor life in a trailer, immoderate in his tastes, violent, and so on), and not only does he turn out to be the effective protector of the black man's home, but he also brings his own lifestyle into that home. The climactic scene of *Lethal Weapon* involves Riggs's combat (in a vaguely kung-fu style) with the archvillain right on Murtaugh's front lawn. In a sense Riggs brings a demonstration of empowered masculinity precisely home in order to correct Murtaugh's wavering masculinity. At least, the implication is that the security of home cannot be guaranteed without the intervention of such a man—an implication that has further, political implications and which is familiar enough in Hollywood, especially in the mid-1980s. This message is underlined by the film's closing scene, in which Murtaugh invites Riggs to share the family's Christmas turkey and Riggs arrives with a dog, which immediately duels with the family's cat. The last dialogue in the movie is Riggs saying that he would "put five on the mutt." Thus the Riggs brand of masculinity is imported into the home as its heroic emblem, but also as a disturbance within it.

In those two ways *Lethal Weapon* undermines or negates its initial dealings with the idea of the "sensitive" male, the eighties man, as he is adumbrated in Murtaugh. The strategy is paralleled in Riggs's development throughout the movie. What the audience knows about him at the beginning is that he is a wildly violent but obviously successful cop who gets transferred to become Murtaugh's partner in part because the movie's police psychologist—a woman, of course—keeps warning that he is becoming dangerously suicidal. In one of this movie's best sequences, shot mostly in very tight close-up, we see Riggs at the point of committing suicide. Like Eastwood's Dirty Harry, he apparently has lost the woman he loved; with his wedding pictures on his lap and his gun at his head, he agonizes and comes within a millisecond of shooting himself. Later he tells Murtaugh that what keeps him from suicide is his job—basically killing the bad guys. His own version of "sensitivity," arising from a definite but unelaborated suffering over a woman, is converted—predictably enough—to the good, to the defense of the nuclear family and the removal of corruption from the civic body.[2]

What is also predictable in *Lethal Weapon* is the way the movie climaxes, as it were, with the two main characters consummating a homoerotic relationship that has been running throughout the movie. Standing very closely one behind the other they draw their guns—Riggs's has earlier been shown to be bigger than Murtaugh's in a scene that perhaps refers to a similar one between Eastwood and Burt Reynolds in *City Heat*—and finish off the villain. This medium shot is also reminiscent of one of the final scenes in *Beverly Hills Cop*, where Eddie Murphy and his older colleague similarly line up one behind the other to simultaneously shoot that movie's villain, a crooked art dealer who is specifically portrayed as gay. Like that movie, *Lethal Weapon* interestingly constructs its "amongst men" by having one of the central characters be African-American. The rather painful prevalence of homophobia in black American culture is thus drawn upon to subvent the general articulation of the Hollywood "amongst men" with an antihomosexual ethic.

Such allegories of the true male spirit, manifested in cooperative relationships and consummated in an act of joint violence, are not of course unusual in Hollywood; nor, as we have seen, is it unusual that one element of such relationships is the simultaneous exercise of homophobia and exorcising of homosexuality or some other kind of "fakery," sexual or otherwise. But what is perhaps most interesting about these two characters is the extent to which their apparent emotional vulnerability is allowed to be portrayed—especially with Riggs in the suicide scene. Certainly for Riggs, this is no mere resentment or frustration with the bureaucracy as it would be in the "Dirty Harry" movies, but something closer to a genuine existential angst. For Hollywood to be portraying explicitly this degree of male vulnerability—in a movie that, moreover, has already committed itself to some kind of discourse about "the eighties man" and male sensitivity—provokes some interesting questions. Why this now, in an era when the dominant political ethos would seem to be antagonistic to such a version of masculinity? What are the aspects of such a move that might empower "the eighties man"? What changes occur in the more traditional or familiar of popular culture's paradigms of gender relations? Is there any sense in which such a portrayal of the eighties man can be functional in a progressive way?

My own implicit answer to at least the last question here is that such a movie, although to some extent internally conflictual, finally succeeds in negating any radical potential it might have included within itself. That conclusion will be unsurprising in many ways. The discourse of left criticism on popular culture—with a few exceptions, such as in moments of Walter Benjamin's work—has chronically consisted in either, on the one hand, a straightforward condemnation of the "false" ideologies foisted by the culture industry upon subjected audiences, or on the other hand, what has always appeared to me as a rather whistling-in-the-dark kind of celebration of the radical energy of both popular cultural artifacts and their mass audiences, often based, as I have suggested before, on a largely uncritical notion of audience pleasure.

This dichotomy certainly does not point to the whole story, but it does seem to me to pose a central and perpetually unresolved critical dilemma: the issue of how to deal with the ubiquitous symptoms of a popular culture that we suspect of both subjecting (in relatively clear ways) and of empowering (in more mysterious ways) the mass audiences of contemporary cultures. To put this contradiction differently: it is relatively simple and even common to read off from the cultural text its "ideological messages" and to critique them, and yet at the same time it is currently politically de rigueur to avoid regarding mass audiences as merely the passive dupes of the overpowering ideological products of their culture.

But to simply assert that subjects are not the dupes of texts or of the cultural formations in which those texts reside does not make it so. It seems important in that context to maintain a critical and oppositional edge capable of recognizing and critiquing the continual structuring of ideological recuperation that the culture can effect. It seems to me still important to try to negotiate a way toward a space from which to view such issues, while maintaining a certain oppositional tendency and while concentrating on the production of meanings around a crucial part of popular culture's ideological range and process, in particular around issues of identity (here, sexual identity in particular). *Lethal Weapon* is in some ways a quintessential case in point, given the way that it subsumes the cultural and discursive phenomenon of "the new man" into an already existing masculinist discourse and thence negates it even while appearing to condone or tolerate it. *Heartbreak Ridge*, especially if located within the narrative of what I have been calling Eastwood's explorations of masculinity, could be said to be performing a similar function.

The ways in which the recuperative operation works are not, of course, confined to the immediate movie texts themselves. There must be, that is, surrounding and subventing discourses that replicate or criticize the gestures of the film text or simply comment upon them. In relation to *Heartbreak Ridge*, those subventional and/or critical discourses tended to concentrate on the movie's relation to the U.S. invasion of Grenada, to American foreign policy, and to war in general. Most such commentaries were written by men, and I will look at those briefly in the next section, "Servicemen." For now, though, it is interesting to see that one other strand of the critical/subventional discourses, this time written by a woman, focused upon the movie's use of this trope of the new man.

Late in 1986, in her syndicated newspaper column,[3] Ellen Goodman specifically addressed *Heartbreak Ridge* for its treatment of masculinity. It is not Eastwood/Highway's action-man persona that is of interest to Goodman. Rather, she picks up on the movie's romance plot. In the town where he is sent in order to train his marine cadets Highway discovers his former wife, who had left him precisely because of what she remembers as his thoughtless and macho behavior and his overcommitment to the lifestyle and ethos of the marines. Highway, determined to get back together with her, begins to look for clues about what went wrong with their marriage. In his spare time he reads women's magazine articles about "relationships," fills in the *Cosmopolitan*-type multiple choice quizzes, pores over the pop-psychology articles about gender roles, and so on. He then attempts to use these in dealing with his ex-wife, asking her, "Did we mutually nurture each other? Did we communicate in a meaningful way in our relationship?" Goodman is impressed to hear these unfamiliar words from the mouth of an Eastwood character and wants to understand them as a positive and hopeful sign that men in the eighties perhaps are willing to "wrestle with new words and emotions" in order to deal with a new generation of women and their demands. Her desire to understand the movie this way clearly coincides with the film's intendment: on his heroic return from Grenada, Highway's former wife takes him back, purely on the grounds that he "really [is] trying to understand." Goodman then generalizes what she sees as this movie's positive point by applying it to other male figures in popular culture who seem to be struggling with the conflict between "macho strength" and the newly acquired "sensitivity" of the eighties men. Such examples of the eighties man, she says—a little to my amazement, I must confess—are Frank Furillo on *Hill Street Blues* and the public persona of Bruce Springsteen.

By leaving aside some of the more dubious aspects of *Heartbreak Ridge* (specifically those—on which the male critics tended to concentrate—involving the invasion of Grenada) and championing its proferring of a new male sensitivity, Goodman effectively misrepresents the movie. This is, after all, a text in which the new male "sensitivity" is in fact presented only to be discarded, or to be undermined by the movie's overall strategies. For instance, Highway's "sensitivity" toward Aggie and her demands is narratively undercut when she pays for it by finally accepting into the home, as it were (as in *Lethal Weapon*), exactly an unreconstructed heroic male. At the end of the movie Highway is still refusing to abandon his marine career—a refusal that had indeed been one of the primary reasons for his wife's leaving him in the first place. In other words, nothing has changed except that the male's courting ritual has promised "sensitivity." Indeed, the problem with this resolution is underscored by the fact that earlier, during their attempts at reconciliation, Aggie had shown a quite firm skepticism about precisely this issue: she accuses him of cynically using the women's magazine discourse as another kind of seduction—an insight that she appears to have forgotten by the movie's end.[4]

Equally, this much-vaunted quality in the Highway character is in contradiction to other movements in the film's rhetoric. The opening sequence shows him, in jail for being drunk and disorderly, delivering himself of a little discourse to his cell mates about the merits of various women he has penetrated while on duty abroad. This scene and many that follow are marked by their extravagant use—even for Hollywood R-rated movies—of obscenities and sexist descriptions of women and their bodies. Similarly, the training of the cadets themselves involves turning them away from being effeminate, fashion-conscious, bejeweled, sexually liberal young men, and toward being the "good men" that the marines demand. One of the sergeant's main strategies in this enterprise is, of course, to impugn his men's sexuality, telling them in various obscene ways that they are gay, and if not gay then mere "pussies" or "ladies."

Here again, just as with *Lethal Weapon*, the spectacle of what Goodman has wanted to see as a "window of vulnerability" being opened in or on the heroic male character is in fact just a lure, a strategy by which the traditional Hollywood male can—without essentially changing—have it all. Both these narratives seem to be not about merely the heroes' triumph over social or political evil, but also and once more over women. A touch of "sensitivity" or vulnerability brings another weapon, a further resiliency to masculinity's dominatory arsenal.

In other words, none of this discourse of male sexuality in the mid-1980s action movies is anything but a lure. Even the problematic of "sensitivity" itself has not been entirely absent from over fifty years of Hollywood action movies. The traditional male hero of these films has always been a divided being, in that the direct expression of his heterosexuality has always been somewhat disjunct from the demonstration of his "action man" qualities. This disjunction has chronically been used to promote the same kind of division of the sexes as we find in these contemporary action movies, where women, in order to be wooed, won, and kept, have to have their "natural" appreciation of "sensitivity," interpersonal communication, and so on flattered by the men to whom that discourse is "naturally" alien. And of course, Hollywood film's male heroes have always been presented as masters of the seductive discourses necessary for the satisfying of women, and equally and simultaneously as the sexist and homophobic masters of the external world (the world of work) and its villains.

Women have, too, always been at the receiving end, as it were, of that mastery. So what's interesting about these particular action movies is that precisely the discourse of "sensitivity" has become here a specific target. As women are perceived to have become more demanding, more independent, more ready to make decisive ruptures in the masculine view of things, and as some men have necessarily become aware of the "rights"—emotional and otherwise—that women have to do these things, so the image of masculinity in the movies has more of which to purge itself, or has to pose itself yet another obstacle to its final triumph. This mode of undermining the "sensitive" man on screen (that is, the mode of seeing him as a further kind of obstacle) and a concomitant increase in the intensity of macho violence act as yet another imaginary—almost cathartic, in an old-fashioned sense—allaying of social contradictions. Audiences know to laugh when Riggs brings his mutt into the settled bourgeois household; they know to laugh when

Eastwood, his face twitching as if to stop from laughing, asks whether his relationship had been a mutually supportive one. And so it goes. Little has changed—except mode—in the more traditional or familiar of popular culture's paradigms of gender relations. The hopeful signs that someone like Goodman grasps at are subsumed under an ever more resilient and even cynical mastery. And the male's assumption of a new masculinity turns out to be, as Aggie had known (but known for hardly long enough), a change in seductive tactics—"you gave up the old frontal attack and tried to goddam outflank me."

If this is indeed the gesture which *Heartbreak Ridge* indulges in or is part of, it becomes additionally interesting as an element in both the narrative of Eastwood's explorations and the narrative of a process that Susan Jeffords has called "the remasculinization of America" after the Vietnam War (1989). I say this without wanting to suggest that those are in fact two ultimately distinct narratives; but I shall deal in the next section with the imbrication of the two narrative strands. Here I simply want to suggest that the movement of Eastwood's concern with the nature of masculinity—even though it does not definitively end here—reaches a certain stage in *Heartbreak Ridge*. It is appropriate to think of the film as an at least provisional stopping point in that it marks the moment where Eastwood's exploration effectively finds a name for itself in "the new man," the "sensitive" male of the 1980s. The movie demonstrates an ability to name the name, to undermine the man who goes by that name, and thence to put aside the exploration. This sets the scene for a certain complacency about issues of gender and sexuality in the last half dozen years or so of Eastwood's filmmaking.

It is intriguing, then, that the exploration should cease with this film about the invasion of Grenada. The mid-1980s were a watershed in the Reagan agenda of "putting the pride back in America" and helping America recover from what George Bush finally named in 1991 as "the Vietnam syndrome," pronouncing it over and done with. We know what preliminary or preparatory part the invasion of Grenada played in that attempt to, as I put it before, win the war to win the Vietnam War. Consequently, we know also the importance of the military man in that effort. In the next short section I will make some remarks about the fantastic or fantasized construction of the authoritative male body in the 1980s, before then turning with a greater degree of literalness to the role of what I have been calling the serviceman in Eastwood films.

Drugs

In an article in *Esquire* in July 1985 (111), it was reported that Eastwood "owns an informal option" on a screenplay called "Sacrilege," worked up by Durk Pearson and Sandy Shaw. These two people had previously been responsible for the best-selling book *Life Extension: A Practical Scientific Approach*, which despite its subtitle can only be described as a somewhat eccentric guide to some of the outer reaches of the world of physical and emotional self-help. Eastwood had figured in the book, under the pseudonym "Mr. Smith," as a devotee of this health program, and Jeffrey Ryder, in his book *Clint Eastwood*, gives an idea of the array of vitamins and drugs that the program encouraged Eastwood to take and that he used daily to increase his physical well-being: choline, selenium, Deanol, Hydergine, DMSO, L-arginine, L-dopa, plain old vitamin C, pyrollidone carboxylic acid, canthaxanthin, RNA, and a "nutrient mix of fifteen or so assorted vitamins and minerals" (12-13).

Pearson's and Shaw's script for "Sacrilege" is apparently a story about a biologist who tries to prevent a nuclear war by cloning a Jesus Christ from the genetic structures found in the bloodstains on the Shroud of Turin. The film has not been made, of course, and so one can only surmise whether Eastwood would have played the biologist or Christ. The *Esquire* report is a little sceptical about "the sanity of this project," but on the other hand it is easy to see that the figures of either this cloned Christ or the concerned biologist who produces him would lend themselves easily to the familiar Eastwood-Hollywood narrative structures where the world is saved by the interventions of single men. There seems to me, in other words, a weird and wonderful appropriateness in the relation of that kind of stereotypical narrative to the kind of biomedical fantasies that Pearson and Shaw's health plan, and Eastwood's accepting of it, bespeaks.

The connection between the aspirations toward the perfect body and the narratives of the perfect male savior are perhaps particularly apt at the cultural moment where America's president was a man whose body appeared—or was intended to appear—to be almost immortal. In so many respects, from the refusal of its hair to go grey, to its ingestion of body and brain "nutrients" similar to those Pearson and Shaw recommend, to its miraculously escaping the ravages of both bullets and diseases, Ronald Reagan's body is in many ways a product (and, of course, in some ways also an origin) of the cultural fantasies that abounded in the 1980s. The messianic role of that body is to regenerate America and turn it from its supposedly reduced state in the world by laying waste to its enemies and giving it the courage to be self-sufficient and industrious once more. In other words, that body is the appropriate or authorized body for the salvation of the American community, inserting itself into the narratives of regeneration that have become so familiar by now.

Reagan's body, after its triumphalist cowboy exit in 1990, disappears into western retirement or hypostasis. The body is mostly hidden from that time on, apart from some moments when the media transgress and peek into its privacy. One such moment is the publication of a picture in the *Star* of Reagan and his wife Nancy bathing at the beach of their retirement home. There the body is puffy but active; its immortality is recalled in its activity, even if its perfection has been allowed to lapse and the bodily flaws allowed to show. But this does not matter so much, because the body has been replaced by another. The same summer that Reagan is shown bathing sees George Bush reprising his role, taking on the task of beginning the narrative over again, or demonstrating the "permanence of the beginning of the world" (Schefer, 73). That is, having fulfilled the narrative promised by the Grenada invasion, by carrying the logic of the narrative to extremes—first in Panama, then in Iraq—Bush overcomes the scare of a sickness in his own body and turns his attention to the domestic—or community—agenda in relation to which these narratives must always provide a moral. Addressing a national convention of the Fraternal Order of Police (in Pittsburgh, 13 Aug. 1991; reported in *Pittsburgh Press*, 14 Aug. 1991) Bush publicizes his

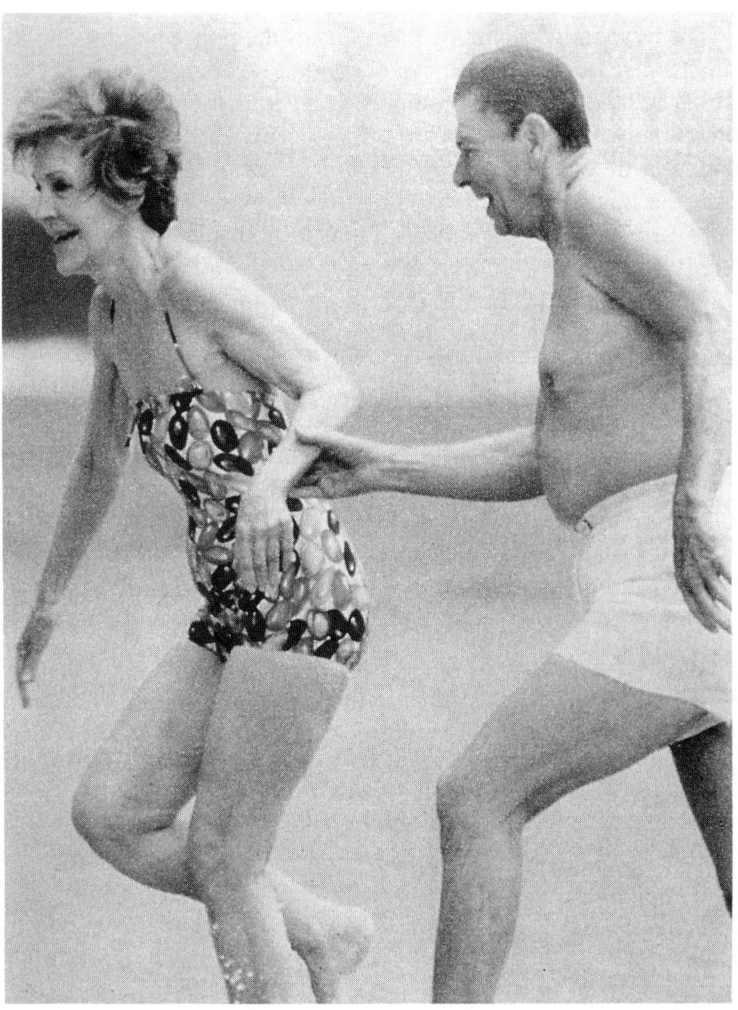

Ronald Reagan: The hypostasized body

domestic agenda of law and order, stressing particularly what had by the time become popularly known as the war on drugs. His speech that day used the threat of drug-related crime on America's streets to justify a repetition of the main points of the argument of *Dirty Harry*: that criminals are not treated harshly enough by courts, that the exclusionary rule needs changing, that victims' rights are too often ignored, and so on.

Bush's speech specifically interpellates the policemen present as servicemen: he says that he cannot condone sending them "into battle handcuffed." Thus, by paraphrasing the line that helped justify the unleashing of unthinkably vicious force against Iraq—unlike the situation in the Vietnam War, American forces would not be made to fight the Iraqis "with one hand tied behind their back"—Bush not only carries further the militarization of the battle against drug-related crime, but also shows the construction of a logic in which the foreign war is parallel to the domestic one. Once the connection is made and once it becomes clear that the application of force both at home and away is guided by the same logic, it is signal that Bush's speech makes clear that the first obligation of his administration is to *punish*.

Servicemen

Clint Eastwood is perhaps not best known for his war movies, but there are several in the Eastwood corpus, specifically two of his early movies, both directed by Brian Hutton and both set in World War II: *Where Eagles Dare* (1969) and *Kelly's Heroes* (1970). One can also think of *Firefox* as a war movie since it is a movie about military things, set in and released during what we call the cold war, and of course there is *Heartbreak Ridge*, which is more recent than any of these and of all Eastwood movies the one most overtly concerned with warfare.

The two earlier movies come from the period where, as I discussed before, Eastwood was taking advantage of the most readily available mode of star promotion at the time: the international blockbuster movie. *Where Eagles Dare* is a film that is almost the epitome of a certain kind of big-budget movie of which the Hollywood studios produced and distributed several in the 1960s and 1970s. These are action adventure movies, usually with a theme from World War II and usually featuring a handful of major stars—for instance, *The Heroes of Telemark* and *The Guns of Navarone*.

In *Where Eagles* Eastwood has second billing to Richard Burton, while additional box-office clout is added through the use of Alistair MacLean as screenwriter. Eastwood's burgeoning reputation as star is solidified by this movie, partly by virtue of his simply appearing alongside Burton and partly because his performance in that context seemed at least creditable to reviewers and audiences.[1] The movie's narrative concerns the penetration and destruction of a German officers' castle in Bavaria by Schaffer (Eastwood) and Smith (Burton) with a small group of commandos and with the help of two women agents. Whatever intrigue there is in the plot derives from the revelation that the enterprise is really being undertaken to discover the identity of some suspected double agents. A large part of the movie is devoted to the spectacular escape of Schaffer and Smith once their job has been done.

As with many movies of this sort the war scenario is of marginal relevance to what happens in the narrative, so that the movie's interest lies mostly in its action sequences and—I would say, merely momentarily—in the intrigue about who is a double agent and who is not. Apart from this, the movie holds little interest except in the way in which the Eastwood and Burton characters are staged. Burton's English character, Smith, is depicted as the leader of the team and as the on-site strategist for the operation, while the American Schaffer is the more physically present member of the pair with no particular intellectual duties. Schaffer's role is perhaps epitomized in a sequence leading up to their escape from the fortress when he and his weaponry hold off wave after wave of German soldiers defending the castle while Smith attempts to organize their escape. The setting of the supposedly refined and masterful actor, Burton in all his Englishness, as the mastermind of the operation, against Eastwood's warrior American is a play upon cultural significations that perhaps have little or no historical substance. Yet the movie's point would seem to be to suggest that it is precisely the alliance between the two men—an alliance between British brains and American brawn—that enables their success in this mission that supposedly can change the course of the war.

Even while this is the case, the alliance—which feminizes all at once Burton/Smith, Englishness, and the qualities of intellect—is played out in the picture's overextended escape sequences precisely to the benefit of the action side of the alliance. It is, in other words, Smith who has to assume Schaffer's characteristics in order to complete the movie, and not the other way around. While I am not suggesting that there is any specific denigration of Burton/Smith and his attributes here, it does seem to be the case that this movie gets pulled, as it were, into the mode of Eastwood/Schaffer, suggesting the priority in this alliance for the hard physical body, this American action man whose physicality and prowess represent the mode of existence that will ultimately save the day. What is effectively put into play here is Burton's high cultural capital as an actor—his connotations of refinement and other such qualities—against Eastwood's relative lack of such qualities and his presignified image as a popular actor; the movie effectively pits, then, images of "high" and "low" culture against each other—even while it suggests that they must be allied—and the narrative ultimately legislates in favor of the "low" culture.

The second war movie that Eastwood stars in under the direction of Brian Hutton, *Kelly's Heroes*, replaces the single and highly invested figure of Burton with a whole group of well-known North American actors like Telly Savalas, Donald Sutherland, and Don Rickles. This replacement entails a different kind of action movie plot but one that is still based upon the notion of an alliance. This time the alliance is among a number of American soldiers whose dissatisfaction with their military lot pulls them together into a kind of antiestablishment venture for their own gain: Eastwood, as Kelly, leads this group of misfit and malcontent soldiers across German lines to steal a consignment of gold for themselves. This narrative plays like a comic version of one of the Leone trilogy, particularly *The Good, the Bad, and the Ugly*, and indeed in one of the final scenes there is a parodical allusion to the corrida showdown from that film. But the movie's primary interest is perhaps in the way that it allows Kelly's men to put aside their duties as patriotic soldiers and to undertake a freelance operation for their own benefit. The script makes explicit reference to the "private enterprise" ideology of these men and begins to sketch out the proposition that the conduct of military operations is nothing but a cover for economic and personal gain.

Most of the reviewers of the film at the time seemed not to have picked up on this "war as private enterprise" theme—although several later commentators do think of the movie as being antiwar, echoing Eastwood himself, who has suggested that the film has "a subtle antiwar message."[2] The specific or overt antiwar message that Hutton might have envisaged for the film may well have been lost because of the refusal of MGM to give him final cut. In any case, it is perhaps more apropos to think of the released version as a commentary on the Vietnam War in particular. This possibility is signaled in several ways, but perhaps most of all in the figure of Oddball, a tank commander played by Sutherland, who in all ways is an anachronism within the film. Sutherland plays Oddball as a drugged, hippy kind of character whose vocabulary is full of 1960s slang (he is particularly fond of discouraging "negative vibes" in his colleagues). Oddball with his eagerness to make a profit out of the war presents a quite cynical image of the U.S. soldier in Vietnam. The allegory that his part subvents is concerned with the way in which the military commanders of the United States are not in control of the forces they unleash on the enemy, and with the idea that it is finally the interests of the free enterprise system that are played out in Vietnam.

The problem with the allegory is that it cannot finally name the villain of the piece. The freelancing soldiers who, as it were, get their capital gains are indeed the heroes of the film's title and the audience's sympathy is thus directed toward them. The general who egotistically garners all the accidental military glory for their initiative is understandably made to look comic and venal, but the men who make a monetary profit here are decidedly not the kind of men who made a profit from the Vietnam War. That is, the ideology of the group of maverick gold seekers does not match up with the true corporate and imperialist interests that benefited from Vietnam.

It is perhaps a little surprising to hear Eastwood complaining about the studio not allowing the movie's supposed antiwar message to emerge, but it is in any case difficult to imagine how the fundamental contradiction that the movie sets up for itself could have been solved or resolved. It may well be that Eastwood's complaints are more to do simply with the situation where the movie's director and its workers have no final control over the product, and less to do with the downplaying of an antiwar message. The making and releasing of this movie is certainly an important event for Eastwood's practical critique of the industry's modes and manners, and it marks an important moment in his drive to have what I described earlier as the homesteader ideology of small business represented in the development of Malpaso. Indeed, one might think it strangely appropriate that this particular movie—whose central contradiction is that its servicemen do not actually serve, even though they are heroic entrepreneurs—should stand as a prime factor in Eastwood's own entrepreneurial development.

A similar kind of tension between the serviceman who does not serve and his nonetheless heroic nature is deployed as the overture to Eastwood's next war movie, *Firefox*, over a decade later. Eastwood there plays Major Gant, who is a former pilot with an exceptionally heroic service record, living the life of a recluse in Alaska and attempting to come to terms with his traumatic experiences in Vietnam. In the opening sequence, as he is out in the woods jogging, he is being hunted down by a helicopter. The scene is an almost literal representation of the fact of his being haunted by the memory of Vietnam, and indeed, the pursuit occasions in him a reliving of those memories in a flashback sequence. Specifically, he had been captured by the Vietcong and rescued at the intervention of such a helicopter, but during the rescue had witnessed the death of a young Vietnamese girl with whom he had just established human contact in the midst of his inhumane treatment at the hands of the Vietcong. It is this particular memory of the war that appears to have caused his debilitation and his retirement, and the helicopter has come searching for him to bring him out of retirement—in other words, to make the serviceman serve again. The premises of this opening sequence are, thus, almost stunningly allegorical in the sense that the 1980s became precisely the time, after more than a decade, that the symbolically traumatized and debilitated American forces were called from their post-Vietnam seclusion and began to serve again.

In that sense the opening of *Firefox* sets up a certain ideological agenda that is to become familiar across the 1980s and into 1991: the right-wing agenda of eradicating the memory of Vietnam by fighting again, but this time winning. The enemy now—as befits the early 1980s and the intensification of cold war rhetoric under the regimes of Reagan, Thatcher, and Kohl—is the Soviet Union. The Soviets have produced a new warplane of untold sophistication which, according to U.S. intelligence officers, threatens to "change the structure of our world." Gant's task is to steal the plane from its base in Russia and fly it back to the West—which he duly does—not only to prevent the structure of the world from changing but, as the script makes explicit, to raise Western morale.

The issue of making the servicemen serve once more is apparent in *Heartbreak Ridge*, also, where Highway's bringing of his company of reluctant recruits to the point of old-fashioned military readiness is the crux of the film. Of course, there the company is made up of servicemen who are debilitated in a different way than Gant had been. *Heartbreak Ridge* proposes that Highway's young soldiers have been softened, turned into "pussies" and "ladies," by contemporary American culture. Their representative in that vein is Stitch, played by Mario Van Peebles, who is shown, for instance, as being much more interested in playing rock music than in doing his soldierly duty. In one of the first encounters between Highway's old-fashioned career marine and Stitch's newfangled American youth, the casualty is Stitch's left ear, from which Highway rips an earring that he sees as signifying Stitch's decadence and softness.

Highway's maintenance of the values of the old marine corps and his refusal to give up or retire is what turns the new and soft generation into real servicemen, though their enemy is a somewhat different one from the one that Gant confronts. Whereas in the early Reagan years the enemy for America was still the Soviet Union, that supposed threat soon officially receded as the administration determined its so-called "get tough" policy in the Caribbean basin, which was to become the preferred site for the ideological and military stand against the threat of communism. With their fundamental rationale lodged in this policy, from the early 1980s onward U.S. forces started to be deployed against a variety of enemies smaller than the Soviet Union, all of them peoples of color: the socialists in Grenada, Qaddafi and the Libyans, Noriega in Panama, and finally the Iraqis.[3] A crude narrative of the same sort can be traced in the passage from *Firefox* to *Heartbreak Ridge*. The servicemen who uphold the idea of American strength and the actuality of U.S. world power awake from the trauma of Vietnam, outflank the Soviets, and turn their firepower on almost helpless targets. All this enables and entails the comment that Highway makes at the end of *Heartbreak Ridge*. After Grenada, Highway can say that America has evened up its losing record in Korea and Vietnam: "Guess we're not 0-1-1 now, huh?"

While it seems easy to implicate both of these movies into such a somewhat crude but nonetheless signal narrative of U.S. foreign policy in the Reagan years and beyond, each has a different relation to what we might call the official discourses that produce that narrative. That is, the actual pragmatic relations of the two movies to both the institutions and the meanings that subvent those official discourses are interesting and can even be formed into a kind of parable.

Firefox can be understood as little more than a fictional playing out of a set of themes and propositions that figure largely in the official discourses of the early Reagan years. The movie's implication into those themes and propositions is demonstrable in many ways, but perhaps not least by its premiere performance in the summer of 1982. *Firefox* opened in Washington as a benefit for the USO. Tickets were priced at $1,000, and the event apparently raised over $125,000 for the USO. It was attended mostly by what *People* magazine (28

Amongst servicemen. (Photo copyright 1982 by Susan McIlhinney; courtesy of *People Weekly*, reprinted by permission.)

June 1982, 28) described as "political heavies," including the then secretaries of defense and of transportation, Caspar Weinberger and Drew Lewis, as well as the utterly ignoble Reagan aide, Ed Meese. At the event, Eastwood posed for photographers wearing a USO baseball cap and shouldering a rifle. The movie itself, with its enacting of the themes I mentioned earlier, drew from Weinberger the comment that it is "exciting and good for morale. *We* won" (quoted in *People*). Both Eastwood and the movie, then, function in this situation as points around which the then prevailing right-wing understanding of America's military destiny and its enemies can be articulated. The individual hero is released from the "exile" of his post-Vietnam trauma, and returns to outwit the cold war enemy. His role as fully operative serviceman is reinstated.

Interestingly, too, the movie articulates with a growing fascination on the part of the right wing for the more fantastic reaches of military-scientific development and application, most evidently displayed in the Reagan administration's controversial spending of billions of dollars on the defense system popularly known as Star Wars. The fantasies that Star Wars was (and in different form still is) intended to fulfill are recalled by the airplane in *Firefox*. The warplane that the Soviets develop but that Gant steals is the epitome of a particular kind of high-tech fantasy: it is a Mach 6 jet, armed with all kinds of defensive and offensive sensor technologies, laser-guided missiles, and various other advanced armaments, but is most remarkable for being directly controllable by the thoughts and voice of the pilot.

The special effects for the filming of the airplane (and its extended dogfight with a second such plane, which the Soviets send to intercept Gant's escape) were done under the supervision of John Dykstra and his Apogee company, who are perhaps best known for having done similar special effects for *Star Wars* (the movie, that is!). Their work for *Firefox* provoked a rash of technical articles and features in the trade press. The movie and its effects also became the basis for the first laser-disc arcade game released by Atari, which featured Eastwood's voice and footage from the movie.[4] It is perhaps not surprising that both the Hollywood industry itself and the allied entertainment industry that Atari represents should be fascinated by the film's special effects.[5] Perhaps it should not be surprising to find also that in the era of Star Wars (the Reagan fantasy, that is) technologies of the kind dreamed of in Dykstra's inventions for the screen are taken seriously as topics of military and scientific research. Eastwood's movie becomes, that is, part of a more generalized fantasy about Star Wars technology. A report in a federal government newsletter called *Government Computer News* in 1987 (13 March, 60) reveals that the movie inspired research into an "ocular attention-sensing interface system (OASIS)." This research, undertaken by a Pennsylvania company called Analytics and funded by NASA and the U.S. Air Force, is intended to produce the technology for commanding machines and other systems, such as fighter cockpit controls. The technology uses infrared cameras to record the operator's eye movements and couples this information with voice commands to speed up control of mechanical devices through microchips. While OASIS itself is not quite what is depicted in *Firefox*, Analytics's president says that "part of our inspiration came from the movie" and that the military and NASA are funding further research into the kind of system, based on transmission of human brainwaves to a computer control, that *is* in the movie's airplane.

It is possible to suggest, then, that on a fairly simple level the high-tech, sci-fi nature of *Firefox* marks its articulation with the discourses of the day, and also that the role of both the film and Eastwood himself in promoting those discourses becomes a political matter. Eastwood confirms something about this when, explaining his decision to premiere *Firefox* in the way that he did, he remarks that "the military cooperated with the making of the film, so we thought that a benefit would be appropriate" (*People*). The benefit is a mutual benefit, and Weinberger also confirms something about it when, mouthing the typical fantasy of the right-wing Reagan male, he praises the film and gloats over "our" winning.

The premiere of *Firefox* effectively constitutes and construes a kind of "amongst men" bonhomie that I think is at best provisional, and even totally phantasmic. That is, while the film does set up a kind of ideal congruence between, on the one hand, the "official" utterances of Reagan's version of the cold war and, on the other hand, the possibilities of a Hollywood-style serviceman drama, such a congruence can only be produced in the phantasmic and even utopian mode of what is essentially or for the most part science fiction. *Firefox* works as an imaginary solution to anxieties over the cold war, over Vietnam and the military power of America, over the integrity of the serviceman. In that sense it is *optative*, capable of producing the euphoric mirage of a solution, and it stands in sharp contrast to Eastwood's later war movie, *Heartbreak Ridge*, which on many levels is retrospective and purports to be a recording of actual events rather than a utopian imagining of events. This latter mode proves to be the more problematical in that its attempt to profer an articulation between official and fictional discourses comes a particular kind of cropper.

On some important levels *Heartbreak Ridge* is, to adopt the language of one article written about it, "an exercise in realism" (*American Cinematographer*, Jan. 1987, 28-36). The climactic sequences of the film purport to depict the actual U.S. invasion of the island of Grenada in 1983, and much of the earlier parts of the film can be taken as "realistic" representations of the training of marines and of the life of a marine camp. The recreation of the invasion was in fact done by exploiting the full-scale training maneuvers of a U.S. marine detachment on the island of Vieques (32). Yet the levels of realism and the actuality of the filming eventually do not help the movie to claim any privileged relation to the actual history, and still less to the official versions of that history, as we shall see.

The invasion itself had been undertaken to oust the supposedly threatening and aggressive faction of the New Jewel Movement, which had seized power from Maurice Bishop, and to prevent the "concerted attempt to transform Grenada into an instrument for Cuban and Soviet objectives."[6] The innocent community that was to be rescued from this self-evidently corrupt regime was a small group of American medical students on the island—although later U.S. justifications for the invasion talked of the need to ensure the safety of about a thousand U.S. citizens. However much they follow the basic narrative of a western in that sense, the official justifications for the invasion are almost transparently factitious, and the exercise itself was perhaps driven more by the need to have U.S. forces begin their rehabilitation than by any pressing political or pragmatic concerns. Indeed, this suggestion is reinforced by J. Hoberman, who points out in his comments on the film that in both the movie and the history of the invasion "the structuring absence is that of the 241 marines who were blown to bits two days earlier in Beirut" (*Village Voice*, 23 Dec. 1986, 82). The general post-Vietnam need to demonstrate the military's effectiveness, and also at the same time to cause a public forgetting of Reagan's ineffectual and ultimately tragic use of the Marines in Lebanon, cannot be discounted as a reason for the alacrity with which the United States undertook this military adventure.

Despite its replication of the official U.S. version of the events of the invasion—particularly its emphasizing the presence of the Communist threat by showing the island garrisoned by Cuban soldiers[7]—and despite the logistical and financial help of the Marine Corps, *Heartbreak Ridge* did not garner the support of the official Reagan mouthpieces in anything like the way that *Firefox* had. The filmmakers and the marines had both expected the movie to become a kind of recruitment device for the U.S. services, in much the way that showings of *Top Gun* had earlier been used by the U.S. Navy as an extended advertisement and as providing a new venue for setting up recruitment tables. But according to *Variety* (26 Nov. 1986, 3), the marines eventually withdrew their support and backed away from exploiting the film in this way.

The Department of Defense asked Warner Brothers, the film's distributor, to omit any reference to or acknowledgment of the support of the marines in the making of the film. The objections that Pentagon officials had to the film centered on the movie's depiction of marines and on the historical accuracy of its account of the invasion. They deplored the movie's "unnecessary and offensive" profanity, and complained that the representations of marines were inaccurate and "stereotyped in a way not characteristic of the Marines today [*sic*]." In relation to the invasion itself, apparently the problem was that the movie "overlooked the role of the Army in the rescue of American students from the island." There was specific objection to a moment in the film when one of Highway's company shoots a Cuban soldier in the back as he flees; "in reality," says the Department of Defense, "a member of the armed forces would be subject to trial by court martial for such an action."[8] In sum, "the Marine Corps views the film as objectionable and believes it does not accurately portray the Marines or their training."

My point is that any conclusion to be drawn, in trying to explain the difference in the relations between *Firefox* and *Heartbreak Ridge* and the official attention of the Reagan government, would have to concern the optative nature of the first and the "realist" nature of the latter. That is, *Firefox* can maintain the support of official reaction precisely because its narrative and representational strategies do not impinge upon the reality of U.S. policy but merely replicate its ideological desires. *Heartbreak Ridge* offers the ideological replication, to be sure, but it also *records* in a certain way an actual historical event. It is the recording of such events—their marking as historical—that the Department of Defense wishes to control, and such an interpretation is not contradicted by the Pentagon's efforts to severely constrain the U.S. reporting media during the invasion itself.

Malpaso's reaction to the withdrawal of Pentagon support for the film is interesting in its own right. Fritz Manes, the movie's executive producer, points out to *Variety* that the objections to the movie come, not from the marines themselves, but from the Department of Defense. He says, "We find it deplorable that the DoD has issued an edict to withdraw its support when not one ranking Marine Corps officer has seen the picture. . . . It's a shame that [the corps] is being put in a position to go along with the DoD edict." The implication in what Manes says is that the top-brass controllers of the Marine Corps are acting irresponsibly in much the same way as Harry Callahan's bureaucratic bosses act toward him. In other words, Manes tries to establish in those few remarks a familiar fissure between the servicemen and the bureaucrats. Here the shape of the standard Hollywood narratives glimmers through, once again directing the political thinking of the movie industry functionary.

Performance and Identification

Acting is more than ranting, raving, crying and rolling around on the ground.

—*Clint Eastwood*

Identification, in fact, is ambivalent from the very first.

—*Freud,* Group Psychology

The *Esquire* feature on Clint Eastwood (14 Mar. 1978) from which the first epigraph is taken is one of the many that have appeared over the years in the tributary media and magazines, celebrating Eastwood as man and as star. In this instance the journalist Jean Valleley follows Eastwood on his daily round at his home in Carmel, seeming to be especially intrigued by his exercise routine and watching him build his body for the hard work that he puts it through when making films. At that point in his life, Eastwood was apparently able to submit himself to two one-hour sessions of exercise every day, including repeated sets of sit-ups, weight training, and work with punching bags. In addition to all this he would play tennis, run, or play golf (the latter of which "I don't consider exercise, all that standing around with a lot of blood in my feet" [39]).

The article justifies the near obsessiveness of Eastwood's fitness routine by repeating the shibboleth about his performances that seems to have so much impressed the tributary media over the years: "He does most of his own stunts, like jumping off a bridge onto a moving bus in *Dirty Harry* and mountain climbing in *The Eiger Sanction*" (40). The body that Eastwood builds for his most typical performances is a body that, as I have suggested, is destined to disappear in the end, and yet it must submit itself along the way to the harsh regimes of the action. It is a body that must at least *appear* to be both powerful enough to be indestructible and experienced and at the same time ordinary enough to be able to disappear. The typical Eastwood performance is, then, a performance of the body as it is carried

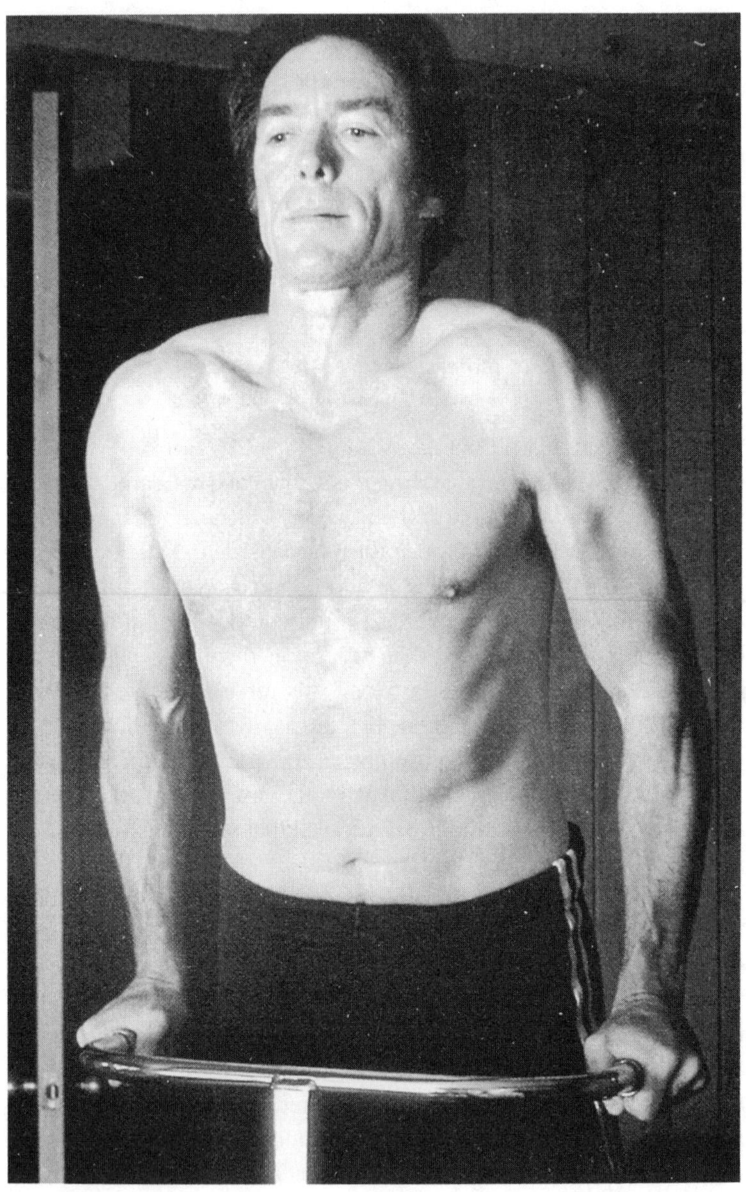

Building the body

through the phases of objectification, destruction, and resolutory hypostasis.

Many critics—and, one might assume, many sectors of Eastwood's audience—have been distinctly unimpressed by his acting, or by his performances as such; they have not failed, however, to be impressed by what very often comes to be known as the "presence" of his body. Some will say, as Pauline Kael does, that there is no acting in an Eastwood performance; of his work in *Magnum Force*, for example, she says, "He isn't an actor, so one could hardly call him a bad actor. He'd have to *do* something before we could consider him bad at it" (*New Yorker*, 14 Jan. 1974, 84). Others will displace the question of his acting onto a question of his mere presence, like Vincent Canby: "Eastwood doesn't act in motion pictures; he is framed in them. . . . [He is] the perfect physical specter haunting a world" (*New York Times*, 3 Oct. 1968); or, "Is it acting? I don't know, but he's the towering figure in [a film's] landscape" (*New York Times,* 22 June 1979). Eastwood himself will respond practically by building his body for its narrative trials and by suggesting (in a wonderfully ambiguous sentence) that "critics think I'm not doing anything, when actually I'm doing it in a different way" (*Esquire*, 14 Mar. 1978, 45).

Acting is actually a notoriously difficult element of filmmaking to account for or to judge. Something of the difficulty of thinking and theorizing its nature can perhaps be illustrated by reference to a couple of moments in Lev Kuleshov's writings. Kuleshov is generally known for having purportedly conducted the editing experiment whereby the same shot of an actor—Mozhukin—is intercut with shots of three different objects—"a plate of soup, a girl, a child's coffin" (1974, 199). The experiment is said to demonstrate that the meaning of a film actor's performance can be considered primarily as a construct of film montage: the famous "Kuleshov effect." But later, in some reminiscences in 1935, Kuleshov appears to retreat somewhat from the consequences of that experiment: "It is not always possible to alter the semantic work of an actor," he says, suggesting that a poor actor, especially, can weaken the effect of montage (193). The difficulty here is, of course, not simply that human expressivity or particular somatic behaviors and reactions are inherently "polysemous, capable of multiple signification" (Naremore 1988, 25). While that is true up to a point, rather more importantly Kuleshov's problem demonstrates that the significance of an actor's performance stands in an uneasy position somewhere between montage and its effect.

That is to say, a given film performance, an actor's activity, mediates in an unpredictable way the relationship between the making and the reading of a film, and is properly outside the total control of either maker or reader. This does not mean, of course, that the performance is in any manner autonomous. What an actor does on set is first of all always directed and coached and furthermore is always dependent on what the camera does and on what the editing process does to his or her activity. Also, more often than not, the actor's activity on set is highly fragmented: it is frequently interrupted, it is repeated and altered in different takes, and it is manipulated on an ad hoc basis by various parts of the film crew (makeup people, lighting crews, and so on).

And by the same token, a film's final audience has a certain interpretative freedom in relation to the image. It might well be the case that "meaning in a film is usually narrowed and held in place by a controlling narrative" (Naremore, 25), which will maintain particular parameters for the viewer to follow (and I would add that the process of intendment is always at work), but an audience's reading will always either exceed or in some other way fail to conform to the proferred meaning. This is particularly obvious if we take into account what we can call the audience's multiple concentration in the case of stars: that is, any given shot of Clint Eastwood will inevitably be submitted to the audience's memory and awareness of his extrafilmic star image, as well as to the particular interfilmic or intertextual resonances of the specific performance being watched, to its relations within the movie in which it appears, and to multiple other factors and codes.

It is perhaps because of this multiplicity of intervening and complicating factors that theoretically interesting and informed examinations of film acting, or of the actor as performer in the movies, have been somewhat thin on the ground and usually rather unsystematic. After Kuleshov and Pudovkin's early, necessarily pragmatic, and somewhat prescriptive efforts, surprisingly little work has been done. Recently, some work in the journal *Screen* has attempted to right the situation, and at the same time Mark Nash has produced his highly interesting television program, *The Acting Tapes* (1984) for Channel 4 in Britain. More recently, James Naremore has written his important book, *Acting in the Cinema* (1988), from which I have already quoted.

Naremore's work stresses that the situation of the actor and the actor's performance derives from a severe contradiction between, on the one hand, a "naturalistic" demand for unity of character and star and, on the other hand, the fragmentational procedures of the cinema apparatus itself. To this contradiction of Naremore's we might add another, namely that the performer—or perhaps better, the performer-text—exists as it were in between filmmaker and viewer, at the mercy of both, and yet is still endowed with a certain agency by filmmakers, viewers, and actors alike. That endowment most often appears, of course, in the evaluative ideology that we all engage in when we talk of good or bad actors—even while we forget or ignore the highly artificial nature and position of film performers within the apparatus. These two primary contradictions (and more than likely, other complications) have helped to make film performance or film acting a problematic and often untheorized category for the ordinary viewer as much as for the critic and scholar.

Much of the available commentary on screen acting depends upon—and in any case almost invariably addresses—the idea that there has been and continues to be in the history of cinema some kind of rivalry or battle between hegemonic or dominant cinema and radical or avant-garde cinemas. That is, discussions of film acting and performance tend to adopt a rather holistic approach to these two traditions, assigning a particular mode or style of film performance to each. Generally the dichotomy is between a Stanislavskian and a Brechtian aesthetic—the first subtending a naturalistic version of performance as expression, the second promising an alienated, fragmented, and artificial performance. Like so many other current issues in cinema theory, the dichotomy has a certain provenance in the pioneering cinematic work of the Soviets, although both of the two modes here ultimately of course have their roots in work in the theater. It is possible to think of Stanislavsky as merely the proponent in cinema of the somewhat hegemonic tradition of naturalism in the theater since the nineteenth century; the Brechtian aesthetic, on the other hand, perhaps harks back to an even older theater and one that Meyerhold is generally credited with having revived in the early part of this century.

The naturalistic tradition in its extreme forms is, of course, an easy target for ridicule—not just because of the Californian ethos it has accrued to itself, but also because it comes across as so self-important and earnest. Yet at the same time some of the most widely recognized "great performances" of recent cinema stem from just this tradition—one might think of, for instance, the work of Meryl Streep and Dustin Hoffman in this regard. As for the so-called Meyerholdian-Brechtian tradition, many of its techniques have reached the dominant cinema and have been appropriated and deployed there easily enough—and one might think of the origin of this appropriation as reaching as far back as the comedies of Charlie Chaplin. But Hollywood cinema in the fifties and sixties, subject to the urge to actually depict social and emotional alienation in so many characters, often produces a kind of miscegenation in the two traditions with performers like Marlon Brando, who can be read as a Stanislavskian who turns out Brechtian performances. Since this dichotomy has in any case rather peremptorily translated its terms from theater, and since the argument can be made that the separateness of the two traditions has been somewhat compromised in contemporary cinema, it is perhaps more profitable to try to consider film performance in its specificity, as this manipulated and manipulating mediation between production and consumption; better, then, to consider it as performance-text.

As I have just mentioned, in general the difficulty in looking at screen performance at the point of its production has a lot to do with the fact that screen performance is highly dependent on factors usually beyond the actor's control. By this, I mean not only to point to the manipulation of performance that occurs in filming and in post-production, but to other factors as well. Some of these have been pointed to by Barry King in "Articulating Stardom" (1985), an article that seems to me to be often less about stardom per se than about the *presence* of actors. King rightly stresses, however, the significance of the fact that actors are necessarily caught up in the whole economic system of Hollywood even before they appear on a set. That is, the film industry can be considered to be in the market for raw materials with which to make specifically designed commodities; thus actors are chosen for their suitability to some preestablished set of types or typologies in terms of physique and demeanor, and these types bear the marks of already signified cultural and cinematic verisimilitudes.

These typologies constitute a large part of what I call the Hollywood imaginary—that is, the system of representations and verisimilitudes in the culture at large to which Hollywood imagines it conforms or aspires to conform. Thus, at any given time very particular kinds of bodies, voices, faces, and demeanors are regarded by the industry as proper. This is a familiar enough point, although it is often forgotten how, as King suggests, these presignifications lead to a de facto "suppression of those elements of the actor's appearance and behavior that are not intended to 'mean' at the level of characterization" or, I would add, at the level of social and cultural significance. But in addition to this conformist urge in the performance marketplace, there is also an industry demand for the unique product, and an urge to have actors represent a certain kind of monopoly over a specifiable field of meanings.

All these factors are of course important in understanding how the actor is produced within this film industry and how the star image in particular is construed within the culture at large. For the moment, however, I shall be concentrating on the performance itself as text and on the actor's place in relation to, as Pudovkin might say, the organic team of filmmakers. This perhaps rather formalist approach will, I hope, lead to some insight into the dialectic of production and consumption of the screen performance, not forgetting that screen appearance and performance are indeed largely issues of spectatorship.

For the sake of analysis, then, it might be helpful to break the film actor's appearance and performance into three elements: the facial, the corporeal, and the vocal. In general the first of these, the facial, is mostly relevant to discussions of the close-up, which is a privileged moment in the process of capturing the spectator's supposed identification with characters and objects. The second, the corporeal, is necessarily implicated into questions of camera work—and here the issue will be the objectification of the actor's body and once again the question of identification; the third, the vocal, is rather difficult to pry away from a discourse on theatrical elocution, but I shall be trying to take the notion of the screen voice as a material and affective entity articulated with the other elements to produce a certain version of the processes of spectatorship. Part of the point with each of these segmentations, as it were, is to problematize the notion of identification as it is most usually deployed in film scholarship.

We might begin by looking again at some of the ways in which Eastwood and his directorial mentor, Don Siegel, deploy the actor's performance. As I mentioned much earlier, across his career Siegel has tended to focus on the male performer most often by means of a preponderance of eye-level shots that feature the torso and head. At the same time, in terms of filming conversations, he employs many medium-length shots of two or more characters; certainly he does this just as often as he uses the more conventional shot/reverse-shot sequencing. Through both these procedures, and others that we have seen, the male torso and face—but especially the face—become the central signifiers of the film, and this seems especially appropriate for Siegel's movies, which are so often concerned with the dynamics of all-male groups of one kind or another. Whereas the classic shot/reverse-shot sequence would partition the viewer's attention and lead to the foregrounding of, say, both male and female leads, Siegel's techniques tend to center on the masculine object. Also, the more conventional sequencing usually motivates particular facial and bodily reactions in a manner that differs from Siegel's techniques. One central purpose of shot/reverse-shot sequencing is that it will render legible the reactions of one character to another. In Siegel, the depiction of reactions is by and large less important than allowing the viewer simply to contemplate the visage and/or bust of the male hero. Without the conventional motivating cues, Siegel's male leads tend to be given as in a sense inscrutable. That is, their expressions and gestures are minimally tied to the action or gestures of others; they thus become, as it were, more inward, orientated toward an apparent "mystery" of a character's "inside."

This tendency on Siegel's part is one of the things that made him such an important director in the last twenty years or so. Compared with other major directors who have such demonstrable curiosity about and concern with masculinity (say, Fritz Lang, Anthony Mann, or Howard Hawkes), Siegel has not only forged his own style in that sense, but has also contributed largely to the formulation of what has become something like an industry standard in the way action movies and their male protagonists are shot. Siegel's use of these particular techniques, even if they are not entirely uniform, necessitates a rather particular hermeneutical process on the part of the spectator. The male character is not only the normal center of the visual field, but is also usually proferred as its mystery. In terms of how Eastwood functions in that setting, we can see in the early films with Siegel the beginnings of the rather static, furrowed face technique that becomes his trademark.

Siegel's elaboration of the Eastwood photo-effect[1] from what it was in the spaghetti western trilogy that made him famous is in the form of an addition. If the Leone movies presented Eastwood's face and body as a kind of tabula rasa onto which the spectator reads nothing but inscrutability, Siegel adds other elements and thickens out somewhat that photo-effect of Eastwood. What he offers is no longer a tabula rasa; he adds an "internal" element to the face that the spectator is called upon to interpret. This internalization of the character's emotion usually promotes a sense of his strength and solidity (that, as much as the pent-up aggressivity of Eastwood's face, is the fundamental proferred point of identification with the Eastwood image). But Siegel's camera work and his editing (over which, as we have seen, he insists upon having a great degree of control) carefully manipulate that image, allowing it to change in what, borrowing Eisenstein's words, we can call "a rising line of annoyance." The Eastwood face, as it changes from repose to a snarl in many almost identical sequences, is not to be read so much as the neurotic or psychotic marker of pent-up violence, as the process whereby an inner strength, even tranquility, defends itself, stakes its claim, proclaims its right to be left alone and undisturbed in its own confidence.

The culmination of this rising line, by which the character's strength changes from being placid and hidden to being annoyed and expressive, is the famous Eastwood snarl (a snarl that is relentless, for example, in *Heartbreak Ridge*, and which constitutes a large part of the "Dirty Harry" persona). Eastwood himself, when he directs, constructs many sequences where the rising line is even more refined, even more the quintessential Eastwood-effect than Siegel himself manages. I think particularly of one sequence in *The Eiger Sanction* where, confronting the sinister spy-boss who is blackmailing him into doing one last job, the Eastwood character's recognition that he is being trapped is shown through a series of close-up reaction shots, each more angry than the last. These kinds of close-ups, then, are an attempt to add something to the Eastwood image as it is transmitted from the Leone movies, and they constitute an addition to the placidity of the No Name figure.

We might see here a confirmation in a certain manner of how the close-up and its representation of the face are described by Gilles Deleuze. The placid close-ups in the Leone films can be seen as instances of what Deleuze calls the "reflecting unity" of the character, and Siegel can be said to have added what Deleuze calls the "reflected unity" (1986). For Deleuze the "reflecting" unity of the close-up is something akin to the face in repose, while the "reflected" is the face as it registers emotion by movement. This simple enough binarization corresponds, in Deleuze's explanation, to a number of others—most usefully, I think, to the distinction between the close-up's *power* in the reflecting unity and its *quality* in the reflected unity. The two are crucial components in the production of affect in the spectator—indeed, they are for Deleuze what gets called in translation the "affection-image." So in terms, for instance, of Leone's close-ups of the No-Name character, these would tend to invoke power rather more than quality, wonder rather than desire, luminosity in preference to intensity; whereas Siegel's and Eastwood's directorial work adds doses of each of these second terms to the Eastwood image.

Deleuze thinks of the close-up and the face as essential features of cinema's effect, and his binaries here are an interesting contribution to thinking about that effect. But for myself, I want to replace the reflecting/reflected unities with slightly different vocabulary, while keeping especially the power/quality dichotomy. This is in part in order to be able to turn away somewhat from Deleuze's implicit metaphor of the screen as mirror. I would replace "reflecting" with contemplative, and "reflected" with reactive; this change in the vocabulary has the benefit of shifting the emphasis away from the kind of identificatory process implied by the first terms. I would also suggest that these elements should be seen not as the *unities* that Deleuze proposes, but rather as merely fragmentary and provisional moments in the production of affect for an audience. That is, while it is important to maintain Deleuze's sense of the production of "affect," it seems to me equally important to stress that the effect of cinema is at its most powerful only through an oscillation between the two poles. Thus Siegel, in adding quality to the power of Eastwood's image, cannot do so by formulaically or mechanically stressing one pole over the other, but rather must oscillate between one moment and another, between contemplative and reactive shots, in such a way that neither is ever fully and unmediatedly a presence.

This oscillation, or the suite of oscillations that occur in the course of a film's treatment of a performer, can be understood as a crucial element for the mobility or multiple attention of the spectator's supposed identificatory relation to the image. The affect that is produced in this oscillation is an ambivalent one—as Freud suggests, "identification is ambivalent from the very first" ([1921] 1959, 37). Film criticism—just like everyday talk about films by filmgoers—often takes for granted the plenitude and efficiency of identificatory processes. This oscillation between power and quality, between contemplative and reactive images, readily opens itself to analogy with one of the fundamental divisions that much film theory either states or implies: a division between, on the one hand, identification with the diegetic world of a movie and, on the other, identification with characters. I will want to take up this division for discussion a little later. For now, I mean simply to stress that the oscillation I am describing necessarily encourages a view of identificatory procedures as ambivalent, split, mobile, and indeed multiple.

I have already looked—in a previous section, "Eastwood Bound"—at some of the ways in which the corporeal level of Eastwood's performances comes to be significant, concentrating on the way that the body in action movies is at first objectified, then tested and experimented upon, and then submitted to a kind of resolutory disappearance or hypostasis. In that narrative track, the first moment of objectification—where Eastwood's body is treated as the object of what Willemen calls "voyeuristic admiration" (1981, 16)—corresponds to the moment of reflective or contemplative power that I have tried to describe for the facial level of performance. The second stage in that process, where the heroic body is beaten and tested before fighting his way back to victory, is clearly akin to the reactive level. And here again, the two elements respond to the temporal movement of the film, where the objectifying moment is usually tied to the establishment of the film's diegetic presence, before the movement of the narrative that always involves that body in a series of reactive activities showing his qualities.

The important point here is that the shift—roughly, from diegetic objectification to narrative reaction—would demand of the spectator different identificatory motions. Outside the realm of psychoanalytical theory it would be impossible to do more than hypothesize what those different motions might be. But one can at least suggest that, as far as the corporeal image is concerned, the question of sexual object-choice might easily be involved, so that what we call identification with the character would necessarily involve the various kinds of mechanisms about which Freud speaks ([1921] 1959 and [1923] 1962, for example). For Freud, identification can follow several different routes. In relation to object-cathexis, identification can serve the aims of *being* the object or *having* it, for instance; thus, an identification with the objectified Eastwood might constitute either the desire to be that person or the desire to possess that person. In the context of a cinema whose codes refuse—in the case of the male spectator—the possibility of a sustained desire for another male object, an identification at the level of the desire to become him would be the more likely, and its function would be exactly to sublimate homosexual desire. But this identificatory mode would itself in any case be provisional, in the sense that the film's movement, as it turned to the tested and experimented body, would then demand a different kind of identification—perhaps no longer a sublimated desire, but the rather looser kind of identification based simply upon a "perception of a common quality shared with some other person who is not an object of the sexual instinct" ([1921] 1959, 38-40).

However hypothetical that particular scenario might be here, it is intended only to suggest once more that a spectator's identification with the heroic protagonist will always be sporadic or provisional, shifting from one moment to the next depending upon the film's movement and its treatment of the object to be identified with. The typical movement followed by Eastwood's films—especially the action movies—can even be said to necessitate as a matter of course a fairly sharp break between different modes of identification. In other words, no simple or uncomplicated identificatory process is encouraged by these movies themselves. One can then complicate the issue further by suggesting that, since identification is always a function of a "subject's" desire and lends itself to that "subject's" purposes, even the motile proferred identificatory points of a movie cannot be guaranteed to be taken up. Identification with such a body is bound in any case to include or take in other moments of identification, which come, not from the particular image given at any specific moment, but from a host of other sources: when we say we are "identifying" with a character portrayed by Eastwood's body, with which intratextual occurrence of that body do we do it? Or are we "identifying" with one or more of those occurrences as they admix with our image of Eastwood the body-builder who does his own stunts? Or perhaps all of these identificatory moments are dependent upon our image of Eastwood as No Name, or as the singer in *Paint Your Wagon*, or the castrated soldier in *Beguiled*.

Among the different kinds of identificatory process that much film theory assumes are the spectator's identification with the gaze of the camera, identification with the figures on screen, and various "point of view" identifications within the film (identification with the looks and reactions of characters as they interact, for example). These are all dependent upon the dynamics and mechanics of *looking*, and in response to that, Stephen Heath, assessing the relay of these identifications and looks, argues that they entail "the impossibility for a film to be *heard*" (1981, 120): "The image is all-powerful (the essence of cinema; people pay to *see* a film), the soundtrack a supplement (often regarded historically as a potential threat to the luminous clarity of the image)" (121). Thus it is that the vocal level of performance receives relatively little attention in film scholarship and is consigned to the interpretation of its content or to remarks upon its elocutionary quality. Of course, to a large extent the vocal level of performance *is* a matter of elocution, or of the nexus of vocal effects obtained through delivery, volume, intonation, pronunciation, and so on. The evaluation of elocution clearly has its roots in stage performance, where, as Naremore points out (47), elocution is a matter of vocal power purveyed as phallic effect or as an effect of presence. There is a certain residue of this effect in screen performance, though it has over the years been necessarily attenuated as the cinema took on its self-styled role of offering the "real" to its audiences. Simultaneously, artificial theatrical and pantomimical vocal performances were more or less squeezed out of Hollywood in the first few years of the talkies by the more demotic speech assumed to fit the realist mode.

Beyond the question of elocution or beyond the technique of particular performers, scriptwriters, and dialogue coaches, the vocal level of performance is perhaps the most difficult one to get at analytically—and this despite the fact that of all the elements of an actor's performance it is the element that is most likely to remain the same, or fairly consistent, across any number of performances. It is probably true to say that, in terms of reception, the voice is most simply understood as part of the system of signifiers that attempts to guarantee the unity of character, and this proferred unity of character is of course tied to a notion of the unity of the body. The apparent naturalness of the voice being grounded in, belonging to, and as it were speaking for the body is, in this sense, the final turn of the screw in the production of a certain effect of the real. Stephen Heath has noted this secondary nature of sound and voice in the cinema and has shown how the visual normally subsumes the vocal. The paradox here, as he points out, is that without sound, movies tend to appear to us as less "realistic": the addition of sound to the body makes it whole and thus adds to the effect of the real (cf. 177 or 190). And yet the visual is maintained as the primary and even the decisive factor for film audiences and film criticism alike, and voices tend to remain in this way more or less unexamined in cinema.

At some levels, of course, the vocal element of performance is not ignored, even if it goes largely unexamined. Spectators will cathect to voices as, for instance, erotic components of film—though there, just as with most other elements of the erotics of popular culture, the attachment is often to highly conventionalized and heavily presignified kinds of voices: Eastwood's drawl, Kathleen Turner's husky voice, the quasi Englishness of Cary Grant's voice, Judy Holliday's whine. The erotic attachment of the voice will lead scholarship to sometimes consider the voice psychoanalytically, as the vehicle of the invocatory drive. Lacan says that the invocatory drive is the closest to the unconscious—it is the one that has the privilege, he says, of never closing (1978, 200). Heath adds to this that it is because of this powerful imaginary effect of the voice that film attempts to subsume the vocal to the visual, deploying its realistic effect but "keeping check of the voice, pacifying it into film" (190). That is, although the voice apparently provides a capstone to the effect of unity in the performance, there is with the voice the potential for identificatory slippage, since its role and possible effects are multiple. As Mary Ann Doane points out in one of the few available theoretical essays on the voice in cinema (1986), psychoanalysis considers the voice as that which at the pre-Oedipal stage enables the "subject" to separate the elements of its field of perceptual experience—the voice heard will separate and distinguish other bodies. At the same time, the voice, as in that of the mother, can be reassuring or pacifying, or as in the case of the father, can mark the most literal imposition of the law of the father. Equally, the voice is not silence, and as Pascal Bonitzer writes, silence itself can be the empty space of fear, where things go on, where activity occurs out of the control and beyond the reassurance of the "subject" (1986). So voices have, in the psychoanalytical account, powerful resonance and multiple significances beyond their actual enunciation.

At the same time the vocal level is perhaps the most privileged aspect of performance in that it bears an exceptional burden in both diegetic and narrative construction. In terms of the latter, vocal performance usually carries the narrative in crucial ways: it describes and explains simultaneously, and "the film comes to a stop when it runs out of words" (Heath, 121). At the diegetic level, the voice is not only the capstone on the unity-effect of the body, but it must be aligned with the diegetic world in terms of its style and appropriateness. When this appropriateness is lacking or badly executed, we recognize not just a bad performance but equally a problem in the diegetic urge for verisimilitude. This is what is at stake, for instance, when Kevin Costner is criticized for his less-than-perfect British accent in *Prince of Thieves*. It is also what happens in Eastwood's case in *White Hunter, Black Heart* (1990). There, playing a film director based on the Irish-American John Huston, he attempts a range of accents and intonations beyond his capabilities: the result is an obstructive foregrounding of precisely his performance, which fails the diegetic demands of the screenplay. A more successful performance in that sense might be his playing of Sergeant Highway in *Heartbreak Ridge*, where the husky, almost croaking growl that he affects for almost the whole movie (it is dropped somewhat for his conversations with his ex-wife) works effectively as an element in the diegetic construction of military life, dovetailing with the cultural verisimilitudes that describe that life and its ethos.

What is important about the vocal level, then, is that it is the crucial point where a spectator's *visual* identificatory processes—always open to oscillation and change in the course of the narrative and the performance—are as it were diverted or perhaps even covered over by an appeal to the "naturalness" of the performing body's relation to its voice. Viewer identification with character or persona is in this sense stabilized by the consistent performance of the voice. The voice, always carefully controlled in film production from both the technical and the performative aspects, adds to other dimensions of performance a point where the security and certainty—the fiction, finally—of identification can be forged. At the same time, or in addition to this, the voice has the task of guaranteeing the supposed unity of the protagonistic body as it engages in its most central function—that of acting as the commutational point between diegetic and narrative constructions in the film.

It is, of course, nothing new to suggest, as I have been doing, that the production effects and the spectatorial affects of cinema are always bound up with the tension between, on the one hand, the intendment of unity and identification and, on the other hand, the oscillating and fragmentational experience of film. This tension is built into the very physics of the cinematic apparatus as it attempts to bind together its twenty-four frames per second, and is built in, also, to the very nature of narrative as it attempts to produce its unity across the bodies and personae of its actors and characters. The same tension is also, one might say, a condition of the "subject" that is perpetually constructing its imaginary between the law of unicity and the multiplicity of desire. The notion of identification—the precise and imprecise uses to which it is put in both film theory and everyday discussion of cinema—is a crucial one in managing this tension. Discussion of Hollywood cinema in particular has often, in my view, taken identificatory processes and intendments to be in the end largely efficacious, as reaching their goal and pulling the spectator into what can only be called a subjected relation to film texts. In that sense, the notion of cinematic identification (especially in writers like Christian Metz and Jean-Louis Baudry, where the spectator's experience of cinema is finally, I would claim, proposed to be that of a repetition of the processes of subject construction)[2] willy-nilly becomes a kind of shorthand for the dominatory effect of cinema.

Now, I am far from suggesting that Hollywood does not have or does not work for that dominatory effect, nor would I deny that identifications occur in the process of viewing. I have merely wanted to suggest that cinema has more difficulty in enforcing identification than is often implied, and that the fragmented nature of performance as it is taken up in the space between diegetic and narrative constructions is an important place to elaborate on the difficulty.[3] The centrality of the performance of a figure like Eastwood derives from what can be called its commutational function between the diegesis and the narrative, its proferred guarantee of the compatibility of those two constructions or fictions. Even while this commutational role relies upon the success of identificatory intendments and upon the "subject's" being understood as the effect of that success, the performance itself is fragmented, demanding different kinds of identificatory motions on the part of the spectator, and in a sense always destined to a certain failure. It is, then, to the moments of failure in identification that I want to accredit a large part of the experience of cinema.

The Meaning of Black

> *People who cannot escape thinking of themselves as white are poorly equipped, if equipped at all, to consider the meaning of black: people who know so little about themselves can face very little in another: and one dare hope for nothing from friends like these.*
>
> —*James Baldwin*

> *Black is the hardest of all tones to keep real. . . . Black is so difficult to keep on film.*
>
> —*Jack Green*

The first epigraph is taken from James Baldwin's *The Devil Finds Work* (1976, 69), which is a powerful attempt to convey the experience of an African-American man struggling to grasp simultaneously three aspects of his existence as a black in America: the cultural power of the Hollywood entertainment industry in relation to black experience, the structural and chronic pervasiveness of white racism in America, and the possibility of hope for black people. The second epigraph comes from an interview with Jack Green, the cinematographer who worked on Eastwood's film about the jazz saxophonist Charlie Parker, *Bird* (Gentry, 7); Green is talking about the difficulties he experienced in trying to ensure that the color black showed up properly on the celluloid in this film whose characters are mostly black and that contains many interior scenes, especially of dark and smoky clubs.

Baldwin is talking about race while Green is talking about color; thus my juxtaposing of their comments is, of course, just a heuristic device, perhaps even a conceit. But the quotations do perhaps point in a strangely apt way to two different aspects of a serious problem in the movie entertainment industry. Baldwin's quotation points to the problem that the *meaning* of race is something that Hollywood, a mostly and chronically white-owned institution and industry, is not equipped to consider; Green's quotation points up in a stunningly literal way the difficulty for the Hollywood apparatus of *representing* "black." I think it is symptomatic that the white cinematographer discusses the problem as a technical issue, as a matter of the capabilities of film technology to give representation to black, while the black observer is left to complain about the white industry's lack of equipment in the realm of meaning. There is a certain incommensurability between the two ways of posing a problem which it will be the task of this section to contemplate.

There can be few people who would contest the fact that there has been a chronic absence of the representation of blackness in Hollywood pictures over the years. Even in the last two years or so, when several movies made by African-Americans have had high public profiles (*New Jack City*, *Jungle Fever*, *Boyz 'n the Hood*, and *Juice*, for example), the position of African-American films in the culture generally is still one of anomaly, of curiosity, and—to say it this way—of minority. This long absence has, of course, been accompanied or symptomatized by multiple problems of representation; that is, an industry that "cannot escape thinking of [itself] as white [is] poorly equipped" to represent blackness or racial difference at all, and still less well equipped to reflect upon its meaning. The Hollywood acceptation of blackness comes, as might be expected, through the medium of a few token stars and a few token movies. In the history of Hollywood cinema one finds the names of a mere handful of blacks elevated to significant status—Paul Robeson or Sidney Poitier, for example. And even in the 1980s and 1990s, it is similarly a handful of names that synecdochally stand for blackness in mainstream cinema—Eddie Murphy or Spike Lee, for instance. And at the level of individual films, again it is just a few that are taken to bespeak African-American experience—films like *Sounder*, *Guess Who's Coming to Dinner*, or *In the Heat of the Night*.

What Baldwin says in *The Devil* of the depiction of African-Americans in the movie *In the Heat of the Night* is perhaps still apropos in relation to most of the roles African-Americans play and of the movies in which they appear. *In the Heat*, he remarks, "helplessly conveys—without confronting—the anguish of a people trapped in a legend. They cannot live within this legend; neither can they step out of it" (67). The legend he refers to is an obstinately vague thing—or perhaps rather, a multivalent thing—in his prose, but it appears to mark a discursive disjuncture whereby African-Americans are submitted to a cinematic discourse that is not of their own making—one marked as much by its absences as anything else—and that equally appears to not correspond or respond to the experience of *their* existence or their own discourses. The cultural verisimilitudes of African-American existences are split off from, are not represented in, the cinematic verisimilitudes that Hollywood allows.

Thus it is that the cultural verisimilitudes that are built into the narrative shape of a film like *In the Heat* will help forge a particular narrative outcome. This film, in which a white southern sheriff has to cooperate with a black northern FBI agent against the diegetic backdrop of a stereotypically southern racist town, necessarily ends with the constitution of the legend, or the myth, of a reconciliation between black man and white man—the only end that will satisfy the white cultural imaginary or that will be appropriate for the flattering of a white audience's hopes and fears. Baldwin describes that forced outcome in terms of its "obligatory fade-out kiss" (67). Of course, no literal kiss occurs between the white and the black man in this film, but this is Baldwin's way of naming the necessary gesture of reconciliation of this movie and of the Hollywood norms; this is the momentary "device desperately needed among a people [i.e. the white audience] for whom so much had to be made possible" (67).

This structural demand of the narrative is hard to disentangle from the codes of cultural verisimilitude that produce it and that it helps produce. Those codes—even, or perhaps especially, in 1967 when *In the Heat* came out—will not "confront the anguish," cannot permit the *meaning* of racial difference to emerge in this "safe" place that has forever been consecrated to the notion of "just entertainment." Ultimately, that is, even where Hollywood attempts to *represent* black, its products will not be allowed to make any gesture toward the *meaning* of racial difference, which is brazenly dissolved into narrative gestures that offer nothing more than a moralistic and sentimental renunciation of the problem of the meaning of racial difference.

The structural move described here is, of course, not applied by Hollywood only to the issue of race, but in fact it appears to be an overriding or overarching maneuver. It is the same gesture I tried to describe in *Tightrope*; both films—and so many others—can do nothing with their central imaginaries and preoccupations except cut them short and submerge them beneath a specious moral intendment. Such an intendment is impelled from elsewhere, from the ideological nexus that says that men and women, or white men and black men, must resolve their differences into a marriage, into a friendship, into a static peace of some kind. As some image of such a relationship comes to be installed, what is renounced—the meaning of difference itself—comes to be seen as nothing more than a temporary or provisional glitch in the production of a new beginning. Such a glitch or problem can be solved always and only by the moralistic and renunciatory gesture of the white male protagonist.

Of course, this kind of collocation of Hollywood's cinematic verisimilitudes, American cultural verisimilitudes, and this narrative of moral renunciation and renewal could always be thought of as a utopian move, one that speaks hope and that stands as a model for a new life. But, on the other hand or in another view, it is in the nature of the commodity character of Hollywood that such a new beginning of the world should be played over and over again, in another film, in another rehearsal of the problem. The problem, that is, is addressed only by repeating it, as if repeating or reaffirming an error enough times will make it look right. And in that replay, the meaning of the problem will always leave its hysterical marks and install its residue of confusion and resistance. Baldwin is one of those spectators who registers all this and who hints at the importance of the struggle that is inevitably set up there between meaning and representation, between the problem and its narrative resolution—a struggle marked by silences, absences, parapraxes, and small twitches. For him, in relation to *In the Heat*, one part of that struggle is constituted around this kiss that does not actually happen: the relation between or amongst men into which the movie resolves elides or suppresses the homoerotic energy and logic of their narrative. At other levels, what Baldwin's writing struggles with is that, finally, "nothing, alas, has been made possible by this obligatory, fade-out kiss, this preposterous adventure: except that white Americans have been encouraged to continue dreaming, and black Americans have been alerted to the necessity of waking up" (69).

Twenty years after Baldwin published *The Devil*, there are, of course, many senses in which black Americans could still wake up—for example, to the fact and meaning of black homosexuality, which Baldwin so patiently explores in much of his writing. But in terms of film culture we seem to be in the midst of one particular kind of waking up where black Americans are engaging in the process of speaking their own meaning in a variety of texts. This is of course not exactly the first time—there has already been such a wave of black films: the much defamed genre of blaxploitation movies in the seventies. The current wave is different from the first, however. The first wave addressed just the question of black representation, and often quite cynically, in the sense that the blaxploitation movies were conceived as a way of attempting to open up the previously underexploited market of the black audience. In this second wave, however, filmmakers are taking advantage of being able to have more control of their enunciation, and their films are thus more able to address the meaning of black rather than just its representation.

No one would suggest that this new wave is overwhelming in size, even if some of its currents have produced some of the most powerful movies of the last few years. But it is a wave that has been fully mediatized, with one result being the visible and audible increase in public exposure for a number of black male filmmakers (I stress their gender only to underline the continuing underrepresentation of black women in the industry). That increase in public exposure and media attention has not been wholly uncontroversial or entirely laudatory. This may in part be a result of the immediate contradiction involved in such a mainstream industry celebrating black in an era of steadily increasing racism at other levels of social and cultural life. At any rate, the controversies attending this new wave have been numerous—from the audience violence around showings of *Boyz 'n the Hood*, to mainstream media attempts to tar Spike Lee as an anti-Semite, debates within the black community about whose experience is actually being represented, controversies over Oscar nominations, and so on. In that context the particular controversy that I want to start from will probably look quite insignificant, but I begin with it because it involves Eastwood and his film about Charlie Parker, *Bird*, and also because I think it in fact not insignificant insofar as it offers the occasion to consider the meaning of the most acceptable (that is, accepted) forms of racism in this country.

The controversy I refer to is a small exchange between Spike Lee and Clint Eastwood, after the release of *Bird* and while Lee was promoting his own jazz film, *Mo' Better Blues*. Lee suggests that filming the life of Charlie Parker would have been better left to a black filmmaker, and passes other negative commentary on Eastwood's film. Eastwood responds to these comments by suggesting that Lee's promoting his own movie by attacking another is unconscionable, reflecting Lee's lack of confidence in his own product. Then he opines that "my being white and doing a story about black people (or vice versa) has no bearing. Mr. Lee is certainly welcome to do a story on Beethoven, and it might be brilliant" (*People Weekly*, 1 Oct. 1990, 114).[1] This exchange between the two is ultimately a quite unpleasant and racist exchange, of course, although that should not in the least prevent us from reading it as precisely an indication of the narrow range of possibilities of public discussion about race and culture in America, where race is supposed by whites like Eastwood to have no bearing.

Lee's objections seem—like Baldwin's utterances before them—to be directed against the simple empirical fact that white America continues to dream, or that it continues by and large to live in a kind of willful ignorance about the meaning of race in the culture, thinking that representation is a more or less neutral issue and one that in any case can be readily manipulated. That ignorance becomes all the more willful in the Reagan-Bush era, where the kind of response that Eastwood makes becomes something akin to a reflex. That is, such comments depend upon a rhetoric about equality that simply attempts to *will* equality into existence or, better, simply asserts the existence of equality in the face of overwhelming empirical evidence to the contrary. The simple fact is that, however much white America may or may not will it to be the case, Lee would probably not be "welcome" to make a film about Beethoven—"brilliant" or otherwise, it would most likely be subjected to the most demanding cultural interrogation—any more than Louis Farakan could become president or Anita Hill be believed by white senators.

Lee's comments, for their part, are predicated on the fact of, and certainly the desirability of, black "ownership" of African-American culture. That predication or claim is one with which I sympathize, although it is clearly the case that, even before Eastwood's film, Charlie Parker and his work did not "belong" to black culture, in the sense that the audience for his music and for jazz in general has mostly been white men, just as the means of its dissemination have been largely white-owned businesses. This is, indeed, something about the jazz music scene that Lee himself addresses in his film, *Mo' Better Blues*, where the two central jazz musicians, Bleek and Shadow, disagree at a party about the cultural position in which that fact places them.

Lee's attack on Eastwood, then, is itself cut through with an assumption that we could quite readily call a fantasy, or indeed a dream. Like most dreams it does not readily open itself to moral judgment but should perhaps be taken only as the expression of a desire. The statement of that desire is scarcely negligible, of course, and can be seen as a kind of strategic interposition of a black desire between the facts of African-American life and the spurious white assumption and assertion of equality. The strategy is not an unusual one, nor one that has not been effective before in other contexts (for example, the same sort of strategy—then called separatism—was a necessary component to feminist demands in the 1970s and 1980s). Yet the strategic demand will always produce its own dialectical response: Eastwood duly supplies this in making his riposte, which is a perfect amalgam of the assumption that white culture belongs to whites and the expression of a readiness to share that ownership in the service of an equality that thereby already exists simply because the readiness has been expressed.

The liberal assumption that Eastwood replicates here—his claim that, like all of liberal Anglo-Euro-American society, he is ready to "welcome" everyone into his better world of equality—simply elides the power relations that white Northern culture has set up and reproduced, and at the same time has the advantage for him of demonstrating his own magnanimity. It is hard to think of *this* as a dream or a fantasy in the way I have suggested that Lee's assumptions are dreamlike or fantastic. Rather what Eastwood's propositions amount to is what we might call the unauthored racism of liberalism, and what I want to do here now is to trace that through some of the particular features of *Bird* and to suggest, not a complete agreement with Lee's point of view exactly, but rather the conviction that such liberal, unauthored racism is constituted in and by the range of narrative and representational strategies that Eastwood has available to himself as a white person making a film about a black man and about black culture.

It is quite possible that in trying to show the limits of some of those narrative and representational strategies, I myself shall fall prey to them—if I have not already. One of the problems of writing this section of the book has been my puzzlement over the meaning of Baldwin's phrase, "People who cannot escape thinking of themselves as white," and I wonder whether he is suggesting that it is my personal responsibility to stop thinking of myself as white, and what the consequences of that could possibly be in racist America. Alternatively, I wonder whether he is simply affirming that I cannot escape thinking of myself as white because the culture will not allow me to. The important point, perhaps, is to not expect to be able to excuse oneself from the limits of either position, but to try, nonetheless, to see how they might operate and perhaps be altered.

The space that *Bird* provides for contemplating questions of race is obviously defined, first of all, by the particular way in which the film establishes its diegetic and its narrative character (roughly speaking, its representations and its proferred meanings). It is mostly to the second that I want to address myself here, broadly considering the way in which the film is narrativized, and only alluding to the question of its diegetic presence. Thus, I begin by considering what kind of narrative is on offer here. At the same time, it is the case that the diegetic frame of the movie is as much a component as the narrativization in the movie's attempt to meet the specification of particular cultural verisimilitudes, and so my second and third concerns are with the way in which the movie tends toward two specific diegetic signifiers in particular: drugs and jazz. Any Hollywoodian diegetic world, however, is finally to be submitted to the intendments of the narrative—usually through the commutation point that the body of the hero constitutes—so I will lastly look at the function of that body in this film.

Donald Bogle, in his foreword to the so-called companion volume to Lee's *Mo' Better Blues*, notices in the history of Hollywood jazz movies the propensity to treat jazz in the frame of "sad-eyed elegies" (Lee and Jones, 24) where the central protagonist has consistently been presented merely as "brooding victim" (23). This is certainly a tendency for which *Bird* offers ample evidence, of course, as it tracks Parker's path toward a death from drugs and alcohol. This sort of "elegy," however, is not at all confined in Hollywood to dealings with jazz, still less to dealings with the lives of African-Americans. Rather, it takes part in a more generalized kind of structure in which a rebellious and romanticized male protagonist struggles against a social world in which he appears to have only a precarious foothold while he attempts to produce something or some effect that is culturally worthwhile. That something is usually—as in *Bird*—art of some sort or genre, and its production is usually halted by the protagonist's failure to win his battle with the culture that ignores or demeans him.

The central fantasy underlying this kind of narrative template is one that *Bird* attaches to with great tenacity as it works to demonstrate the notion that particular kinds of human achievement, most often art, can transcend the sadness and defeat of the personal struggle. In *Bird* what is supposed to be transcended by this narrative is quite simply Parker's circumstantial relation to the problem of racism in America. This kind of fantasy is, in fact, nicely satirized in another of Lee's movies, *Do the Right Thing*, when one of the Italian-Americans tries to explain to Mookie how people like Prince, Magic Johnson, Eddie Murphy, and other black celebrities are "black, but they're not really black, they're more than black—it's different." This same demeaning logic, more sedately and sophisticatedly articulated, to be sure—also drives *Bird*—a logic entailing that the achievement should be so remarkable in and of itself that the conditions under which it was effected and its subsequent relation to those conditions may be disregarded.

In the case of *Bird* the proposition is that Parker lived and worked in a culture where it has no bearing that he is black, but only that he produced his monumental and revolutionary achievements in music. The historically racist conditions of his production can be alluded to only in the most utterly devolved fashion. Thus, the only moment when the segregated America of Parker's time is directly represented is when his band is touring the South and they confront the problem of passing off Red Rodney, their white trumpet player, as an albino black in clubs where blacks take the dance floor and whites are confined to cramped balconies away from the action. What happens in that section is complex in that it is a reversal of a certain kind: the site of segregation is the black community, which, we are to assume, will not accept a white man into it. The meaning of segregation is thus altered in this representation. This is a rhetorical formation that might be familiar to us today, where, in a sick parody of the term *racism*, African-Americans are increasingly often accused of *reverse* racism. Meanwhile Parker himself passes through the whole film almost as if he were not black. There is one moment in the film, where Parker and his white wife, Chan, are out dancing, when a few short disapproving looks emanate from a group of whites watching them, but this disapproval is brief and silent, and is in any case almost immediately overridden by the musicianly solidarity of the white players in the dance band who have gladly noticed Parker's presence.

Apart from this short moment, which in itself again elides the issue of race by reference to Parker as artist, no other character and no narrative situation directly represents Parker's blackness as having significance until the coroner in the movie's final sequence examines Parker's dead body. The coroner's mention there of Parker's race is put on record as merely an objective fact—one more way of assuring the audience that race "has no bearing."[2]

So *Bird* in fact elides the question of race and the conditions of racism in the name of Parker's production of his art. Furthermore, this narrative tells us that the particular kind of hero that Parker is can be immediately drawn into a specific discourse of Euro-American views of the artist: the traditional romantic narrative of the tortured and tragic artistic genius who prematurely self-destructs. This is, to be sure, a kind of subordinate narrative in Hollywood—that is, a narrative formation that is feasible for Hollywood in that it fits with common codes of verisimilitude, but one infrequently used, perhaps precisely because of its contingency to the tradition of high art. But by and large, when Hollywood wishes to approach the question of art, it is this structure that facilitates the effort.

That romantic ideology is exhibited to a tee in *Bird*, and its meaning is underscored by Eastwood himself when he wonders aloud for the benefit of reporters about the "irony" of how Parker was so disciplined in his music and yet so undisciplined in his personal life (*Variety*, 28 Sept. 1988, 10). The disorder of Parker's life and the drugs that led to his death are seen in this movie not as products of any particular cultural matrix—certainly not connected in any way to racism; rather they are seen precisely as personal problems, simply the product of the strain and tension of genius having to live in the world. So the narrative template of the self-destructive romantic artist here squeezes the meaning of Parker's life into an individualized drama where the social, cultural, and political components of such a drama are elided. The function of such a structure in *Bird* is perhaps more than usually irresponsible in that what is most efficiently elided, what "has no bearing," is the racism and the race relations that cut across the life of the real Charlie Parker. The argument I am proposing here, then, is that the representational elision of racism, or the white assertion of its nonmeaning, must in fact be considered a prime component of racist structures.

This kind of primary elision by no means legislates against the insertion into the film's diegetic world of already existing signifiers of racism. Thus, the diegetic presence of *Bird* is in part constituted by a heavy emphasis on Parker's drug habit. The connection between black masculinity and drugs is, of course, one that has become almost indefeasible by the moment of the release of *Bird* and has been one of the central signifiers around which the Reagan-Bush administrations have waged their war against African-Americans. *Bird* underscores the place of drugs in black culture, confirming in that sense the white view of that culture—and indeed, even giving it a historical dimension. The diegetic presence of drug dependency is established in the first main narrative sequence of the film, where Parker tries to kill himself with iodine, and is stressed in the movie right through to its end, where the doctor attending his death remarks on the premature decadence of Parker's body.

Drugs are narrativized, then, as the instrument of Parker's demise, and as the prime component of his inability to successfully deal with the struggle between his life and his art. The romantic and revolutionary genius that we are to believe Parker to be is at risk in the movie, not from the world of racism or from white ownership and manipulation, but simply from himself and from his "undisciplined" relationship with drugs. Eastwood has claimed that *Bird* is "not meant to be propagandistic towards Bird's drug problems and excesses. It was not meant as a 'just say no message' " (*Variety*, 28 Sept. 1988, 10). The evidence from the film itself, however, suggests otherwise. One might look, for instance, at Dizzy Gillespie's portrayal as a kind of role model in his refusal to use or condone drugs, but one whose rectitude Parker cannot emulate. Equally, the end titles of the film praise Red Rodney for his having led a "drug-free life" after Parker's death; the importance is underscored of the fact that one of the film's major subplots consists in this white man's struggle to remain uncontaminated by the black man's habit. If there is a moral censure of the undisciplined genius already built into the structure of the romantic tragic artist narrative, drugs indeed become the occasion of that censure here.

It is perhaps interesting to compare Eastwood's determined stress on the place of drugs in Parker's world with the absence of drugs from the diegetic world of Spike Lee's jazz movie, *Mo' Better*. Despite the clear cultural expectation that Lee, as a black filmmaker, *should* represent drugs in his movies about African-American life, he has by and large refrained from doing so (the major exception now being, of course, the stunning sequence in the crack house in *Jungle Fever*). One might speculate that Lee's refusal in this respect is a kind of resistance to the fact that the expectations and demands placed on him in this respect, in that they bespeak the cultural assumption about black culture's being defined by its relation to drugs, are racist.[3] At any rate, the comparison between Lee's gesture and Eastwood's at least illuminates the determination with which the issue of drugs appears in Eastwood's film, replicating the white cultural verisimilitudes whereby black culture is defined by its relation to drugs and because of which it is both pitied and condemned. Lee's refusal, on the other hand, to adopt the "sad-eyed elegy" approach in his jazz movie and the absence of drugs from both the diegesis and the narrative produce the upbeat ending to *Mo' Better*, where Bleek's struggle does not end in his demise but with his establishing a family. This ending could be criticized for many reasons, and perhaps not least for its sentimentality, but its gesture, so distant from Eastwood's, can perhaps be seen in the light of another of James Baldwin's utterances: "It was not *we* who were supposed to *die out*: this was, of all notions, the most forbidden, and we learned this from the cradle. Every trial, every beating, every drop of the blood, every tear, were meant to be used by us for a day that was coming—for a day that was certainly coming, absolutely certainly, certainly coming: not for us, perhaps, but for our children" (19). Eastwood's movie, then, simply focuses on the black protagonist's descent and upon the decadence that is tracked through the movie as a matter of indiscipline in relation to drugs. What that focus, that representational decision, makes absent is any examination of the meaning of racial difference itself.

If drugs are diegetically stressed in *Bird*, there is an accompanying absence that also has a significant effect on the movie's intendment in terms of "the race issue." That, strange as it may be to say so, is the absence of Charlie Parker's music. A large part of Eastwood's desire to make *Bird* apparently derived from his long-standing affection for jazz and from his conviction that in the movies "jazz had never been shown as the real, true American art. A jazz movie has never been made by anybody who really liked jazz" (*Esquire*, Oct. 1988, 136). The dissemination of Parker's music, then, becomes one of the central motives for making the film. Yet the music that Parker made, its evolution throughout Parker's career, and its status as the revolutionary art of a genius are never explicated in this movie. That is, the music is not narrativized—except in the one sporadic sense that other musicians are at first shown to be unable to understand his music and later are shown to adulate it. But by and large the genesis and evolution of the music is not tracked, and the extensive use of the music is by and large merely diegetic.

In that sense, Parker's music is absent from *Bird*'s narrative. But it is also absent in a different and more symptomatic way. The musical sound track is equally interesting as an engineering project and as a representation of Parker's music. That is, Parker's original sound has been maintained for the movie only by way of his solos, and these have been extensively remastered. The music of Parker's sidemen has been completely elided in that it has been rerecorded and engineered by contemporary jazz musicians under the supervision of Lennie Niehaus. The process is briefly described in an *Esquire* article by Gary Giddins:

> To build up the sound of [Parker's original] recordings, Eastwood's techs separated the alto from the accompanying instruments, which he wiped off the tracks. He brought in musicians to overdub drums, bass, piano and trumpet, then laid it out in stereo. We brought in Monty Alexander, Ray Brown, John Guerin, Walter Davis, Barry Harris, Ron Carter, and others. Dizzy [Gillespie] wasn't available so we had Jon Faddis play Dizzy's solos, and a pretty good imitation of Howard McGhee too. (Oct. 1988, 142)[4]

The reasons for Eastwood's undertaking this revision of Parker's music are said to be technological. The recordings that Parker has left do not match the wide capabilities of contemporary Hollywood sound technology. In the process of revamping Parker's music, then, a "new and improved" version of Parker's music must be produced, displacing in many respects the music that was supposed to be Eastwood's inspiration for making the film. Parker's own recordings as they have come down to us are not adequate to the technological standards of the industry and must be corrected, to update them and deprive them of their historical resonance. One might be reminded in this context of Adorno's observation, made in his essay on jazz, that "the image of the technical world possesses an ahistorical aspect that enables it to serve as a mythical mirage of eternity" (1987, 125);

the technologically manufactured "image" of Parker's music in this movie draws it closer to the transcendent status of art, while at the same time depriving it of its history and its authenticity. All of this constitutes, of course, another kind of elision and another facet of Hollywood's difficulty in representing the color black.

That the music is treated as primarily a diegetic phenomenon by Eastwood (that is, it is not fully narrativized but simply helps to present the "world" of the film) is perhaps underscored when Peter Watrous reports (*New York Times*, 3 Oct. 1988, C21) on one of Eastwood's reasons for revamping the music. Eastwood apparently "feared that the juxtaposition of the thin sounds of the [original] recordings with Mr. Whitaker's large presence on screen would have been too jarring, risking the visceral excitement of a live performance that he was trying to capture." Now the body of the central protagonist in Hollywood always constitutes a crucial point in the attempt to meld diegetic elements to a narrative and to assimilate thence the diegesis to whatever cultural verisimilitudes are being played to. Forest Whitaker's body in *Bird* is an interesting instance of this principle, particularly in the ways it carries the two diegetic phenomena I have been discussing—drugs and music—into the romantic hero narrative structure.

A major part of Whitaker's performance as Parker is the result of the cinematographic techniques used in relation to his body. Parker/Whitaker's body is a major emphasis of the movie, forming a bulking and looming presence throughout. This effect is achieved, not simply by dint of Whitaker's own size, but equally through the extensive use of backlighting and by the construction of large areas of dark and shadow in the image. The mode of shooting has been described by Green as operating "with the idea that *Bird* was a black and white film that we just happened to be shooting with color stock" (Gentry, 3); thus fill lights are by and large not used in many scenes, and the key lighting is designed to cast shadows, these being left "very hard, well-defined and dark" (5). Against these elaborate shadows, Whitaker's features are often almost indiscernible and his huge body is often left as simply a presence, an indistinct spectacle. The opening sequence in which Parker tries to commit suicide provides a good example of these effects, as does the ending sequence of his death in the apartment of the so-called jazz baroness, Nica de Koenigswater—both scenes attaching the indistinct image of Parker to the idea of his self-destruction. In the former scene, the direction establishes perhaps the most extreme image of Whitaker's body in the whole film: the scene in Parker's and Chan's living room is lit by little more than the concentrated light in two rear windows, against which is silhouetted Whitaker's bulky body (stripped to its underwear and shot from a long angle to emphasize its fat). But the effects are at their most powerful in the film's many scenes of the clubs where Parker plays his music.

Whitaker's body in those club scenes is attached to Parker's music in a form of stasis. In other words, he there becomes simply a diegetic spectacle that functions not only as a halt in the flow of the narrative, but also as a refusal to narrativize the music. But what seems to me more interesting about this presentation of the body is the way its detail, its features and its expressions, become almost indiscernible. This is of course to be expected; a deliberate effort to darken the scene in general and also at the same time to depict the body of a black man within it will inevitably produce a somewhat indistinct image. The technological and ideological difficulty of representing the color black, of keeping it on film, is here exacerbated with much deliberateness.

One aspect of this deliberateness that cannot be overlooked is that many of the techniques used to treat Whitaker's body are the very same ones that have been made familiar in numerous other Eastwood films over the years, but in those movies the body so treated—Eastwood's—is the exact antithesis of Whitaker's. The extensive use of backlighting, for instance, in relation to Eastwood's body has always been used in order to silhouette his lean and muscular frame, to promote his body as an all-powerful shape and presence, his face's sharp features and the steady encratic gaze of his eyes, the almost perfect agelessness of his body and face, his whiteness. In *Bird*, Whitaker is all the bodily things that Eastwood is not and, in our culture, could never be. His silhouette is broad and portly, his face pudgy and ill defined, his eyes either obscured or rendered shifty, his physical being given over to the point of its demise, where a doctor mistakes its thirty-four-year-old frame for that of a sixty-year-old, and he is black. Whereas all those filmic techniques of Eastwood and his cinematographers have always constituted the manufacturing process of Eastwood's significance in the culture, here they have been deployed to diminish and darken a black body, which is shown to be

Backlit Bird: Forest Whitaker

exactly the antithesis of Eastwood's own, and to depict its descent and decadence.[5]

To understand what is happening here with Eastwood's forming of Whitaker's body, it might be informative to refer the process back to a comment Eastwood makes during the promotion of *Bird*. Recounting his enthusiasm for jazz while he was growing up, he says, "I think I was really a black guy in a white body" (*Newsweek*, 31 Oct. 1988, 68). Whatever the particular imaginary that Eastwood is addressing there, it might not be too fanciful to suggest that this film—of which he has said, "I wanted to make this badly [*sic*]" (*Variety*, 28 Sept. 1988, 10)—figures that "black guy" and speaks for him, marking a clear distance between his own white guy's body and the black man inside it, whose appearance means all the things that Eastwood cannot. This formation is strongly reminiscent of what Homi Bhabha says of the colonialist's relation to the body of his subaltern other. The white man both desires to and fears to resemble the black body, and it is this ambivalence that is a primary component of the racist gaze. "Black skin," Bhabha says, "splits under the racist gaze, displaced into signs of bestiality, genitalia, grotesquerie, which reveal the phobic myth of the undifferentiated whole white body" (132-33).

While it would not be true to suggest that such "signs of bestiality, genitalia, and grotesquerie" are quite the products of the gaze in *Bird*,[6] it is clear that the particular kind of representation that I have been tracking through the movie establishes Parker's blackness as a matter of decadence and dissolution, and that those signs bear a significant relation to the way in which Eastwood's own body both represents and signifies whiteness.[7] Indeed, it could be said that, for many years in American culture, Eastwood's body has acted as the very type of the "undifferentiated whole white body," and that *Bird* functions as a privileged moment of its phobic expression.

Auteur-Father

When you get to the end, you don't want to have 'em say, "Well, he did fifteen cop dramas and twenty westerns, and that's it."
—*Clint Eastwood*

There is the beginning of a shift in the shape of Eastwood's public image that roughly coincides with the release of *Pale Rider* in 1985 and *Heartbreak Ridge* in 1986. The first of these two movies constitutes, as I have argued (see "Restitution"), the reconstruction of the western genre after the damage done to it by the first big movies of Eastwood's career, and it is a film that resolves into what is almost the exact type of the western. *Heartbreak*, by the same token, is perfectly consonant with Hollywood's general project of fusing cultural and cinematic verisimilitudes; despite the disagreement between Malpaso and the Department of Defense mentioned earlier (see "Servicemen"), that project remains. With these movies (the first especially), Eastwood begins to receive attention from the tributary media that, in degree, he has not seen since the days of the spaghetti westerns and the "Harry" movies, and that, in kind, he has not seen before at all. That is, the restitutional gesture that *Pale Rider* constitutes seems to have concentrated the attention of the media on Eastwood to an unprecedented degree. The years 1985 and 1986 saw an unusually high number of major spreads on the star in the press: from *Rolling Stone* and the *New York Times Sunday Magazine*, through *Us* and *Newsweek*, to *50 Plus*, Eastwood was feted on a regular basis.

That degree of media attention increased even further during 1986, when he began campaigning for office as mayor of Carmel—an episode I shall look at later. But in relation to Eastwood the filmmaker, it could be surmised that the media were responding to the clear reestablishment of the classic Hollywood parameters in *Pale Rider*, or that they were simply joining *Heartbreak* on the bandwagon of Reagan-era support for military adventurism, so-called patriotism, and so on. Or else the new attention might have been encouraged by the fact that Eastwood, making his first serious attempt to win a prize at the Cannes film festival with *Pale Rider* in 1985, was now self-consciously beginning to take advantage of the higher critical esteem in which his product is held in Europe, and that this gesture provoked the American media to begin to take his work more seriously. Indeed, one of the major articles on Eastwood during these years is entitled, "Clint Eastwood, Seriously," by John Vinocur, and is constructed around his early-1985 promotional tour around Europe (*New York Times Magazine*, 24 Feb. 1985, 16ff); another, in *Newsweek* (22 July 1985, 48ff.) specifically tries to claim him as "an American icon," stressing throughout the ways he and his films embody the so-called traditional American values. But aside from the sheer amount of coverage Eastwood receives at this time, the nature of the attention is also interesting and different. The article by Vinocur in the *New York Times Magazine* marks the change in an exemplary way, making much of the fact of its own gesture; that is, it wonders throughout about this man who has been "treated as a third-rater for so long, respected so late" and who has become "terribly significant, almost overnight."

Actually, the process of installing Eastwood as a major figure in the canon of American filmmakers had begun some time before, although it had never gathered much steam. A few critics and reviewers in the late 1970s and early 1980s had begun to see his work as an important contribution to American cinema. His 1979 collaboration with Siegel, *Escape from Alcatraz*, garnered especial credit from the critics. Vincent Canby, even though he is still undecided about the value of Eastwood's acting ("Is it acting? I don't know, but he's the towering figure in [the film's] landscape"), says that *Alcatraz* contains "more evident skill and knowledge of movie making in any one frame of it than there are in most other American films around at the moment" (*New York Times*, 22 June 1979). But it is also around this time that Eastwood's own directorial work, rather than specifically his acting, begins to be regarded as significant enough, and firmly enough located within the tradition of American film, to allow him some accolades. For example, the introduction of the term *auteur* to describe him comes in 1978 ("Clint Eastwood, Auteur," *Film Com-*

ment, Jan., 24ff.), in the context of an article that takes very seriously his skill and intentions as a director.

These are, as I say, early moments in the establishment of Eastwood as auteur and as a serious figure in film. The confirmation ceremony takes place in the mid-1980s, attended by articles such as one in the *Los Angeles Times* that bears the headline: "Auteurity Figure at the Helm" (18 May 1985). And the process has carried on into the present, its ineluctability marked by the fact that it survives despite the relative lack of success of all the movies Eastwood has made since *Heartbreak*. This critical acceptance, flying in the face of this box-office fate, has become almost entrenched, and the role of respected auteur seems to have stuck. A retrospective of his movies at the Walker Art Center in Minneapolis in 1990 was by no means the first by such a major "highbrow" institution (the National Film Theater in London and the Museum of Modern Art in New York, for instance, had already run such retrospectives in the 1980s). This one featured a symposium led by Eastwood himself, accompanied by a critical account of his career by the film journalist Richard Schickel. That account claims that "he has created one of the most interesting and substantial bodies of work in postwar American film," an accomplishment achieved "incrementally, in an increasingly complex body of work, and inferentially through the honorable and patient conduct of his entire career" (1990). Here Schickel sets out the basic and necessary terms of a description of an auteur (the body of work, its complexity, its substance, and so on), and adds to it some of the optional qualities of an auteur (his honorable and patient—his moral—character).

One of the functions of the notion of the auteur, as it is practiced in both the tributary media and the industry itself, is to guarantee the legitimacy of the Hollywood text and to preserve its tradition. The man who can be given the title of auteur must have spent a certain apprenticeship in the industry before becoming one of its master craftsmen and one of the guardians of its tradition. It is the recognition of this long apprenticeship on Eastwood's part that is the essence of Vinocur's account, cited above, as well as of Schickel's genetic view of Eastwood's progress. Eastwood is seen to have put in enough hard work and to have paid his dues to be considered a craftsman; equally to the point, he has demonstrated his ability to preserve the tradition by defending and replicating it.

There seems to me to be a quite clear relationship between the establishment of this new canonical figure in the last few years and the aesthetic and values of the classic Hollywood era. That aesthetic is, as has been demonstrated frequently, a realist aesthetic that draws many of its values from nineteenth-century literary narratives, but at the same time it stresses the function of the auteur-director as craftsman (perhaps reflecting Hollywood's inability to embrace fully the notion of the artist or to accede to the condition of art, as it champions the artisanal over the "properly" artistic) and as safeguarder of a tradition. It is no accident, at any rate, that the canonization of Eastwood accompanies the process of "restitution" that I described in relation to his westerns (where the integrity of a tradition is upheld and safeguarded against the threat of what we might call the postmodern westerns). Indeed, even as far back as 1979, when his movies are praised it is because they supposedly allow spectators to "rediscover the simple classic pleasures of moviegoing" (*Time*, 2 July 1979, 22-23).

It is preferable, too, as Schickel makes plain, that the auteur should be able to show his credentials as a responsible and decent man, in addition to being the preferred kind of artisan. Just as the narrative verisimilitudes that the auteur is assumed to successfully replicate point movies toward the established state of heterosexual partnership and to the values of home and family, so the auteur himself is produced in the tributary media as one who as nearly as possible embodies those values. Slight concessions and certain rhetorical moves have to be made in Eastwood's case, since his real-life role as husband and father is somewhat compromised. After his long marriage to Maggie Johnson (lasting from 1953 until its informal breakup in the late 1970s), Eastwood lived with his frequent co-star Sondra Locke for a number of years. That relationship ended in 1988. If that pattern is not ideal for the kind of cultural narratives that I am pointing to, it is not especially scandalous, either. And in any case, one crucial part of it can be readily recuperated: Eastwood's role as caring and responsible father.

In other words, the authority of the auteur is increased insofar as he can be seen as a real father, and not just a symbolic one. The burden of forging that construction is taken on by the tributary media. An early instance of that production comes in the emblematically titled article, "A Tough Guy's Tenderest Role" (*Redbook*, Nov. 1983,

82ff.). There, before his breakup with Locke, Eastwood is shown as essentially a family man, despite the irregularity of his family. The journalist visits Eastwood on set to watch him combine his work with caring for both his children, Alison (ten years old at the time) and Kyle (fourteen). The article ends, after portraying him as responsible and loving, by suggesting that "when he's ready to retire and do real-life stuff, maybe someone will send him a script about single fatherhood, the toughest role yet. He's got that one down pat." The same kind of article appears in 1989—*after* the breakup with Locke but saying essentially the same things as the 1983 article about his role as father and building itself around the same rhetorical dichotomy of "tough guy"/tender father ("Not-so-tough Talk from Clint Eastwood," *Ladies' Home Journal*, June, 38ff.). Both articles, that is, portray this responsible family man in contrast to the stereotypical media image of his acting roles. Neither of them openly avows its part in constructing the auteur-as-father image; however, within the general cultural text that Eastwood has become, each contributes to that image at a crucial point. The first one helps prepare the way, as it were, for his canonization as auteur, and the second helps to reconsolidate that image after the much-publicized and quite damaging media coverage of the end of his and Locke's relationship.

What can perhaps be seen as the full achievement of this process, the final signifier in Eastwood's elevation to auteur-father, came in late 1988, when two major institutions chose to memorialize the Eastwood corpus by establishing archival collections to preserve various materials from Eastwood's life and career. The first is at Wesleyan University in Connecticut, which is largely a repository of memorabilia from his career, and the other, at the Museum of Modern Art in New York, is an archive for prints of all his movies. Reacting to the establishment of these collections, Eastwood remarks, "I think the preservation of films the way they were intended to be shown the first time is like any good item, whether a piece of antique furniture or a painting on the wall, you want to preserve it in its original state as much as possible." There, in a sufficiently modest and depersonalized manner, he gives his consent to the importance of preserving his oeuvre. With regard to the artifacts, he is a little more ambivalent: "Special is in the eye of the beholder. Some of the stuff might be more special to an archive than to me. I'm never too much at looking back. I'm always in today and tomorrow." But on the other hand, "There's a poncho that's close to my heart. It sort of started me off. It'll be in there" (*New York Times*, 6 Sept. 1988). Thus, even as he partially refuses to accept the touch of morbidity, the hint of his death, that comes with this memorializing process, he recognizes the value of the retrospection.

Attendant upon this process of canonization, retrospection, and preservation is the possibility of Eastwood's death, the recognition that a career has in some sense passed, or passed on. This is mostly offset, of course, by the general tone of celebration that the process overtly adopts, but this hint of death gives rise to something else. That is, the looking back over a career and the looking forward to its end endows Eastwood with a certain kind of liberty or freedom from constraint in the production of the last part of his oeuvre. That liberty helps in part explain the nature of the movies that have followed the moment of his canonization, and I will talk about those movies a little further on. However, the freedom that might normally accrue to such a newly established auteur-father is compromised to a degree by two major events in Eastwood's offscreen life during the latter part of the 1980s. The first of these is his stint as mayor of Carmel, his hometown in California, and the second is the ending of his relationship with Sondra Locke.

The first of these two events might be thought of as in many ways an extension of, or a kind of logical consequence of, Eastwood's elevation to the figure of grand old father in American cinema, and his being understood as a kind of guardian of the values that attend and are promulgated by the cinematic codes. Or rather, perhaps it can be seen to promise the playing out in the real world of the motifs of one of Eastwood's principal movie roles: the avenging hero who rescues the community from nefarious influences and revitalizes civic courage and solidarity. The role of small-town mayor is perhaps not so glamorous as the avenging hero's role, but Eastwood seems to have entered his campaign and his subsequent term in office with that look about him. He was sworn in for a two-year term on 15 April 1986, after having a few days earlier gained 72 percent of the vote (there were 4,142 registered voters).[1] He is rumored to have spent twenty-four thousand dollars on a telephone poll before declaring his candidacy and displacing the incumbent mayor, Charlotte Townsend. Speculation about Eastwood's reasons for running always include the fact that the previous council had refused to give him planning permission for an office complex near the restaurant of which he is part owner, the Hog's Breath Inn. That refusal appears consistent with the policies of Townsend, who had been a conservationist leader, considering Carmel as a village that should maintain its old character (no neon signs, parking meters, traffic lights, or house numbers) and placing great emphasis on a 1929 council resolution that had specifically subordinated business and commerce to the residential character of the town.

Eastwood's campaign against Townsend was one that was relatively familiar in the Reagan era, based as it was on the claim that government was too oppressive and that a better balance needed to be struck between commercial and other interests. Like much of Reagan's manifesto, Eastwood's was built on the assumption that the prime interests of the community could best be served by readjusting the relation of commercial interests to other interests. Despite making these points in his campaign, Eastwood claimed, "I am not pro-business. I never have been," and instead presented himself as wanting only to end local "bickering and to stop arbitrary and capricious council decisions." In this regard, after his victory Eastwood himself drew the comparison between what he had done in film and what he had stood for in his campaigning: "[Dirty Harry] was always fighting bureaucracy. I guess in real life I've been fighting it too. . . . Now maybe we can get back to simplifying our problems." His first act in office was to revamp the planning commission, and this helped to open the way to rolling back a number of what he called "punitive ordinances" that had inhibited various kinds of development and commercial and touristic expansion in the town.[2] In that sense there does seem to have been some kind of revenge motive at work in Eastwood's tenure as mayor, as well as a definite probusiness stance; certainly, the commercial center that he had been refused permission to build figured as just part of a large number of new buildings and building projects in Carmel by 1989.

On other political issues Eastwood's stance seems to have been quite difficult to identify, with at least one opponent reckoning that he was simply "a mayor without a vision." In one instance, he appeared to not quite know what he was doing: supposedly lobbying on behalf of a county supervisors group against a tax plan of California governor Deukmejian, he nonetheless appeared in the media giving his approval of the same plan. Opponents also charged him with conflict of interest in a case where, according to the *Los Angeles Times*, his "architect applied for a water meter permit for a commercial building site Eastwood owned, only hours before a building moratorium was slapped on the city by the local water board" (10 April 1988, 32). Eastwood denied any impropriety or use of inside information, and in his denial took the opportunity to lash out at his critics—a tendency that appears to have earned him more enemies. In terms of his personal behavior as mayor, Eastwood seems to have been quite authoritarian on some occasions: for example, he reputedly used "his gavel like a gun" in council meetings and was often disdainful and sneering toward his opponents. During his tenure he wrote a regular column, "Mayor's Report," for the local newspaper, the *Carmel Pine Cone*, and, particularly toward the end of his term, used it quite brazenly to condemn and ridicule opponents, including one candidate in the upcoming election to replace him. "He's a vindictive man. You don't want to get on his hit list" appears not to have been an uncommon opinion in Carmel.

But final opinions of Eastwood's performance vary. A group called the Carmel Residents Association, with about five hundred members, was formed specifically to counter him and his policies; although on the other hand and predictably enough, the local Rotary Club honored him with an award for having "substantially contributed to the quality of life in Carmel." The fairest assessment of his administration is perhaps simply to say that it was generally sympathetic to a degree of commercialization in a town that had chronically resisted it, and that his handling of issues was by no means universally approved. He himself presumably reckoned that he had achieved what he set out to do. Having taken civic control for a while, he moved on and did not run for a second term: "I think our greatest contribution was we got things done; we got things moving again," he claimed, and then offered a politician's stereotypical rationale for retirement by saying that he needed to return to his paternal role and spend more time with his children.

His retirement from local politics and his continual refusal of notions that his stint as mayor was a prelude to higher office constituted a certain disappointment for much of the media. Throughout his year as mayor, various suggestions were put forward to say that he either should or would run for higher office in California or for president. He persistently claimed, "My political ambitions start and stop with

Carmel," and so far he has been as good as his word. Yet his one year in office inevitably stirred up the intriguing prospect of some amalgam of his fictional roles coming to life, as it were. Apart from the very minor symptom of "Eastwood for President" T-shirts becoming widely available in 1987, the media often speculated about his political future, sometimes seriously, sometimes humorously. For example, a sidebar to an article in *U.S. News and World Report* considering the Republican candidates for the 1988 elections leaves open the possibility of Eastwood's entering the race, while at the same time keeping a comic distance on the prospect: "The mayor's fans claim he is more macho than Bush, more popular than Kemp, more conservative than Dole, richer than Du Pont, less holy than Robertson, and at 6 foot 4 inches, nearly a foot taller than Baker" (2 Feb. 1987, 26).

I would speculate that a certain degree of media and public disappointment and even continued hopeful expectation attend Eastwood's decision to limit his ambitions to this one stint as mayor. The years of the Reagan presidency and their construction by the media tended to advance many of the propositions that the films of Clint Eastwood are popularly understood to embody. While I have been trying to complexify an understanding of those films, the effort has been all along to show how the hysterical text, as it were, is always brought around to the moment of hypostasization in which the savior-hero disappears, only to reemerge in another time and place to begin the world over again. The hero's hypostasis always has at least two possible figurations: he can disappear into the wilderness, leaving his little son Joey (or his little daughter Megan) crying for his return, or else his body can figuratively disappear into the heterosexual couple and he can become there the domestic patriarch. In either figuration a certain temporary halt is reached and the promise of a return tantalizingly proferred. The real-life Eastwood offers no hope of a real-life return, but instead promises only to stay by the side of his real-life "family" and attend to his proper, now fully prepared role as auteur. But in fact all does not go well for the auteur-father when he attempts to flesh out that double role. The second issue that complicates and even questions his suitability for the role occurs almost on the heels of his retirement from politics: the end of his relationship with Sondra Locke and her "palimony" suit against him.

By all accounts Eastwood's and Locke's relationship began in 1977 during the filming of *Gauntlet*, Locke's second film for Malpaso (the first being *Josey Wales*). A 1978 feature in *People Weekly* (13 Feb.) reported on persistent rumors that their affair had broken up Eastwood's marriage to Maggie Johnson, which had lasted since 1953 (the ending of that marriage reportedly resulted in Eastwood's paying out a $25 million settlement in 1980). Locke and Eastwood lived together from 1979 until the breakup, which resulted in Locke bringing a "palimony" case to proceedings in April 1989. Appropriately enough, the substance of the suit concerned issues of fatherhood and paternity. The most spectacular complaints that Locke apparently made are that she had wanted to have children with him, but that Eastwood had forced her to have two abortions and, subsequently, to undergo a sterilization procedure. Eastwood, for his part, riposted that in fact he desired to have children with Locke and that her claims were fabricated. Eastwood's response to the suit, as it has been reported in the media, does not seem to deny that he ejected her from their home.

To speculate on what is the truth about this relationship is, needless to say, not part of my aim here. Indeed, the "truth" in that sense will always be nothing other than the legal fiction that eventually emerges from the settlement of the case. What is at stake here for me, on the other hand, is the way in which the signifiers of the case are taken up and disseminated in the culture at large, and how meanings—as distinct from facts—are thereby constructed and circulated. In this case, those meanings had a relatively brief moment of circulation. That is, after the initially extensive media coverage of the suit and after a series of tabloid expansions of it, the case seems to have disappeared from our screens. Indeed, as I write in 1992, I have not been able even to confirm whether or not the case has been settled.[3] There is a passing mention of a settlement on the gossip page of the *Houston Chronicle* (12 Jan. 1992, Z6); there the suggestion is that the "suit was quietly settled," but no further details are given. What, on the other hand, seems interesting and apt about the case as it has been reported in both the mainstream and the tabloid press is the way it does damage to the carefully constructed meaning and image of Eastwood as auteur-father that I have been discussing so far. It is not only the immediate details of the case that cause this damage, but the way in which the tabloids in particular have extended the issue into other questions about Eastwood's personal life and the ramifications of this in terms of his gender politics and his persona. That is, while the case itself revolves largely around the issue of the alleged abortions and sterilization and thus around the question of Eastwood's paternal and patriarchal roles, those issues have been amplified exponentially by the tabloids, like the *Star* and the *Globe*.

The issues contested between Eastwood and Locke are appropriately tabulated in a *National Enquirer* article (16 May 1989) on opposing pages (as is habitual—and legally necessary—in such reports, most of the information is given through the mouths of supposed "close friends" of each of the parties). The story on Locke's side is basically that her life with Eastwood had ultimately deprived her of "her chance at motherhood" and that she had wanted both marriage and children, but that Eastwood "enjoyed his independence" too much to marry her. Locke's story, then, constructs her as a woman who had, out of love, chosen to give in to her man's demands, but whose attachment to the ideals of marriage and motherhood—especially in the face of Eastwood's many alleged affairs—finally outweighed her submissive love. On the other side, Eastwood's rebutting story denies that he had forced the abortions and sterilization, affirms that he "loves kids," and then attempts to counterattack by portraying Locke as a gold digger and a liar who, among her other transgressions, remained married to someone else even while Eastwood was supporting her. Both stories thus appeal to very familiar paradigms and verisimilitudes about gender roles in this culture, but most important for my purposes here are the images of Eastwood as baby-killer, as a man unwilling to commit to the full responsibility of wife and family, as a philanderer, and so on.

Even while the more "respectable" press (*People Weekly*, 7 Aug. 1989, for example) corroborated much of the factual detail of Locke's case, the same kind of undermining of Eastwood's newly acquired status as auteur-father continued for quite a while in other tabloid stories, with their aggressive accusations about Eastwood's past. The *National Enquirer* (11 July 1989) produced the claim that he had kept a "secret" family for twenty-five years. In that story Roxanne Tunis, who worked with him as an extra on *Rawhide* in 1959, was reported to have reared Eastwood's "love child," Kimber, for all those years with his financial support. Kimber is now reported to have a son herself, named Clinton. The *Globe* (27 June 1989) tried to offer some reasons for the breakup by reporting that Eastwood dumped Locke in order to begin a relationship with Bernadette Peters, his co-star in *Pink Cadillac*, who implicitly was aligned with Locke in the sense that she supposedly would not entertain a steady relationship with Eastwood "until he clears up this mess with Sondra" and could fully commit himself. And the *Globe* tried to compete with the *Enquirer* stories with its emotive headline: "Clint Eastwood Killed My Grandchildren" (25 July 1989). The accompanying story reported on Locke's mother's anger over the abortions that Locke allegedly underwent at Eastwood's behest. After that the *Star* (27 Feb. 1990) speculated on a relationship between Eastwood and a woman called Jacelyn Allen Reeves, a neighbor of his in Carmel—in the story's headline Eastwood "unveils" this woman. Reeves has two children whom Eastwood purportedly looks after, in addition to giving Reeves four thousand dollars a month. Reeves was reported as being keen to "snare" Eastwood, but was portrayed as better than Locke in the sense that she apparently would not resort to a paternity suit to keep him; instead she simply resolved to keep fit in order to keep up with him and keep him interested.

What is at stake in most of these accounts is, of course, no simple prurient curiosity about Eastwood's "private life," but an obsession—which we can properly call cultural—condensing for a moment around this particular man: an obsession about fatherhood and its responsibilities, and on a more abstruse level, male potency. Eastwood emerges from this series of articles as condemned: he is turned from being previously regarded as a respectable and responsible, traditionally caring father and husband-lover, and becomes instead a man whose sexual adventurism has been habitual and has left in its wake children and financial obligations rather than emotional responsibilities. The role of the various women in all of this is reduced to being part of the band of those who want to "snare" him and pull him into the proper place of responsibility and care.

Some of the damage that all these articles inevitably do to Eastwood's image gets to be recuperated in various ways. For instance, Eastwood won a judgment against the British tabloid newspaper, the *News of the World*, and a printed apology from them after they claimed that he had fathered an illegitimate child in the 1960s (see *Variety*, 16-22 Aug. 1989, 7). Just as important as any legalistic remedy in the attempt to recuperate himself is Eastwood's access to various tributary media platforms that can be exploited to advertise, as it were, his own preferred image. The article I have already mentioned from *Ladies' Home Journal*, "Not-so-tough Talk," is an interesting example of this sort of recuperative gesture, especially in its timing: it is dated June 1989, about the time of Locke's suit, and yet contains Eastwood's insistence that his relationship with Locke is strong, and also asserts as unproblematically as is imaginable his proper paternal conscientiousness.

A later recuperative gesture, published some time after the tabloids went to town on him, is Eastwood's interview with *Elle* magazine in April 1990. The interview is mostly concerned with discussing the "impotent virility" that the interviewer claims is being portrayed in Eastwood's latest project, *White Hunter, Black Heart* (1990), but its last page mentions Eastwood's relation to "feminism." It should be said, first, that the implicit definition of the term is quite vapid here; it seems to refer only to the presence of "strong" women characters in Eastwood's films, and cannot recognize that feminism might have more to say about a mode of representation where those women characters exist simply as a "catalyst for the male role" (126). Nonetheless, in his own terms and that of the interviewer (another man), the discussion of feminism first allows him to claim, "I have always been extremely profeminist," attempting to undo in a single stroke much of the damage that he has recently suffered. Then, in perhaps the most brazen move in the article's attempt to recuperate Eastwood, the question of abortion is brought up and along with it, inevitably enough, the unmentioned question of Locke's charges. Eastwood proposes that feminists are looking at issues much more intelligently than they once did, "the abortion issue especially, because it affects both men and women equally, and because people are saying, 'I'm not going to let any political or religious group take those rights away.' " The interviewer follows up this remark by suggesting, "It's entirely in keeping with Eastwood's personal politics that he should be prochoice—his career is a testament to self-determination." Again, whatever the "truth" about Eastwood's "personal politics," these remarks all have the clear aim of facilitating the rehabilitation of Eastwood the man after doubts about his gender politics have emerged from the debacle with Locke.

What I have been describing here, then, is a particular cultural process that goes toward the construction of what we might call "the meaning of Clint Eastwood" over the course of the last seven or eight years. This quite complex process elaborates on a set of signifiers around issues and questions of paternity and responsibility. As Eastwood becomes auteur-father in the tradition of American film, questions get asked about his ability or inability to correspond to the cultural verisimilitudes of that new role. His life outside of film is put under the microscope—in the first instance this is with his own connivance, to be sure, as he campaigns to become mayor of Carmel; while in the second instance, the breakup with Locke, he has less control over the scrutiny. In the aftermath to the latter of these events, it is his paternity—the question of his commitment to the next generation, if I can say it that way—that comes to be at stake. All this occurs in the same cultural and media sites as the process of canonization, retrospection, and memorializing that I have spoken about. At the same time, too, Eastwood continues to make films, and it is to these that I now turn.

Between 1986's *Heartbreak* and 1990 Eastwood released five movies: *Bird* (1988), *The Dead Pool* (1988), *Pink Cadillac* (1989), *White Hunter, Black Heart* (1990), and *The Rookie* (1990). Three of these five are primarily "commercial" movies—*Dead Pool* is the fifth "Dirty Harry" movie, *Cadillac* is a comedy, and *Rookie* is another cop movie. The other two are instances of Eastwood's producing and directing movies that, sitting between more commercial efforts, are often taken to be his more "serious" and "expressive" works. All five movies are relatively unsuccessful in box-office terms, as I have noted before. *Cadillac*, for instance, "grossed only $4.4 million and could take no better than fifth place [in its first week]. Audience surveys show that even diehard Eastwood fans do not like the movie, and industry sources are calling it the first casualty of the summer" (*New York Times*, 31 May 1989). These relative failures all fall within the time period during which, as I have been suggesting, Eastwood becomes auteur-father. The discrepancy between their fate at the box office and the elevation of Eastwood to auteur-father could perhaps have something to do with the kind of faltering of that new reputation that I have described. At the same time, each of these films marks a relative departure for Eastwood; each in its way attempts to do something that audiences have not seen Eastwood do before as he takes advantage of the liberty with which his new and elevated position endows him.

Dead Pool is the necessary first gesture undertaken under the aegis of that liberty. It is a "Dirty Harry" movie, to be sure, but it is equally obviously a gesture of farewell to those movies. As the TV movie critics Siskel and Ebert note in their broadcast review of the film, it is Dirty Harry's "swan song," by which they appear to mean that the comic and sardonic and almost cynical treatment of what is essentially the same diegetic and narrative structures that have been used in all the "Harry" movies suggests that Eastwood has "finished with Harry." It is indeed the case that Eastwood looks remarkably older in this movie than in the other "Harry" movies, and plays all the old trademarks of those movies without much verve or apparent conviction. The film's only exceptionally inventive sequence can itself be read as a sardonic commentary on the formula of the "Harry" films: that is, the film's obligatory car chase sequence is conducted with a miniature, electronically-guided car, filled with explosives. Like so many others in the film, this sequence turns the relative seriousness of the previous movies into an almost farcical display.

The fundamental gesture of the movie, then, is easy to think of as a disavowal of a certain sort, and such a gesture is in fact built in to one of its central significations. That is, the movie's narrative discourse attempts to provide a critique of the very media to which it is itself essentially one more contribution. The claim or proposition built into the narrative is that media representations and reporting of violence and social problems leads to their exacerbation. The argument seems to be that such media forms are dangerous impediments to the forces of law and order: some render the society more violent, others make it more difficult for the law to do its job of eradicating crime and violence.[4] The movie tries hard—flirting at length with this theme of the decadent effects of the media—but finally it can never grapple with such an issue because, evidently, it is itself part of the problem. The recreational violence of this movie—and indeed that of the other "Harry" movies to which it refers—stands in an uneasy relation to an attempt to critique horror movies, television journalism's prurience and bloodthirstiness, and the general moral ineptitude of the entertainment industry and its tributary media. The incongruity is in fact underlined when Harry cynically kills the movie's psychotic villain with an enormous harpoon gun. He also makes an accompanying verbal joke—"he's hanging around back there"—which contrasts sharply with what might be called the angst or the earnest attempt to purvey the importance of certain moral decisions that end the other "Harry" movies. *Dead Pool* is, thus, in many respects nothing more than a hypocritical censorious act on the part of the father, critiquing the media and acting as a kind of warning to everyone that the world is going to hell. But, like many such paternal pronouncements, its moral seriousness is radically compromised by its participation in the same phenomenon. The articulation of the film's own implication in the same practices with its collapse into self-parody and broad comedy turns that gesture of the father into something relatively meaningless.[5] Indeed, if the film has any great significance, it seems to me to reside in the fact that it marks a certain exhaustion of the Harry character at precisely the moment when Eastwood's elevation and canonization would seem to imply that a different kind of work might be expected of him. It is in that sense that I mean that this film is a necessary gesture, because it clears away (at least for the moment) and takes a distanced perspective upon the career that precedes it. It is, in fact, its own kind of retrospective.

If the paternalistic gesture of *Dead Pool* emerges in its censoriousness toward the media of which it is itself a part, the same trope appears in much more literal ways at other moments in the course of these few years. It appears, in fact, almost unprovoked in certain contexts, as if it were the point of an obsession. For example, the newspaper advertisements for *Cadillac* feature an image of Eastwood's head with sunglasses; each side of the glasses reflects an identical image of his co-star Bernadette Peters with a baby in her arms—a baby who scarcely turns up in the movie itself and certainly plays no part in constructing its discourse. But it is perhaps in and around *The Rookie* that the father-figure comes most prominently and even literally to the fore.

This movie is another cop movie and one whose diegetic world and narrative is so close to the standard "Harry" constructs that it could easily have been a "Harry" movie. However, it is in fact structured principally around one component of those previous movies—the relation of the Eastwood character to his partner. In this case, the narrative does not demand (as it has done in all the "Harry" movies) that the partner—the rookie played by Charlie Sheen—should die before the end of the movie. Instead of that formulaic maneuver, *Rookie* tracks the rookie partner's growing into the job that the older cop is about to vacate. This process of the younger partner's matura-

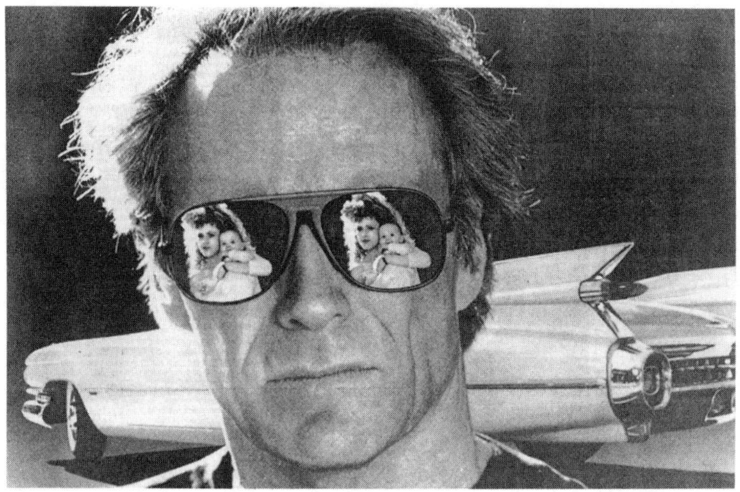

Advertisement for *Pink Cadillac*

tion, his taking over of the role of the father, is pointed up by the film's very title, in that it names the younger partner rather than the older one. Equally, the process is summarized in the opening and closing sequences of the film. In the first, Eastwood's Nick Pulovski, the father in this context, is introduced to his new partner by his superior officer; in the final scene, Pulovski has been hypostasized, promoted to a desk job, so it is now his task to introduce his rookie son, who has now sufficiently grown up, to *his* new partner. The paternal function of Pulovski is clear, but it is interesting to note as well that the paternal function of Eastwood himself is fully implicated into this movie. The cable television company Home Box Office produced a thirty-minute program on the making of *Rookie* and broadcast it in 1991. That program, and the media in general, made much of the fact that the movie's son, Charlie Sheen, was having difficulty disciplining his relationship to drugs and alcohol—until the shooting of this movie, when Eastwood took him in hand and, in effect, repeated the process of inducting the younger man into the proper responsibilities and behaviors of adulthood.[6]

It is easy, as I have hinted, to think of these later years of Eastwood's career as being marked by what is almost akin to an obsession about this issue of paternity and its responsibility. It is true that as a motif the issue has been present in much of his work; one thinks especially of the fictional relation to Mordecai in *High Plains*, or the complicated and ambivalent relation between Block and his two girls in *Tightrope*—and in that movie there is an even more resonant significance in that one of them is played by his real daughter, Alison. But I think the motif becomes more and more apparent—more and more obsessional—at the point where Eastwood is elevated and canonized into auteur-father. It is in that light, certainly, that it is tempting to understand the penultimate film that Eastwood has made, *White Hunter, Black Heart*.

This film is based on a roman à clef by Peter Viertel, who was the screenwriter during John Huston's shooting of *The African Queen* (1951). The novel and Eastwood's film tell the story of an aging film director, John Wilson, who, while engaged to shoot a film in Africa, becomes obsessed with the idea of killing an elephant. The film tracks his obsession and the concomitant abandonment of his responsibilities to the film, its crew, and its producers. The story turns out badly when Wilson's obsession directly leads to the death of his African tracker Kivu (played by Boy Mathias Chuma); confronted with his best opportunity to actually shoot his elephant, Wilson decides not to. Immediately thereafter, the elephant threatens to attack in order to protect its young, and Kivu, trying to distract the elephant from the white hunters, is fatally mauled by it. The movie ends with Wilson returning to make his movie; he has returned to the village and confronted the villagers' message—white hunter, black heart—and realized his responsibility: his responsibility for Kivu's death and his responsibility toward making his film. The last shot of *White Hunter* is of Wilson in the director's chair, forcing himself to mutter the word "Action."

The affective core of *White Hunter* is supposed to be exactly this coming to responsibility of the male obsessed by his need to escape responsibilities. Wilson demonstrates this need to escape in many different ways: his urge to scorn his audience of "eighty-five million popcorn eaters," his penchant to turn against his friends and supporters, his willingness to abandon everything for the hunt, and finally the inability to shoot that directly causes Kivu's death. And yet the actual proof of his finally coming to responsibility is scant in *White Hunter*: all that is proferred is the sense of a man who has been humiliated and shaken by realizing his implication in a death, and the prospect of his returning as an altered man to the work that he does. All of this is perhaps little more than a familiar modernist fantasy about obsessive masculinity, with all its Hemingwayesque overtones. But whatever interest the movie holds is not so much in this modernist fable itself, but in two other aspects of the film: first, that it constitutes a turn on Eastwood's part to a consideration of exactly the figure I have been trying to describe in this section, the auteur-father, and second that this is played out in the context of an African adventure.

Eastwood's turn here, then, is primarily back to Hollywood, to its tradition and its history as they are displayed in the figure of Huston, a grand old master of the sort that Eastwood has been encouraged now to deem himself. That is not to say that the film is autobiographical in any sense, but it does draw upon the established image of Huston as auteur to consolidate that of Eastwood as auteur. In some of the tributary media's discussion of the film, Eastwood makes it clear that, even though he personally does not think of Wilson/Huston's hunting obsession as very "progressive," nonetheless he agrees "with a lot of the things that Wilson says about the need to take risks without bending to the dictates of the public, and about the compromises of the creative artist" (*Le Monde*, 10 May 1990, 89-90; my translation). The movie then encourages an understanding of Eastwood himself, of his own career and persona, as being somehow close to the figure that Wilson/Huston cuts; and it addresses directly some of the issues that arise around the question of the auteur's freedom and his responsibility toward his work and its audience. *White Hunter* thus becomes, if not a meditation upon, then at least an assertion of, Eastwood's own role as "creative artist" and auteur. Of course, the conduct of such a retrospective look, of such a self-reflexive performance, is made available by the liberty that the role of auteur has delivered; thus, the film can be read as a kind of moral fable whereby the new auteur warns himself that he must take on the responsibilities that come with that new freedom.

It is interesting, to say the least, that this drama must be played out across African bodies, shot on the African continent as a way of displacing the drama of responsibility to another scene. It is almost as if the auteur-father can consider the question of his responsibility only in the context in which he does not actually live and which, as we see both literally and figuratively, is effectively too much for him or in which he is out of his depth. But this renders it, of course, a scene where the drama of responsibility can be *played*, precisely; a scene that is proposed as the site of adventure and exoticism where things count differently. In that sense this is a scene of a strange kind of experimental safety in which the auteur-father can learn his lessons, can make his warning gestures to himself, without answering for them except to himself.

Eastwood's career effectively began with the spaghetti westerns and their almost postmodernist gesture of irruption into the fixed generic modes of the western, their setting up of the dramatic irresponsibility of the No Name character, and their introduction of the presence of the Hispanic other into the heart of the American drama. So one might consider that there is something peculiarly apt about the way *White Hunter* (which I am taking as a provisional moment of cessation in Eastwood's career, the last movie he makes before 1992's *Unforgiven*) not only returns to an essentially modernist "art" narrative and replays an intensified drama of masculine responsibility, but also and at the same time projects these onto a diegetic world where the black other is the symptom of a displacement. Kivu becomes the sacrificial figure through which the white male hero, the auteur-father, will remind himself, will warn himself, of his responsibilities: responsibilities that, finally, are to the role itself. The auteur-father makes his movie. He mutters the word "Action" and announces the closure of all the hysterical dramas, all the obsessions, all the self-doubting stories of the patriarch turning in upon himself, and all the narrative tests that he has therefore gone through, and he becomes a director.

Coda

Clint Eastwood's newest movie, a western called *Unforgiven* (1992), broke industry records for an August release when it opened: it took $15 million in its first weekend, and went on to pick up over $55 million on the domestic market in just a month. *Entertainment Weekly* attributed the film's initial success to "a strong trailer," and, indeed, *Unforgiven*'s prepublicity and its reviews were encouraging. Even if many of the press reviews expressed minor criticisms about one or another aspect of the movie, most of them were unexpectedly laudatory. Westerns had been supposed dead; older actors like Eastwood's co-stars Richard Harris, Gene Hackman, and Morgan Freeman were thought to be having difficulty getting good roles; Eastwood himself was apparently "on his way to dignified semiretirement" (28 Aug. 1992, 7); and he had had little box-office success for six years or so. But such negative auguries appear to have been easily transcended.

The press reviews paved the way for the film's opening success. Their general consensus was that *Unforgiven* is an unusual, "revisionist" western that reworks the traditional significations of the genre and, indeed, Eastwood's own work in westerns (it bears comparison in many respects to *High Plains Drifter* particularly). But the most signal claims made by the reviewers for this film suggest that it is a complex and meaningful work whose artistic qualities tend to transcend its generic condition: the proposition is that *Unforgiven* constitutes a profound character study that carefully examines the moral issues of conscience and guilt in the context of the bloody ethos of the gunfighter or of the West in general. Perhaps the most convinced reviewer in this vein is Peter Travers in *Rolling Stone*, who concludes that this is the "most provocative western of Eastwood's career. . . . Eastwood gives *Unforgiven* a tragic stature that puts his own filmmaking past in critical and moral perspective. In three decades of climbing into the saddle, Eastwood has never ridden so tall" (20 Aug. 1992, 55-57). Other reviewers agree that the film exhibits these dimensions of moral investigation and critical self-reflexiveness—dimensions that, in the understanding of the tributary media, can elevate a film beyond mere generic status to the status of art. The film's print advertisements in fact quote Rex Reed from the *New York Observer*, who apparently feels that *Unforgiven* is "a profound work of art." Even in the *New Yorker*, the magazine that has so often been the launching pad for Pauline Kael's relentless assaults on Eastwood, the word is positive. The reviewer on this occasion, Michael Sragow, particularly admires the complexity of the characters and praises the performances of the male stars, and "this time Eastwood even does a good job directing Eastwood." The review ends by noticing that *Unforgiven* is dedicated to Eastwood's directorial mentors, Siegel and Leone, and suggests that Eastwood has honored them "by going his own way" (10 Aug. 1992, 70-71).

The reviews, then, offer the sense that the movie goes beyond the ordinary western, that its complexity and profundity endow it with the status of art, and that it is a fitting culmination if not of Eastwood's career then at least of his work in westerns. Eastwood himself endorses such a view when he proclaims that "I'm not sure this will be my last western, but if it is, it'll be the perfect one" (*New York Times*, 6 Aug. 1992, B3).[1] All these high opinions of the movie are interesting in that they help garner audiences, but they also help provide an apposite coda to the narrative that I have been sketching out in this book. The elevation of Eastwood to auteur-father had been predicated upon his ability to sustain and regulate the traditions of Hollywood and upon his becoming their artisanal guardian. With this new movie his status is enhanced even more on the grounds that he himself has gone further by adding an original contribution to American cinema; he has at the same time surpassed his mentors by following a new direction; and he has shown himself worthy of being considered as an artist rather than simply as a solid journeyman, functionary, or serviceman.

As I have suggested before, the achievement of such status would demand at minimum the connivance of the reviewers, but in this case the elevation is significantly aided by another kind of publicity that the film receives. That is, in late July 1992 ABC television broadcast a thirty-minute documentary entitled "Eastwood & Co.: Making *Unforgiven*."[2] The producer, writer, and director of this piece of work is none other than Richard Schickel, who has already, as we have seen, proposed himself as the mouthpiece for Eastwood's greatness—a veritable Ruskin to Eastwood's Turner. Schickel's documentary touches on many of the aspects of Eastwood's work that I have looked at in this book. There is particular stress on the intimate way that Eastwood and his crew of Malpaso veterans worked together on location. *Unforgiven* was shot entirely on location in Alberta, Canada, and in the space of only fifty-two days, following the familiar speedy pattern of Malpaso films. Schickel's commentary makes much of the "almost instinctive" communication between director and the large number of his crew who have worked with him on many previous movies; the implication is that this "small-business" way of working and the "family" atmosphere it encourages are exemplary for their efficiency and for fostering a productive atmosphere among Eastwood's men. There appear to be no women in positions of responsibility on this production—certainly the documentary interviews only men and ignores the film's several actresses—and the male ethos is alluded to by Eastwood himself when, commenting on his directorial role, he says that his crew is "a platoon and [I'm] the platoon leader." There is perhaps a certain irony in the documentary's lauding of these happy labor relations between director and veteran Malpaso crew since *Unforgiven* is Eastwood's first film for many years that is not actually produced by Malpaso. This is because the company is not party to Canadian labor and union agreements, whereas the credited producer, Warner Brothers, is.

The documentary also underscores the efficacy of Eastwood's directing of his actors. The overt claim here is that his natural empathy with actors enables him to direct them more efficiently and sympathetically; a more silent assumption is that Eastwood's own acting ranks with those of his co-stars, Richard Harris, Gene Hackman, and Morgan Freeman. Plaudits from these men for Eastwood's directing effectively foreclose upon any residual questions about the quality of his own acting abilities. Showing the director at work and foregrounding his apparently unique abilities are, however, only part of the documentary's aim. Much is made also of Eastwood's meticulous adherence to the ideologies of realism and "authenticity" that guide the aesthetics of the Hollywood tradition. And the documentary also casts a glance back across Eastwood's career to show its shape and consistency—even managing to spot a speck of originality in an early bit-part he played for a TV episode of *Maverick*. But most important, the documentary goes out of its way to advertise the very same characteristics in the film that the critics and reviewers in their turn talk about. That is, it makes identical claims for the seriousness and the moral reflexiveness—the "purpose," in Hackman's word—that are to become the film's selling points.

In the film Eastwood plays William Munny, an old and retired gunman who was once reputed for his exceptional ruthlessness but who has been reformed by his now-dead wife and devotes himself to bringing up his two children on his isolated and impoverished pig farm. Munny is tempted out of retirement by the lure of a bounty offered by prostitutes in Big Whiskey who want retribution for the mutilation of one of their number. Munny and two companions, Ned Logan (Morgan Freeman) and the Schofield Kid (Jaimz Woolvet), set out for the bounty and thus to test the iron rule of the town's sheriff (Gene Hackman). Having being badly beaten by the sheriff as a warning to give up the bounty hunting, Munny nonetheless kills—mercilessly, though quite inefficiently—the first of the two bounty targets after Logan has been unable to bring himself to do it. The second victim is shot point-blank while relieving himself in an outhouse; this time the killer is the Kid, who, after displaying excessive bravado and bloodthirstiness before the fact, promptly feels the horror of his act and forgoes his share of the bounty. The movie's climax consists in Munny's hunting down and murdering the sheriff who has captured, tortured, and executed Logan, despite the fact that he had played no part in the killings.[3]

The claims for the complexity and ambiguity of the film are a little difficult to fathom. That is, if there were any particular ambiguity here it might concern, first, the motivation of Munny as he decides to take up his old profession again, and second, the determination of his bloodthirsty murder of the sheriff. But the first of these is rather simplistically explained by the film: Munny takes on the job in order to get money and remove himself and his children from their miserable circumstances; the role of serviceman subvents the role of father in a quite familiar way. The second is so structured into the regular codes of the western that it almost needs no explanation: Munny's friend has to be avenged. In these ways the movie is quite straightforward and even familiar.

As to the question of the complexity of the characters' conscience and the investigation of the consequences of violence—both of which are issues that the reviews and the Schickel documentary alike claim to be central to the movie's power—the scenario in fact provides Munny with very little opportunity to reflect upon such sentiments and consequences. Rather, he simply exhibits, first, a sententious devotion to his dead wife's principles, and subsequently, the cold-bloodedness of a murderer and avenger. The film's discourse does not even attempt to explain the gap between these; all that intervenes between the two is a period of feverish visions, brought on by Munny's beating at the hands of the sheriff, when he hallucinates the faces of people he has killed and experiences his own fear of death. The only real display of conscience in the movie is when the Schofield Kid reactively (rather than reflectively) feels the horror of having killed a man. Munny's only response to the Kid's discomfiture is to utter banalities: "It's a terrible thing to kill a man. You take away everything he's got ... and everything he's ever going to have." Munny himself finally does not show any conscience, or any signs of being tormented, as he cold-bloodedly finishes off the sheriff. While it might be true—as Schickel's commentary points out—that the film's murders and violence are "never random" within the logic of the narrative, it is difficult to support the claim that this film, which finishes with the sheriff's murder, investigates the "consequential nature of murder."

Indeed, like *Dead Pool* before it, *Unforgiven* suffers from being unable to criticize convincingly the very violence that it itself is involved in and that it does not shrink from re-representing. This inability also compromises one of the other strands of this supposedly thoughtful film. That is, through the character of Beauchamp, a writer of penny dreadfuls about the West (played by Saul Rubinek), the film's first part provides a critique of the mythologizing of the West and its fabled gunmen. This demystification is actually enacted in the encounter between the sheriff and another bounty hunter, English Bob (Richard Harris), when the sheriff rudely dismantles the latter's claims to fame for Beauchamp's benefit. The sheriff offers a supposedly "truthful" version of the West: its cowardly and vicious protagonists, its guns that don't work, its drunken and inept gunfights, and the like. In other words, the sheriff stands for a correction of the representations of the West that Beauchamp peddles. Rather than read *Unforgiven* as some of the critics do when they claim that this "revisionism" indicates that the film is joining with Beauchamp's and the sheriff's demythologizing attempt, one might just as easily understand it in a quite opposite way. That is, the film's discourse in this regard demonstrates that, whatever kinds of revisionism are attempted (even if "truthful"), the mystified, mythological (and vicious) "spirit of the West" always returns. In other words, *Unforgiven* depicts the fiction returning in overpowering form to literally blow away the demythologizing truthfulness of the sheriff.

However difficult it might be to credit the kinds of claims the tributary media make for this film, it is nonetheless the case that only a few reviewers were unwilling to subvent them. One exception was the review in *Entertainment Weekly* where the prevailing view of the film's profundity is contradicted with the observation and complaint that "we're supposed to look at Clint, doing the same cold-blooded shoot-'em-up number he has done for 20 years, and think . . . ah, moral ambiguity! A tragic figure! . . . Not quite" (14 Aug. 1992, 39). However, this kind of reading looks as if it might remain a minority view so long as respected critics like Vincent Canby will propose that this is Eastwood's "richest, most satisfying performance since the underrated, politically lunatic *Heartbreak Ridge*. There's no one like him" (*New York Times*, 7 Aug. 1992, B1). Canby's review was preceded the day before by a half-page feature on Eastwood that suggests that *Unforgiven* "may emerge as the most significant [film] of his career." Significantly, in my view, this article reports that the film's producer, Warner Brothers, "is saying the film has the potential for Academy Awards" (6 Aug. 1992, B3). An Oscar would, of course, constitute the perfect capstone to the career whose narrative I have sketched out in this book, and it would represent the desired recognition of the prophet in his own land, a quarter century after his Italian interventions. On Jay Leno's late-night TV talk show just after the opening of *Unforgiven*, the host was fulsome in his praise of the film and predicted that it would indeed earn Eastwood an Oscar; his guest's only reaction was a broad grin.

Notes

SUBALTERN SPAGHETTI

1. Not much has been written about Eastwood and his *Rawhide* days (but see chapter 4 of Brauer's book on TV westerns [1975] for some comments on *Rawhide*), nor anything that I can discover about his admittedly rather forgettable early movies. My choice here has been to start with the moment when Eastwood's international reputation in film begins.

2. Frayling critiques some of the contemporaneous criticism of the spaghettis under the heading "The 'cultural roots' controversy." That is, the critical claims about inauthenticity revolve, in his reading, around a sense that the true Americanness of the western and its roots in the frontier tradition of American thought and action is finally unavailable to the spaghetti filmmakers because they are not themselves Americans.

The critical fortune of the spaghettis has somewhat improved since their release in the late 1960s—perhaps as a result both of their clear popularity with American audiences and of Clint Eastwood's subsequent success. And yet their reputation remains somewhat dubious in scholarly circles, in much the same way as various other forms of colonial, third world, and ethnic cultural products never quite escape a condescending critical view from the North: thus even Frayling, a committed champion of spaghettis, at one point throws up his hands in disbelief at what he sees as their determination to become more bizarre with every production.

3. Asked about one aspect of his films in particular—the dirty and unkempt appearance of his lead characters—Leone says, "I have consulted historical documents and can assure you that they were a lot dirtier in reality. . . . Historically, my vision is the more correct" (Simsolo 1973, 31).

4. For an account of this, see Bordwell, Staiger, and Thompson (1985), especially parts 5 and 7 by Staiger.

5. For a typical account of the "New Hollywood," see Jacobs (1977).

6. For useful information and readings on *caudillaje* in relation to film and literature, see Sullivan (1990).

7. It perhaps should not be necessary in the 1990s to recall that the unfortunately ubiquitous use of the word *Indians* to refer to Native Americans is racist. However, I use the word here to refer to Hollywood representations of Native American people and peoples. Berkhofer has effectively elaborated the history of how the term *Indians*

has been deployed ideologically "to stereotype the manifold lives of Native Americans" (1978, 196).

GENRE

1. Perhaps the most influential exponents of myth criticism and the western have been Warshow (1962) and Cawelti (no date). The latter proposes that westerns can be defined primarily by their representation of an "epic moment" of American history, and along with Warshow, tackles the western by defining its formulaic features—such as Warshow's idea that a real western will represent a hero who recognizes that his "code" can be maintained only through violence. Homans (1962) basically follows such critics and provides a clear example of their interventions when he defines myth as follows: "By myth I mean three things. First of all, it is a story whose basic patterns of character, plot and detail are repeated again and again, and can be so recognized. Secondly the story embodies and sets forth certain meanings about what is good and bad, right and wrong. . . . And thirdly, some of these meanings are veiled by the story, so that one can affirm them without overtly acknowledging them" (87).

2. One of the most blatant examples of this kind of criticism must be Toll's chapter on the significance of westerns (1982). This kind of formulation—that westerns reflect particular moments and conditions in U.S. capitalism—is used with limited success by Wright (1975) in his attempt to meld a structuralist methodology with a Marxist approach. Wright also uses the notion of myth in a more than usually sophisticated way, suggesting that myths are signifying constructs that a society "needs" as a way of communicating with itself (this might mean: as a way of transmitting ideological messages that will explain and legitimate particular social structures through the realm of fiction). For him myths "correspond" to or "relate" to structural formations of twentieth-century capitalism; for instance, he sees the classic western plot, as embodied in *Shane* or *Dodge City*, as reflections of an ideal bourgeois society (153). The main problem, for me, with Wright's book on westerns is not so much the reflection theory implicit in it, but its dependence upon a fixed and even essentialist notion of what the genre actually is: there are "standard images that define the Western myth" (14), and many movies that might be received as Westerns are for him mere distortions of an overarching western essence (see 13). The logic of reflection theory would seem to legislate against such an essence.

3. Reagan presents himself as "riding into the sunset" after his successfully and single-handedly rallying the community (America) against the "bad guys" (variously the Soviets, the Sandinistas, Colonel Qaddafi, etc.). See the *New York Times*, 7 Nov. 1988, A1, for a simperingly complicit rendering of Reagan's elaborately staged campaign tour.

4. The nature and consequences of the exercise of such "professional values" and codes is interestingly taken up in relation to television in Alvarado and Tulloch (1983): "Every performance text is marked by a potential heterogeneity of 'meanings' (attached to its various codes) which it is the task of the dominant member of the production team to make coherent by mobilising 'professional' values" (250). An emphasis on such "professional values" is, of course, consonant with my sense that the text produces intendments.

5. Bennett and Woolacott's definition of this potentially useful term is somewhat unhelpful; according to them reading formations are "those specific determinations which bear in upon, mould and configure the relations between texts and readers in determinant conditions of reading. It refers, specifically, to the intertextual relations

which prevail in a particular context, thereby activating a given body of texts by ordering the relations between them in a specific way such that their reading is always-already cued in specific directions that are not given by those 'texts themselves' as entities separable from such relations" (1987, 64). The clumsy prose is obfuscatory, but the passage might nonetheless be salvaged and amended by suggesting that it is not only or necessarily a given body of *texts* that is activated in and by a given intertextual setup, but also (or even, rather) a set of *discourses* and *imaginary relations*. This latter addition helps to provide a necessary subjective element to Bennett and Woolacott's sense of the production of meaning, and the former emphasizes that meanings are not produced only in the structures of some pregiven and delimited set of texts, but rather are engaged and taken up in a variety of discourses that do not all necessarily belong to the particular (e.g., cinematic) institution under discussion.

RESTITUTION

1. Both reviews are quoted from *Film Facts* 11, no. 20 (1968): 325.

2. Among the westerns Sturges had directed are *Gunfight at the OK Corral* (1957), *The Law and Jake Wade* (1958), *The Last Train from Gun Hill* (1958), *The Magnificent Seven* (1960), and *Hour of the Gun* (1967).

3. For some accounts of Native American struggles in these years, see Matthiessen's work in *Indian Country* (1984) and his listing of source materials in *In the Spirit of Crazy Horse* (1983).

4. A good instance of the evolutionary notion of genre is Schatz (1981).

5. There have been, of course exceptions, from *Broken Arrow* (1950) to *Dances with Wolves* (1991), even perhaps including Eastwood's *Outlaw Josey Wales*. But few such exceptions escape the trap of representing Native Americans by deploying the concept of the noble savage, which, as a representation, is perhaps as damaging as no representation at all (see Drinnon 1980).

6. "*High Plains Drifter* is an incontestably narcissistic film, right on the edge of megalomania" (Guérif, 1986, 95).

7. At the same time as it presents this vision of harmonious community, the film might not readily escape the political appurtenance of its origins. That is, as Mellen reports, the novel on which the movie is based, ostensibly by Forrest Carter, was in fact written by one Asa Carter. Carter was a speechwriter for George Wallace and "the very person who drafted Wallace's inaugural speech in 1963 in which he uttered 'Segregation now! Segregation tomorrow! Segregation forever!' " Mellen mentions this and other details about Carter to point up the movie's pro-Confederacy "nostalgia for the racist, feudal past" (1977, 301), which is certainly an element in the diegesis.

Also, to problematize the movie's vision further, we might recall that in one supposedly comic moment Wales falls asleep while Lone Watie catalogs for him the historic wrongs that have been done to Native Americans. A more profound indication might not be found of the way that the white American subject generally becomes bored by "politics"; politics is always the concern of other people.

8. During the 1980s there were continual indications in the trade press and in interviews with Eastwood that he wanted to make another western before he retired. As I completed the writing of this book, Eastwood released *Unforgiven*, a western in which he stars with Gene Hackman and Morgan Freeman. For a brief account of this film and its relation to the arguments I am making, see the final section of the book, "Coda."

9. *Pale Rider* grossed over $9 million in its first weekend (*USA Today*, 2 July 1985) and had done more than three times that amount of business after three weeks. By January 1988 it had become, in the North American market, the highest grossing of all the westerns with which Eastwood has been associated before *Unforgiven*.

10. Perhaps the least savory of these is *The Cowboys* (1971), as I have already mentioned. The extremist right-wing politics that guide that movie turn to the certain kind of bitter and morbid self-consciousness of 1976's *The Shootist*, via the reckless violence of *Rooster Cogburn* in 1975. A strident annoyance emanates from Wayne and his movies in his final years, and it can perhaps best be understood as a symptom, not only of the cancer that finally killed him, but also of his inability to turn the western back to its proper paths. It is in this regard that Eastwood becomes Wayne's proper "heir" (a significance that the tributary media have often assigned to him), completing the job of restitution that the father could not manage.

11. See my earlier remarks in "Genre"; also, Rogin's book *Ronald Reagan, the Movie* entertainingly examines Reagan's discourse as it is related to his own movie career and sense of himself (1987).

12. See the report in *New York Times*, 10 April 1987, A18. Secretary of the Interior, Donald P. Hodel, had recruited Charles Bronson, Lou Gosset, and Clint Eastwood for a series of television spots in the department's "Take Pride in America" campaign. These stereotyped "tough guys" are mobilized against vandals and thoughtless users of public lands and parks. Eastwood glares at the camera and snarls, "These people who are abusing our public lands can either clean up their act or get out of town." The report quotes a Department of the Interior source: "The macho image these spokesmen project is intended to put a negative social stigma on those who might abuse public lands."

AT THE SMITHSONIAN

1. There are many such histories, but perhaps still the most stunning and depressing exposure of the racism inherent in white America's perennial empire building—from early colonization to Vietnam—is Drinnon's *Facing West* (1980). The information and argument in that book, along with Todorov's very different approach and emphasis in *The Conquest of America* (1984), are all the more relevant in the wake of the 1992 celebrations in the United States of Columbus's arrival in America.

2. See *New York Times*, 26 May 1991, sec. 2, 1; *Manchester Guardian Weekly*, 30 June 1991, 25; and a widely syndicated column by Alexander Cockburn. I have used quotations made from other sources in these three accounts.

HOMESTEADERS

1. The figure $87 million is given in "Ruling Stars," *Stills*, June/July 1985. This must be a worldwide figure, since the domestic rental figure is given by *Variety* in 1988 as $51.9 million.

2. *Firefox*'s domestic returns by 1988 are reported in *Variety*'s list as $25 million.

3. See Zmijewsky and Pfeiffer, for instance, where an account is given of the five-month shooting schedule in a tiny mountain town in Oregon, incessantly delayed by the fact that "everything and everyone had to be flown in by plane or helicopter at great expense," and so on (1988, 96-97).

4. Bach reports that United Artists executive Danny Rissner told him that "there had been some unpleasantness between Eastwood and UA over the company's handling of [*Thunderbolt*], and the actor had sworn he would never work for UA again" (1986, 83).

5. *Breezy*'s lack of success was measured by *Variety* (24 May 1979, 4) by its thirty-three-day first run in New York, where it earned only $16,099, set against the $37,899 Universal had spent promoting it in that market. Universal later made efforts to revive the film in "four walls" showings with scarcely more success. *Variety* suggests this was done to try to answer Eastwood's complaints. Since then, the film has all but disappeared.

6. This quotation and the next, as well as much of the information in the following paragraphs, come from *Stills*, June/July 1985.

7. Eastwood has commented upon the replacement of Kaufman as director and writer of *Josey Wales* in an interview with David Thomson, *Film Comment* 5/6 (1984): 69.

8. True enough, they do not, or rather cannot, check Eastwood's accounts because the company is private and refuses to divulge financial information. My phone inquiries to Malpaso's publicity offices in 1991 and 1992 provoked a certain degree of hostility and a refusal to supply any financial information or more than the most meager details of Malpaso's current setup or ownership.

9. Gomery's figure of $4.2 billion for Hollywood revenues appears to relate to 1988 (1989, 94).

MISOGYNY

1. These are, notably, Clarens (1980), Kaminsky (1974b), Kass (1975), and Lovell (1975).

2. It is perhaps worth noting that when other directors have done this in the "classical" Hollywood period (directors like Alfred Hitchcock and John Huston), their motive was primarily to avoid the mangling of their films in postproduction by the studios. With Eastwood and Malpaso, that aesthetic concern has been allied with an economic motive.

3. Albert Maltz won Academy Awards for documentary films in the 1940s and wrote the screenplay for Jules Dassin's *The Naked City* (1948). He was blacklisted for refusing to testify about his links to Communism and did not work in Hollywood until 1970. With Irene Kamp, he also wrote the screenplay to *The Beguiled* under the pseudonym John B. Sherry.

4. *Variety*'s 1988 list demands domestic returns of at least $4 million to the distributors.

JUST ENTERTAINMENT

1. See Tulloch (1990) for an account and critique of the "uses and gratifications" approach.

2. See Modleski (1991, 35-45), for an examination of the assumptions that inform some feminist uses of "ethnographic" criticism.

3. Kael is quoted in Kass (1975, 147), along with other detractors of the film's politics, like Garrett Epps in the *Harvard Crimson* talking of the "fascist propaganda and sado-masochistic wet dreams."

4. See, for example, Brown (1975). Brown particularly stresses the peculiarly American nature of vigilantism, tracing it from early colonial times right through to Lyndon Johnson's foreign policy as it was affected by his propinquity to a heritage of Texan vigilantism. Or, for a version of vigilantism that attempts to idealize it as a mode of seeking political and social change, see Culberson's execrably written *Vigilantism*

(1990). Locke's dicta rationalizing private violence are in *Two Treatises on Government.*

5. For provocative readings of those psychological structures see particularly Reich (1946) and Theweleit (1987).

6. Given the cultural importance of the idea of the author, it might appear reasonable that filmwriters should also be asked to take a role in defining the intention of movies. That they are not—or very rarely are—is perhaps explained by the processes of production. Siegel himself, when asked to comment on this elision of writers, says as much: "Well, let's take *Dirty Harry* as an example; by the time I came on the picture there had already been seven screenplays done, each changed because a different director came on the project, or someone, an executive or star, didn't like the version. By the time I came on it, it was hard to tell who had contributed what. Then Dean Riesner worked with me on a script for Clint, making great use of the original screenplay by Harry Julian Fink. So, the credit for the picture's writing went to Dean Riesner and Harry Julian Fink" (quoted in Kaminsky 1974b, 293-94). In fact the screenplay credits were made to Riesner, Fink, and Fink's wife, Rita, and an additional story credit given to both Finks.

7. I have drawn the quotations from Eastwood that I am using in this section from Kaminsky (1974a), but they originally appeared in several different places, notably in a *Playboy* interview (Feb. 1974) and a British Broadcasting Corporation show in 1977.

THE OPPOSITE OF FASCISM

1. See Simsolo (1990): "Nous sommes dans le réalisme, le tangible, l'idéologie nette et explicatif sans équivoque" (73).

2. One part of Milius's self-presentation can be found in a *Playboy* interview (Feb. 1974, 79ff.) attendant upon the release of *Dillinger*. Clarens is inclined to think that Milius's politics were in fact little more than posturing: "too calculated to convince any but the most dedicated flower-child and too outrageous to alarm any but the most liberal film critic" (307). One might, on the other hand, be skeptical that Milius could be so consistently insincere over the years.

PAULINE'S KNEE, HARRY'S WAR

1. I take the term most directly from Rabinowitz's excellent book on three women filmmakers (1990).

2. Further evidence is provided in the spectacle of Eastwood, in the last half dozen years or so, responding to various critical promotions by appearing to take himself seriously as an "auteur" and assiduously courting the critical establishment (especially the French), perhaps in search of a Palme d'or from Cannes or an Oscar from Hollywood. See my later section, "Auteur-Father."

3. See particularly John Vinocur, "Clint Eastwood, Seriously," *New York Times Magazine*, 24 Feb. 1985. While Vinocur's article does not make the right-wing case for Eastwood so brazenly as Grenier's, it does have its kinship with Grenier's positions, and it also contains perhaps the most unconscionable and craven answer to the question, "Is Dirty Harry fascist?" that I have yet seen: "Ask the black audience," says Vinocur.

4. Grenier's account of Eastwood's life appears to be drawn from the much less tendentious account in Zmijewsky and Pfeiffer (1988; first printed in 1982).

5. For information on Gritz's adventures into Laos in 1982 to rescue supposed American MIAs see *Newsweek*, 14 Feb. 1983, 30, and *People Weekly*, 28 Mar. 1983, 102. The latter article claims that "Gritz secured five-figure donations from actors William

Shatner and Clint Eastwood. Gritz explains that while Eastwood's contribution was simply a donation, Shatner purchased the film rights to some of his earlier war adventures." Gritz retired from the Special Forces in 1979, after twenty-two years in the services, and has over sixty decorations. It was never clear whether the operations in Laos had the backing of the Reagan administration, even though the public facade was the statement that Gritz was an embarrassment to the administration and a danger to the interests of any surviving MIAs. Gritz nonetheless claims to have been helped by the Intelligence Support Activity that, by Mark Perry's account (*Nation*, 17 Jan. 1987), was part of Oliver North's secret operations network in the years leading up to the Iran-contra affair. Gritz appears in a further mystery (reported in *Nation*, 7 May 1988, 634), this time over the purported involvement of CIA officials in drug-running out of Burma. One of the claims made by Gritz's associates is that drug smuggling was occurring in 1976 when George Bush was head of the CIA.

AMONGST MEN

1. While I am deploying Cameron and Frazer's work here because it seems appropriate to the production of cultural narratives in which such a masculine sexuality is proferred and constructed, there are implications to their argument about which I have to be a bit more hesitant. In particular, they take as the starting point for their investigations the fact that there is no history, nor indeed much fictional representation, of female sexual killers. This leads them to infer and imply that all men are potentially capable of sexual murder while all women are not. Although even this might feasibly be true, it strikes me that the construction of the categories "all men" and "all women" is dangerous and even indicates a relapse into the kind of essentialism that they impugn so well in other writers' and theorists' accounts of the lust to kill.

2. Perhaps the only other particularly noteworthy aspect of it is the shooting of the final sequence on the island of Alcatraz. The island and its prison had been more or less abandoned since the occupation by Native Americans in 1969.

3. Zmijewsky and Pfeiffer report that the movie had a budget of $5 million. Its 1988 North American rental income reached nearly $18 million, according to *Variety*.

4. "Amongst men" is a shorthand way of designating the combined logics of what Irigaray (1985) calls "hommosexuality" and what Sedgwick (1985) designates "homosociality." Perhaps the primary feature of the "amongst men" is that it is a logic that allows male subjects to assume that power need be brokered only through or with another male subject and in a homoerotic struggle that obfuscates its own sexual dimension. Its multiple other effects would obviously include—as is aptly shown in this scene—the simultaneous playing out of the struggle across the woman's body and the exclusion of the woman. Further relevant discussion occurs in the section "Gay Subtext."

GAY SUBTEXT

1. In reading this film, I agree with and repeat many of Wood's points, even while coming to slightly differing conclusions. All subsequent quotations from Wood (1986) are from 230-33, unless noted. Wood's own arguments are often akin to those of Biskind (1974). While both treatments see many of the same things in the film, Biskind attacks it for being anti-*hetero*sexual; Wood sees it, as I have quoted, as an "honorable exception" among Hollywood buddy movies on the grounds that it allows for the appearance of homosexual meanings in a relatively overt way.

EASTWOOD BOUND

1. Compare Douglas's remarks on Natty Bumppo (1988, 346), or Baldwin's remarks on America as emblematized by Steinbeck's Lennie (1976).

2. Studlar, too, investigates "the masochist's disavowal of phallic power" (1988, 16) in her readings of some of the Von Sternberg–Dietrich collaborations, such as *Blonde Venus*; unlike Silverman, however, she is concerned to use masochism as a way of intellectually displacing the phallic schemas that so much film theory assumes. Although one has considerable sympathy with such an effort, Studlar's is insufficient insofar as she is led to posit masochism as a kind of Ur-sexuality in which sexual difference is ultimately elided. The masochistic turn, in her version, does more than push toward denarrativization, as in Bersani, but actually desexualizes insofar as the privileged figuration of masochism becomes in her account the androgyne. This leaves Studlar with the unfulfilled task of explaining how and why sexual difference emerges. Indeed, her way of taking masochism back to the pre-Oedipal does seem to assume the Oedipal; thus masochism serves the function of countering exactly the thing that by her argument it should have rendered impossible—that is, the phallic schemas of sexual difference. Silverman's brief argument against Studlar seems pretty near the mark: Studlar's "is a determinedly apolitical reading of masochism, which comes close to grounding that perversion in biology" (1988, 66).

3. To be precise, Mayne ends her article "Walking the 'Tightrope' of Feminism and Male Desire" with the following claim from which I have extrapolated here: "But there is a fit between theory and narrative, and the intersection of feminism and male desire needs to be thought, and rethought, by submitting theory to the test of narrative" (1988, 70).

4. My point here is akin to something Adams says in her brilliant essay, "Of Female Bondage" (1989): "Think of the masochist in particular; though he may appear as victim he is in fact in charge. He is the stage manager in charge of the scenery, the costumes and the roles" (253).

5. A similar kind of critique of the use of the trope of masochism comes in Modleski's book, *Feminism without Women* (1991), especially the chapter titled "A Father Is Being Beaten." Modleski seems to me correct in her sense that the fashionable deployment of male masochism encourages the secret reimportation of the father, rather more than it produces a feminist masculinity. She suggests that the masochistic project will be "doomed to failure, from a feminist point of view, unless the father is frankly confronted and the entire dialectic of abjection and the law worked through; otherwise . . . the father will always remain in force as the major, if hidden, point of reference—and he may in fact be expected at any time to emerge from hiding with a vengeance"(70). See my article "Vas" (1988b) for another kind of attempt to shift the terms of the debate away from any masochistic model.

BURLESQUE BODY

1. Even what might appear at first blush to be obvious exceptions—like *Tootsie*, for example—are finally unable to *accept* their own representation of a feminized man and are continually undercutting its subversion. Indeed, *Tootsie* is perhaps especially problematic in this respect, shot through as it is with the anger of the unemployed man. But I do like to recall one remarkably pure (and even innocent) moment of male masochism in the (aptly titled) TV series *Bewitched*, where the male lead character,

Darrin, is threatened by a spell that would make him pregnant, and he thoughtfully reacts by realizing that he would have to have his pelvis removed.

LETHAL WEAPONS

1. A reasonably representative sample of such articles, which both set up the concept of the "new man" and also question it, might be the following: "Does the New Woman Really Want the New Man?" *Working Woman*, May 1985, 54-56; "The Book on Men's Studies," *Newsweek*, 28 Apr. 1986, 79; "The New New Man," *Mademoiselle*, Aug. 1986; and "Has the 1980s Man Become Superwimp to Superwoman?" *USA Today*, 26 Nov. 1986.

2. See Modleski (1991, 141-45) for similar comments on this movie; her initial aim seems to be to show how in this movie and its sequel, "both heterosexuality and homoeroticism (are) clearly connected with male bodily fears," and to show how what I am calling the sensitivity theme in the movie finally "pulls back from the brink to reveal [Riggs] as more firmly in charge than ever." The interest of Modleski's interpretations resides in the way she then takes them up into more general arguments about the relations among masculinity, feminism, and popular culture.

3. My quotations are from Ellen Goodman, "A Nurturing Eastwood?" *Boston Globe*, 23 Dec. 1986.

4. Modleski's reading of this film suggests that what is disturbing about it is the way that the female characters, like Aggie, are given the role of rejecting the "feminism" contained in the *Cosmopolitan* discourse: "the heroine herself is made to invalidate the language the man is using to try to communicate in her terms. . . . [T]he film purveys a profoundly misogynist vision which it works to get women to share" (1991, 65). Another view of this might be less sanguine about the *Cosmopolitan* discourse's being understood as "feminist" in the first place; equally, another interpretation might suggest that Aggie—by dint of her place in a certain class, one where the bourgeois slatherings of the glossy magazine can have no real purchase on her own experience in gendered relations—precisely recognizes the vapidity of that discourse.

SERVICEMEN

1. For instance, Rex Reed in *Women's Wear Daily* says that the movie has "brilliant acting" (quoted in Zmijewsky and Pfeiffer 1988, 91). The *Variety* reviewer suggests that "Eastwood seems a little wooden in the early scenes, but snaps out of it when the action starts piling up" (quoted in *Film Facts* 12:5 [1969], 109).

2. Eastwood makes this comment in his 1974 *Playboy* interview. Simsolo, as usual, repeats the party line: "a grinding antiwar parable" (1990, 34).

3. For basic information on the rationales and justifications of U.S. foreign policy in the third world, see the accounts offered in Schraeder (1989), most of which are devoted to showing how the United States might maintain its supposed "leadership" role in the third world.

4. See *Vending Times*, April 1984, 64. No financial information is given here about the deal between Atari and Malpaso. Deals between the video game industry and Hollywood and television are presumably not all that uncommon, but the comments by Atari's president for coin-operated games, Charles Paul, that are included in this article are interesting: he suggests that there is a growing similarity in the way movies and arcade games are produced. His observation is based on the similarities in both production and aesthetic: "Each is a collaborative effort involving the efforts of large num-

bers of people on both the technical and creative sides," and the games "strive for the realism that is possible in movies."

5. Dykstra and his crew (including Don Trumbull, the name most often associated with the special effects in *Star Wars*) explain their work in *American Cinematographer*, Sept. 1982, 912ff. See, too, Thomas Wayne's short article, "Filming 'Firefox'," *Air Progress* 44 (1982): 28-9.

6. This quotation is from the propaganda of the Reagan administration, *Grenada: A Preliminary Report* (Washington, D.C.: Departments of State and Defense, 1983). This report not only details the operation itself, but lays out the justifications used by the United States for the invasion. See especially page 2.

7. Official U.S. reports such as the one mentioned in the previous note claim that there were about nine hundred military advisors on Grenada at the time of the invasion, most of them from Cuba.

8. While it is true that the U.S. military will sometimes court-martial servicemen for this kind of action, it is also true that they are often slow to do so and quite lenient in sentencing. Still, one cannot help but wonder whether the U.S. massacre of fleeing Iraqi soldiers on the infamous "highway to hell" during the Gulf War ought not have provoked some similar determination from the Department of Defense.

PERFORMANCE AND IDENTIFICATION

1. I take this term from Ellis (1982, 93), where it is used to describe only the signifying effect of a star's image in marketing.

2. See, for instance, Baudry (1986) and Metz (1975), where the case for such working of the cinematic apparatus is most elaborated. Heath, too, gives extensive accounts of this (e.g., 1980, 120 or 147), and Ellis provides a cogent and concise version of what is being claimed (1982, 41-45). Despite the general usefulness that psychoanalytical theory undoubtedly has had for film studies, it has always seemed to me that this kind of position too readily subsumes the cinematic experience under the master code of Lacan's account of the subject's entry into the symbolic realm, and thence in a way does no more than allegorize the spectator's activity. Experience of the cinema is by this account always a repetition, a kind of reactivation of subjective formation—always in that sense a mythical formation. See my brief critique of this tendency (1988a, 33-34).

3. Burch, who deploys the diegesis/narrative distinction to great effect in his study of early cinema, notes the place of the "lecturer" in early film as a sort of precursor to the mechanism whereby the protagonistic body acts as the commutational point between the two constructions (e.g., 1990, 154). However, Burch's work here tends to replicate the theses of Metz and others that suggest that the kind of identifications I have been talking about are processes of "secondary identification." For this school of thought—and indeed for much current film scholarship—the spectator's "primary identification" is with the gaze of the camera. In Metz's terms, such an identification is in fact with the spectator "him/herself, with him/herself as a pure act of perception. . . . [A]s he/she identifies with him/herself as look, the spectator can do no other than identify with the camera too" (1975, 51). This kind of primary identification, Burch implies, is appropriate to the spectator's grasp of diegetic presence, whereas the secondary identifications pertain to the narrative. In my view such a distinction is hard to maintain, given the way in which the commutational body is as it were divided between diegetic and narrative functioning. At any rate, without arguing the case further here, I would suggest that the notion of the spectator's "primary" identification with the gaze

of the camera and with him/herself as pure perception is one of the most dubious claims of Metz and his followers, even if it is by now a shibboleth in film studies.

MEANING OF BLACK

1. The *People Weekly* article referred to here does not quote Lee's original attack (which I heard only on a television program), but his point of view is represented in his own words in the "companion volume" to *Mo' Better Blues* (Lee and Jones 1990, 39-40). The same volume also has Donald Bogle's foreword, which critiques *Bird* in the context of a history of jazz movies and expands greatly on Lee's own negative reaction (23-29). Bogle's encyclopedia of blacks and film and TV is a fine corrective to the standard reference books (1988).

2. One might read other moments in the film as alluding to American racism—in particular, an exchange between Parker and a character based on the expatriate Sidney Bechet. The following dialogue occurs after Parker declines an invitation to work permanently in Europe: "I'm not running from my own country." "Your country?" "Mine, whether they like it or not." The problem here, of course, is that nothing in the film motivates any such remark for the Parker character.

3. Lee's response to a *Penthouse* interviewer's question about the absence of drugs in *Do the Right Thing* might be understood to contradict this insofar as he views "the race issue" and the drugs issue as separable. He says, "I'm getting a lot of questions about the absence of drugs. . . . Of course drugs are prevalent, but adding that issue to this film would dilute the race issue" (*Penthouse*, Aug. 1989, 16 and 140). It nonetheless remains the case that Lee registers here the expectation that he should portray drugs.

4. A fuller account of the production of this new and improved Parker music is given by Peter Watrous in the *New York Times* (3 Oct. 1988, C21 and 26). Like the majority of reviews that mention the rerecording, Watrous is quite positive about this new representation. A less positive commentary—one that attempts to delve into the meaning of the new work—is Stanley Crouch's article, "Bird Land" (*New Republic*, 27 Feb. 1989, 25-31). Crouch quotes, for instance, Doris Parker (Charlie's third wife), who is said to have remarked to Eastwood that "Charlie didn't play by himself. When you take him away from his real musicians, you destroy what inspired him to play what he did" (27).

5. It is possible that the process I am trying to describe has its analogue in Eastwood's casting in the first place: "I wanted to use unknown players, no name faces" (*Esquire*, Oct. 1988, 136).

6. But Paul Sandro has pointed out to me how the cinematography produces Parker's saxophone as a kind of weird and distorted substitute for the white hero's gun.

7. One of Eastwood's least successful films, *Honkytonk Man* (1983), has already ventured into the kind of narrative of which *Bird* is a quite elaborated version, except *Honkytonk* uses Eastwood's white body instead of a black body at its center. *Honkytonk* similarly concerns a musician who pursues the goal of fame and recognition, only to be cut short by an untimely death. Many of the elements that I have described in *Bird* are present in this movie, too. Yet there are significant differences that illuminate some of the choices that the later movie makes, and that perhaps can be used to show how a narrative structure that is similar can produce a somewhat different meaning.

Honkytonk is the story of Red Stovell, a honky-tonk singer who is given the opportunity to audition for the Grand Old Opry show in Nashville. Set in the Depression era, the film is mostly made up of a sort of picaresque narrative that relates Red's journey to Nashville, through various difficulties and adventures, in the company of a small collection of fellow travelers. It begins with his visiting his relatives, a family of sharecroppers, from among whom he takes his teenage nephew, Hoss, and the grandfather. They are later joined by a teenage girl, Marleen, with whom Red becomes sexually involved. Red's audition is ruined by the sudden onset of the terminal stages of tuberculosis, which has been alluded to by his coughing fits in a number of scenes. The last few days of his life are spent recording his songs for posterity; his death is thus to become the beginning of his fame, designated to "make something of him" by allowing his recordings to reach beyond the grave (literally, in the sense that at his funeral we hear his first hit song played on a car radio).

The first obvious difference between this film and *Bird* is that the protagonist is white rural poor rather than black and that his music is country rather than jazz. Country, of course, is a genre almost exclusively dedicated to the travails of Red's class—the white rural poor—and is perhaps the "whitest" of American popular musical genres. In a gesture different from that of *Bird*, this movie does narrativize the music in the sense that it is proferred as the fitting expression of the experience of Red and his class. The movie spends a good amount of time in giving details of that existence and its hardships; there is, for instance, a long scene in which the grandfather explains to Hoss the history of the opening up of the Cherokee strip to white settlers in 1893. Equally, the travails of the family and its difficulties in deciding whether or not to move to the next promised land, California, are examined. Among all this, Red's music is offered as an intrinsic, expressive component of Depression-era life, of sharecropping and cotton picking in the Midwest. The narrative of Red's efforts to have his music heard are interlocked with these diegetic constructions in a way that is not done in *Bird*.

Red's fate is also dealt with very differently than Parker's. Essentially, Parker is blamed for his own fate, but right from the beginning *Honkytonk* allows—sentimentally, to be sure—that Red's lack of discipline in relation to alcohol has a cause that is not his fault. The tuberculosis that will kill him (and that will also ensure his fame) not only is given as not his to control, but also allows the film to portray him as bravely struggling against the affliction. The sympathy for Red that is the film's central intendment is elaborated early on in the film when Hoss's mother explains to him that Red is sick and says, "You can't blame him—it's not his fault."

In this context, where the narrative does not blame Red for his own victimization, possibilities are left open to Red that are not repeated with the black man in *Bird*. For instance, at his death Red will not be alone, but in the company of the boy Hoss (to whom he is explicitly handing on his talents) and the girl Marleen (whom he has impregnated in his dying days). Even though Red does indeed die, the film thus gives him the same kind of possibilities that Lee has claimed for his black musician in *Mo' Better Blues*; such possibilities are not given to Parker. Red is offered as the victim of misfortune and of the world's asperity, rather than as someone who could possibly have had more positive agency in his fate. That is, the white hero here is proferred as ultimately not degenerate—as against Parker whose degeneracy defines him for *Bird*.

AUTEUR-FATHER

1. The national and international press coverage of Eastwood's campaign, his election, and his term in office was massive, and often repetitive, so here I cite only some of the more definitive American accounts that I have consulted for information and

quotations in the following part of the section. In chronological order: *People Weekly*, 17 Mar. 1986, 49; *Wall Street Journal*, 19 Mar. 1986, 1; *New York Times*, 25 Mar. 1986, A20; *Washington Post*, 1 Apr. 1986, A3; *Christian Science Monitor*, 7 Apr. 1986, 1; *Newsweek*, 7 Apr. 1986, 42; *Time*, 7 Apr. 1986, 30; *Us*, 7 Apr. 1986, 20; *Los Angeles Times*, 9 Apr. 1986, sec. 1, 1; *New York Times*, 10 Apr. 1986, A20; *Life*, July 1986, 98; *Los Angeles Times*, 1 Oct. 1986, sec. 1, 3; *Editor and Publisher*, 13 Dec. 1986, 19; *Los Angeles Times*, 19 Dec. 1986, sec. 1, 26; *Time*, 6 Apr. 1987, 34; *Los Angeles Times*, 28 May 1987, sec. 1, 3; *New York Times*, 1 Sept. 1987, A10; *Saturday Evening Post*, Sept. 1987, 42; *San Francisco Examiner*, 27 Dec. 1987, B1; *Los Angeles Times*, 10 Apr. 1988, sec. 1, 3; *Los Angeles Times*, 8 Dec. 1988, sec. 1, 3; and *California*, Dec. 1989, 12.

2. Among the actions that Eastwood took against these supposedly punitive ordinances, the one that the media most fancied was his overturning of an ordinance against fast food in Carmel, which, among other things, had disallowed the eating of ice-cream cones in the street. Other ordinances he overturned included one about which he remarked, "If you've read that ordinance, it's like Adolf Hitler knocking on your door." The ordinance in question prevented homeowners from building second kitchens in order to be able to rent out parts of their houses. These and other actions seem to have been directed toward a deregulation of everyday life in Carmel that would improve the climate for business and private enterprise. Most of his other interventions seemed geared toward the expansion of building projects in the town. He approved the building of new parking lots and access stairs to Carmel's beach, and instituted plans for a library expansion. He also abolished a zoning ordinance that had been intended to inhibit development by imposing principles of architectural uniformity on building plans. While all of these steps encouraged—and produced—the desired developmental expansion, Eastwood threw a bone to his antidevelopment opponents by himself purchasing a local site, a twenty-two-acre ranch, for about $5 million, supposedly in order to keep it out of the hands of developers. (The property was actually bought by an Eastwood production company, Tehama Productions, about which I can glean no further information.)

3. Again Malpaso has been of no help in answering this question. One can assume, I think, that there has been a deliberate effort on the part of Eastwood and his associates to keep the issue away from the public eye—partly by way of the proverbial "chilling effect" of lawsuits such as that taken out against the *News of the World*. The claim of a publicity person at one of the major tabloids (whom I telephoned in 1992 and who insisted on anonymity) is that there has been extensive pressure on publications such as hers to ignore this issue.

4. The film takes the rather unusual step of "quoting" some of the Hollywood products of which it disapproves. For instance, we are shown the film's psychotic villain watching the opening to one of Larry Cohen's better-known slasher flicks.

5. The problem is multiplied if we consider the difference between the villains of the previous "Harry" movies and the villain of this one. First of all, the audience is not introduced to this villain in any detail; he appears from nowhere almost (apart from a few shots of his apartment that do not reveal his identity). Second, he turns out to be pathologically insane more than he is simply criminal. That is, while the other, previous villains were shown to have some kind of social and/or political fault, this one has turned to murder as the result simply of psychosis. In that sense Harry's determination in tracking him down to kill him appears almost mean-spirited: the villain's fate really should not be a shoot-out with Harry, but confinement in a psychiatric ward.

6. While concern for those kinds of responsibilities traverses the movie and its broader text, another responsibility is ignored. The film is cut through with a racist discourse whose supposed humor appears to rely upon the prospect of the Hispanic actor Raul Julia playing a Teutonic villain. The film's racism, especially coming after *Bird*, sits uneasily with the fact that the NAACP had very recently given Eastwood an Image Award for providing people of color with serious and respectable roles in his films (see *Crisis Magazine*, Feb. 1989).

CODA

1. *Entertainment Weekly* reports that Eastwood is working on yet another film, though not a western: *In the Line of Fire*, directed by Wolfgang Petersen and starring Eastwood with John Malkovich. This will be produced by Columbia Pictures and will be the first non-Warner movie Eastwood has made for many a year.

2. The documentary was also shown later a number of times as a filler program on the American Movie Classics cable channel.

3. A longer discussion of the movie would necessitate consideration of the significance of the fact that Logan's being black is not mentioned at all in the movie—a playing out, perhaps, of the proposition (discussed earlier in this book) that race "has no bearing."

Bibliography

Adams, Parveen. 1990. "Of Female Bondage." In *Between Feminism and Psychoanalysis*, edited by T. Brennan. New York: Routledge.

Adorno, Theodor. 1987. *Prisms*. Cambridge, Mass.: MIT Press.

______. 1990. "The Culture Industry Reconsidered." In *Critical Theory and Society*, edited by S. Bronner and D. Kellner. New York: Routledge.

Agan, Patrick. 1975. *Clint Eastwood: The Man behind the Myth*. New York: Pyramid.

Alvarado, Manuel, and Tulloch, John. 1983. *Doctor Who: The Unfolding Text*. New York: St. Martin's Press.

Bach, Steven. 1986. *Final Cut*. New York: New American Library.

Baldwin, James. 1976. *The Devil Finds Work*. New York: Dell.

Baudry, Jean-Louis. 1986. "Ideological Effects of the Basic Cinematographic Apparatus." In *Narrative, Apparatus, Ideology*, edited by P. Rosen. New York: Columbia University Press.

Baym, Nina. 1985. "Dramas of Beset Manhood." In *The New Feminist Criticism*, edited by E. Showalter. New York: Pantheon.

Bennett, Tony, and Woolacott, Janet. 1987. *Bond and Beyond*. New York: Methuen.

Berkhofer, Robert F. 1978. *The White Man's Indian*. New York: Knopf.

Bersani, Leo. 1986. *The Freudian Body*. New York: Columbia University Press.

Bhabha, Homi. 1984. "Of Mimicry and Man: The Ambivalence of Colonial Discourse." *October* 28: 125-33.

Biskind, Peter. 1974. "Tightass and Cocksucker." *Jump Cut*, Nov. 1974.

Bogle, Donald. 1988. *Blacks in American Film and Television*. New York: Garland.

Bondanella, Peter. 1983. *Italian Cinema from Neorealism to the Present*. New York: Ungar.

Bonitzer, Pascal. 1986. "The Silences of the Voice." In *Narrative, Apparatus, Ideology*, edited by P. Rosen. New York: Columbia University Press.

Bibliography

Bordwell, David; Staiger, Janet; and Thompson, Kristin. 1985. *The Classical Hollywood Cinema*. New York: Columbia University Press.

Brauer, Ralph. 1975. *The Horse, the Gun, the Piece of Property*. Bowling Green, Ohio: Bowling Green State University Popular Press.

Brown, Richard M. 1975. *Strain of Violence: Historical Studies of American Violence and Vigilantism*. New York: Oxford University Press.

Burch, Noel. 1990. *Life to Those Shadows*. Berkeley: University of California Press.

Burnett, Ron. 1985, "The Tightrope of Male Fantasy." *Framework* 26-27: 76-85.

Buscombe, Edward, ed. 1988. *The BFI Companion to the Western*. New York: Atheneum.

Cameron, Deborah, and Frazer, Elizabeth. 1987. *The Lust to Kill*. London: Polity.

Cawelti, John. n.d. *The Six-Gun Mystique*. Bowling Green: Bowling Green State University Popular Press.

Clarens, Carlos. 1980. *Crime Movies*. New York: Norton.

Cole, Gerald, and Williams, Peter. 1983. *Clint Eastwood*. London: Allen.

Culberson, William C. 1990. *Vigilantism*. Westport, Conn.: Greenwood Press.

Cumbow, Robert C. 1987. *Once upon a Time: The Films of Sergio Leone*. Metuchen, N.J.: Scarecrow.

Deleuze, Gilles. 1986. *Cinema 1: The Movement-Image*. Minneapolis: University of Minnesota Press.

Doane, Mary Ann. 1986. "The Voice in the Cinema: The Articulation of Body and Space." In *Narrative, Apparatus, Ideology*, edited by P. Rosen. New York: Columbia University Press.

Douglas, Ann. 1988. *The Feminization of American Culture*. New York: Anchor.

Douglas, Peter. 1974. *Clint Eastwood: Movin' On*. Chicago: Regnery.

Downing, David, and Herman, Gary. 1977. *Clint Eastwood: All-American Anti-Hero*. London: Quick Fox.

Drinnon, Richard. 1980. *Facing West: The Metaphysics of Indian-Hating and Empire-Building*. Minneapolis: University of Minnesota Press.

Ellis, John. 1982. *Visible Fictions*. London: Routledge and Kegan Paul.

Erlich, Victor. 1981. *Russian Formalism*. London: Yale University Press.

Ferrari, Philippe. 1980. *Clint Eastwood*. Paris: Solar.

Frank, Alan. 1982. *Clint Eastwood*. New York: Exeter.

Frayling, Christopher. 1981. *Spaghetti Westerns*. London: Routledge and Kegan Paul.

Freud, Sigmund. [1921] 1959. *Group Psychology and the Analysis of the Ego*. New York: Norton.

______. [1923] 1962. *The Ego and the Id*. New York: Norton.

______. [1924] 1963. "The Economic Problem in Masochism." In *General Psychological Theory*. New York: Collier.

Bibliography

Genette, Gérard. 1969. *Figures III*. Paris: Seuil.

Gentry, Rick. 1989. "Jack N. Green: An Interview." *Post Script* 8(2): 2-20.

Gomery, Douglas. 1989. "Hollywood's Business." In *American Media*, edited by P. Cook, D. Gomery, and L. Lichty. Washington, D.C.: Wilson Center Press.

Guback, Thomas. 1969. *The International Film Industry*. Bloomington: Indiana University Press.

Guérif, François. 1986. *Clint Eastwood*. New York: St. Martin's Press.

Hardy, Phil. 1983. *The Western*. London: Arum.

Heath, Stephen. 1981. *Questions of Cinema*. Bloomington: Indiana University Press.

Hirsch, E. D., Jr. 1967. *Validity in Interpretation*. New Haven, Conn.: Yale University Press.

Hirschman, Albert O. 1991. *The Rhetoric of Reaction*. Cambridge, Mass.: Belknap.

Homans, Peter. 1962. "Puritanism Revisited." *Studies in Public Communication* 3: 73-84.

Irigaray, Luce. 1985. *This Sex Which Is Not One*. Ithaca, N.Y.: Cornell University Press.

Jacobs, Diane. 1977. *Hollywood Renaissance*. New York: Tantivy.

Jeffords, Susan. 1989. *The Remasculinization of America*. Bloomington: Indiana University Press.

Johnstone, Iain. 1981. *The Man with No Name*. New York: Morrow Quill.

Kael, Pauline. 1973. *Deeper into Movies*. Boston: Atlantic Monthly Press.

Kaminsky, Stuart. 1974a. *Clint Eastwood*. New York: New American Library.

______. 1974b. *Don Siegel: Director*. New York: Curtis.

Kass, Judith M. 1975. *Don Siegel*. London: Tantivy.

Kellner, Douglas, and Ryan, Michael. 1988. *Camera Politica*. Bloomington: Indiana University Press.

King, Barry. 1985. "Articulating Stardom." *Screen* 26(5): 27-50.

Kristeva, Julia. 1980. *Desire in Language*. New York: Columbia University Press.

Kuleshov, Lev. 1973. *Kuleshov on Film*. Ed. and trans. R. Levaco. Berkeley: University of California Press.

Lacan, Jacques. 1978. *The Four Fundamental Concepts of Psycho-Analysis*. New York: Norton.

Lee, Spike, and Jones, Lisa. 1990. *Mo' Better Blues*. New York: Fireside.

Lovell, Alan. 1975. *Don Siegel*. London: British Film Institute.

Matthiessen, Peter. 1983. *In the Spirit of Crazy Horse*. New York: Viking.

______. 1984. *Indian Country*. New York: Viking.

Mayne, Judith. 1988. "Walking the 'Tightrope' of Feminism and Male Desire." In *Men in Feminism*, edited by A. Jardine and P. Smith. New York: Methuen.

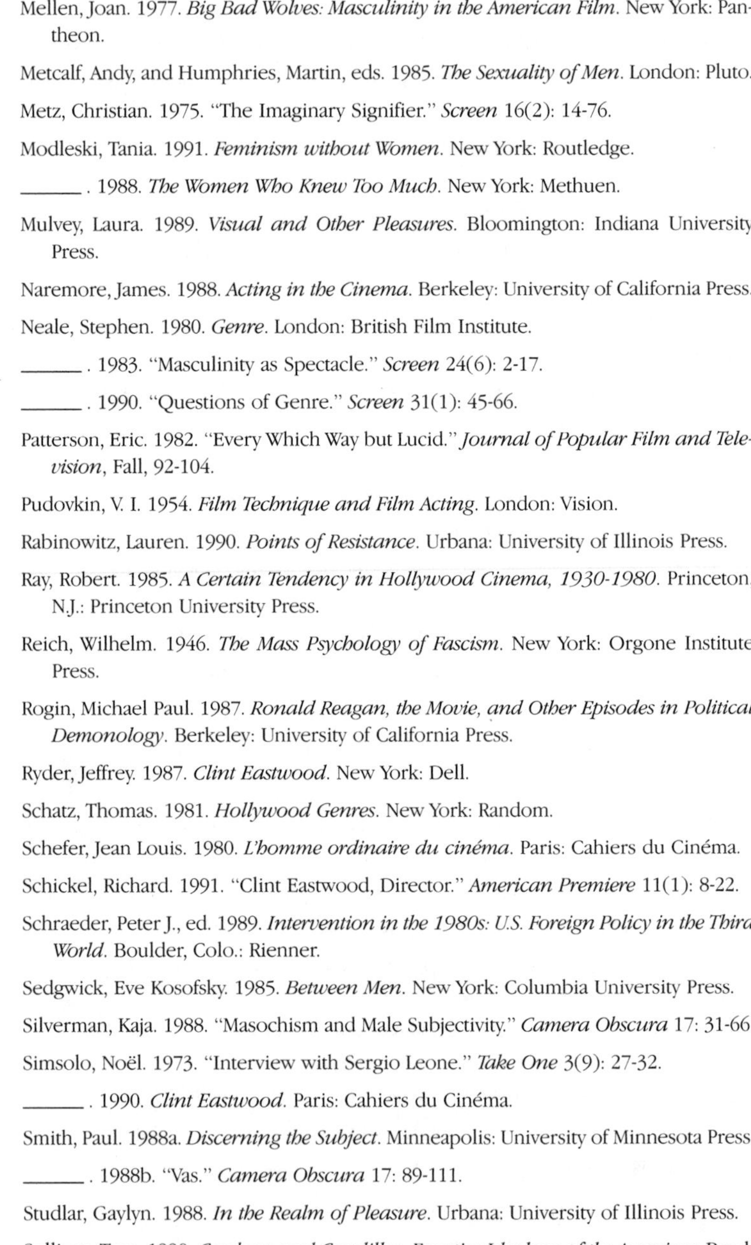

Bibliography

Mellen, Joan. 1977. *Big Bad Wolves: Masculinity in the American Film*. New York: Pantheon.

Metcalf, Andy, and Humphries, Martin, eds. 1985. *The Sexuality of Men*. London: Pluto.

Metz, Christian. 1975. "The Imaginary Signifier." *Screen* 16(2): 14-76.

Modleski, Tania. 1991. *Feminism without Women*. New York: Routledge.

______. 1988. *The Women Who Knew Too Much*. New York: Methuen.

Mulvey, Laura. 1989. *Visual and Other Pleasures*. Bloomington: Indiana University Press.

Naremore, James. 1988. *Acting in the Cinema*. Berkeley: University of California Press.

Neale, Stephen. 1980. *Genre*. London: British Film Institute.

______. 1983. "Masculinity as Spectacle." *Screen* 24(6): 2-17.

______. 1990. "Questions of Genre." *Screen* 31(1): 45-66.

Patterson, Eric. 1982. "Every Which Way but Lucid." *Journal of Popular Film and Television*, Fall, 92-104.

Pudovkin, V. I. 1954. *Film Technique and Film Acting*. London: Vision.

Rabinowitz, Lauren. 1990. *Points of Resistance*. Urbana: University of Illinois Press.

Ray, Robert. 1985. *A Certain Tendency in Hollywood Cinema, 1930-1980*. Princeton, N.J.: Princeton University Press.

Reich, Wilhelm. 1946. *The Mass Psychology of Fascism*. New York: Orgone Institute Press.

Rogin, Michael Paul. 1987. *Ronald Reagan, the Movie, and Other Episodes in Political Demonology*. Berkeley: University of California Press.

Ryder, Jeffrey. 1987. *Clint Eastwood*. New York: Dell.

Schatz, Thomas. 1981. *Hollywood Genres*. New York: Random.

Schefer, Jean Louis. 1980. *L'homme ordinaire du cinéma*. Paris: Cahiers du Cinéma.

Schickel, Richard. 1991. "Clint Eastwood, Director." *American Premiere* 11(1): 8-22.

Schraeder, Peter J., ed. 1989. *Intervention in the 1980s: U.S. Foreign Policy in the Third World*. Boulder, Colo.: Rienner.

Sedgwick, Eve Kosofsky. 1985. *Between Men*. New York: Columbia University Press.

Silverman, Kaja. 1988. "Masochism and Male Subjectivity." *Camera Obscura* 17: 31-66.

Simsolo, Noël. 1973. "Interview with Sergio Leone." *Take One* 3(9): 27-32.

______. 1990. *Clint Eastwood*. Paris: Cahiers du Cinéma.

Smith, Paul. 1988a. *Discerning the Subject*. Minneapolis: University of Minnesota Press.

______. 1988b. "Vas." *Camera Obscura* 17: 89-111.

Studlar, Gaylyn. 1988. *In the Realm of Pleasure*. Urbana: University of Illinois Press.

Sullivan, Tom. 1990. *Cowboys and Caudillos: Frontier Ideology of the Americas*. Bowling Green: Bowling Green State University Popular Press.

Bibliography

Tahimik, Kidlat. 1989. "Cups-of-Gas Filmmaking vs. Full Tank-cum-Credit Card Filmmaking." *Discourse* 11(2): 81-87.

Theweleit, Klaus. 1987. *Male Fantasies*. Vol. 1. Minneapolis: University of Minnesota Press.

Todorov, Tzvetan. 1977. *The Poetics of Prose*. Ithaca, N.Y.: Cornell University Press.

______. 1981. *Introduction to Poetics*. Brighton: Harvester.

______. 1984. *The Conquest of America*. New York: Harper and Row.

Toll, Robert C. 1982. *The Entertainment Machine*. Oxford: Oxford University Press.

Tulloch, John. 1990. *Television Drama*. New York: Routledge.

Warshow, Robert. 1962. *The Immediate Experience*. Garden City, N.Y.: Doubleday.

Whitman, Mark. 1973. *The Films of Clint Eastwood*. Isle of Wight: BCW.

Willemen, Paul. 1981. "Looking at the Male." *Framework* 15-17: 16.

Wood, Robin. 1986. *Hollywood from Vietnam to Reagan*. New York: Columbia University Press.

Wright, Will. 1975. *Six Guns and Society*. Berkeley: University of California Press.

Zmijewsky, Boris, and Pfeiffer, Lee. 1988. *The Films of Clint Eastwood*. Secaucus, N.J.: Citadel.

Index

Paul Smith is associate professor of literary and cultural studies at Carnegie Mellon. He is the author of *Pound Revised* and *Discerning the Subject* and a coeditor, with Alice Jardine, of *Men in Feminism*.